In Search of

THE LOST

ORIENT

In Search of

THE LOST ORIENT

AN INTERVIEW

———∞∞∞———

Olivier Roy

As Interviewed by Jean-Louis Schlegel

Translated by C. Jon Delogu

Columbia University Press

———

New York

Columbia University Press
Publishers Since 1893
New York   Chichester, West Sussex
cup.columbia.edu

Copyright © 2014 Éditions du Seuil
English translation © 2017 Columbia University Press

Library of Congress Cataloging-in-Publication Data
Names: Roy, Olivier, 1949– author. | Schlegel, Jean-Louis, interviewer.
Title: In search of the lost Orient : an interview with Jean-Louis Schlegel /
Olivier Roy ; translated by C. Jon Delogu.
Other titles: En quête de l'Orient perdu. English
Description: New York : Columbia University Press, 2017. | Includes
bibliographical references.
Identifiers: LCCN 2017003802 | ISBN 9780231179348 (cloth : alk. paper) |
ISBN 9780231542036 (e-book)
Subjects: LCSH: Islam and politics. | Religion and culture—Islamic countries. |
Political culture—Islamic countries. | Civil society—Islamic countries. | Islamic
countries—Politics and government. | Political scientists—France—Interviews.
Classification: LCC BP173.7 .S388 2017 | DDC 909/.09767—dc23
LC record available at https://lccn.loc.gov/2017003802

Columbia University Press books are printed
on permanent and durable acid-free paper.

Printed in the United States of America

Cover image: Photograph by Chantal Lobato

CONTENTS

PART III
THE AFGHAN DECADE

PART IV
THE CENTRAL ASIA DECADE

PART V
CULTURES AND THE UNIVERSALLY HUMAN:
TOWARD *HOLY IGNORANCE*

FOREWORD

Olivier Mongin and Jean-Louis Schlegel

OLIVIER ROY HAS a list of books, articles, and other research projects that speaks for itself. Therefore, it is not really necessary to introduce in the customary way this global public intellectual. As publishers of his books and essays for many years, we would instead like to offer this book of interviews as a way to retrace his highly original career path. Roy got his start as a novice student of Persian during university preparatory studies at the Lycée Louis-le-Grand when revolutionary Maoism was at full boil in Paris. Today he holds a research and teaching position at the prestigious European University Institute in Florence. Over these many years, Roy gradually has become one of the most frequently cited French specialists on the Middle East and Central Asia. But also one of the most debated, because he does not keep his lamp under a basket or hidden under a cloak of neutral academic prose, nor has he refused higher-visibility media attention that goes beyond the polite recognition within traditionally organized academic institutions. The reason is simple: as the author of one of the very first books on Afghanistan, published in 1985, his path has been nothing like the typical university progression from student to savant.

Oliver Roy is first of all a traveler who looked to the East, a hardy walker who climbed to the passes that led from Pakistan to the Afghan mountains and into the most inaccessible regions near the Russian border—and all at a time when hippies arriving in Kabul routinely went along the southern route through India. They let others pursue the northern route through an Afghanistan that was still at peace in the 1970s, though unknown and "savage." Later, at the end of that decade, and especially after the Soviet invasion in 1979, the country entered a time of very rough and protracted war, as stories in this book attest. The 1980s rapidly transformed the country where the young student and later teacher had done some idyllic traveling—journeys that, at least in the beginning, were almost like children's dreams of finding oneself in an Orient that was still unexplored and wild. This lost Orient is above all the unexplored and still traditional Afghanistan of the early '70s, when Kabul was still a Western dream. Afterward, that peaceful Afghanistan disappeared behind the rapid changes brought on by war. In this book, the reader will become acquainted with Roy the traveler, who, searching for virgin territories, finds modern war and then becomes, perhaps unconsciously at first, a researcher gathering rare information about zones others have abandoned. He becomes curious about the lay of the land—regarding both the invader's forms of combat and the modes of resistance by locals—in a country typically described as "medieval" and "tribal." The reader will also learn of the rise of jihad—both the word and the act—in the country where al-Qaeda establishes its base of operations in the 1980s. Afghanistan would eventually become the knotted point of intersection of all Western concerns—not to mention that at the start of the twenty-first century it remains the world's leading producer of opium.

This traveler-researcher's unique experience in the country led him to be listened to more attentively than some of his future colleagues when representatives from the Pentagon or from French intelligence services came to ask questions about conflicts there. During the 1990s, he expands his knowledge of these "land-mined territories"—traveling through the post-Soviet nations, which are confronting the prospect of becoming independent, modern nation-states, while remaining in many ways Soviet creations. Roy is invited to join an official mission to Tajikistan and ends up filling an international political post in Dushanbe for several months. This stay presented him with the opportunity to pursue his research throughout this new Central Asia that was then just emerging.

Besides freely exploring a vast territory, Roy had his own way of working and thinking that was shaped by his formative early years as a philosophy professor in Dreux at the end of the 1970s, a post he obtained after completing a dissertation under the direction of Yvon Belaval on "Leibnitz and China." Roy was never afraid of forging surprising new concepts, starting with "the failure of political Islam," which would become the title of a book that scandalized many who believe in only an essentialist, uniform, and immobile Islam. From that time onward, the point was to change the understanding of events that were disrupting the Muslim regions of the world—an understanding that was often frozen, marked by an unshakeable culturalism according to which cultures were static entities with clear differences. The events of September 11 proved Roy was right about the global, universal disruptions that until then had been perceived as taking place only at the center and on the margins of the East—Near, Middle, and Far—with secondary repercussions for countries of immigration.

The high school philosophy professor of the 1970s was also a politically engaged figure who had gone through what in France are called the antitotalitarian currents (see, for example, his relationship with Doctors Without Borders). He was closely associated with the journals *Libre* and *Passé-Présent*, and therefore with Claude Lefort, who served on the editorial board of *Esprit*. Roy knew well the writings of Michel Seurat (now deceased), who was always rereading Hobbes to try and understand the unprecedented mechanisms of domination in Syria. Roy developed a political spirit (which does not mean exactly militant, though there was a bit of that) and didn't back down from some battles in France. In the 1980s in Dreux, he witnesses the rise of the National Front. How was resistance to this Far Right wave to be organized? He seized on it as an occasion to entirely rethink the conditions of immigration in France, of France's oddly particular *laïcité* model, and of French and European Islam. It is striking to notice how this decidedly lay researcher is completely open about his own progressively more secular path that his Protestant origins played an important role in shaping. Religion and religious phenomena come to occupy the center of his anthropological, social, and political curiosity—but without the presuppositions (prejudices perhaps?) of an ideological *laïcité* that is once again very present across the French intellectual landscape. As Roy sees it, this ideological filter has impeded new thinking, notably about the revolutionary events of the Arab Spring. It's in this context that the publication of his book about the evolution of globalized religion, *La sainte ignorance* appeared as a strikingly original event.[1]

Starting in the 1970s already, in collaboration with his friends Jacques Rancière and Patrice Vermeren at the journal *Les révoltes logiques* and with Miguel Abensour, who would play a large role in introducing the Frankfurt school in France, Roy investigated the professor figure and all those who claimed to possess a solid grip on knowledge merely by occupying the places and institutions where that knowledge was supposed to be held. Granted, the European University Institute in Florence where he now teaches could be viewed with raised eyebrows as precisely one such place, but one could also see in this late relationship a fitting ironic ruse of history. Roy is not whimsically donning different caps—that of the activist, the academic expert, the field researcher, and the university power broker. It is the tension he maintains between these roles which is productive, as he explains at one moment when reflecting on his position as expert council to politicians. His career has been consistently atypical, even iconoclastic, a fact which has occasionally drawn him into some polemical turmoil of no real interest. This unusual path is the key to understanding the inventive character of a long and exceptional current of research pursued by a free man.

As a follow-up to an extensive and exciting interview in *Esprit* from 2002 that gave everyone the desire to one day "go farther,"[2] this book's sole purpose is to convey a better understanding of a specific human and intellectual itinerary that takes place amid many events of considerable importance in the late twentieth and early twenty-first centuries, events that are constantly unfolding in the background or on the side and that cannot be ignored and certainly not undone or eliminated.

PART I
PREAMBLE

Chapter 1

HITCHHIKING FROM PARIS TO KABUL

A Look Back at a Departure

It's May 1969. You are in your *khâgne*[1] preparatory year at the Lycée Louis-le-Grand, you're nineteen, and you've just passed the written portion of the *concours* (exam competition) to get into the École normale supérieure. You don't wait for the results and instead start hitchhiking to Afghanistan in early June before the oral exams. Did you think you weren't going to make it to the oral portion of the *concours*, or did you just leave without worrying about what would happen?

I LEFT WITHOUT worrying. I'd basically given up on the idea of taking the orals, and therefore on the whole *concours*. I just needed to pass the written part to get credit for my two years of studies. When I learned that I had qualified to take the oral exams, and even ranked quite high among the qualifiers, I was already in Kabul.

Actually, I had been preparing this trip for two years. In the summer of 1968, after one year of *hypokhâgne* at Louis-le-Grand, I had hitchhiked to Turkey, and as soon as I got back I had made up my mind to prepare "the grand tour," a longer hitchhiking journey the following spring to Afghanistan. While preparing for the competitive exam to get into Normale sup' and for the "revolution" (keep in mind May '68 had just happened), I bought myself a copy of *Teach Yourself Persian* (it was a Penguin book—there was no French equivalent) and in the evening in my dorm room after eleven P.M., I studied Persian without the slightest idea of the pronunciation because the book didn't come with records, and besides I didn't have a turntable and cassettes didn't exist yet. The Persian spoken in Afghanistan is the same Persian that's spoken in Iran with few differences like those that separate Québec French from French in France. Even though I've never spoken any language very well, I've always been fascinated by all languages. In fact, I used to jump at any opportunity to begin a new language, even though I'd usually drop it once it started getting too complicated. With every language, I got stuck on one particular thing—in Kurdish and Pashto it was ergative constructions, in Turkish it was deverbal nouns, and in Italian the conditional tense!

What did you do in Afghanistan?

Once I got there, I traveled around the whole country by bus, hitchhiking, and on foot. It was a magical time—all the more so when I discovered that after hitchhiking all across Turkey and Iran my Persian was actually more or less working with the people I was meeting and that I was able to speak and figure things out on my own. In about four and a half weeks, I had arrived at the Afghan border. The world was less dangerous then than it is today, so crossing the border was a relatively simple matter and I never had my stuff inspected or stolen. A French citizen in those days could travel from Paris to Kabul without a visa, except if you went through Bulgaria.

Why did you choose Afghanistan at that moment in your life?

When you're traveling, you always come across people who come from some country farther away. That's the way it was in Turkey the year before. I met people who were returning from Afghanistan, and still farther there was Nepal. Those were the days when people would go to India, Nepal, or Kathmandu to get high. Personally, that was not my goal. Hashish never interested me, and so I didn't really want to mix with those who were traveling along the route to India even if, of course, I came across hippies in hotels and hostels who lived the festive side of 1968 that I had not experienced in Paris. Trekkers like me, with our backpacks and our hair still short, returned after doing our circuitous routes. The hippies were on the road for years living on fifty cents a day as they pursued their "peace and love" dreams in Kabul and Kathmandu. But there were also junkies, though not many yet in 1969, who had moved on to hard drugs. These junkies worked their way into the same migratory flows even if everyone else fled them. Of course, an entire economy gradually built up along this route with cheap transportation networks run by locals and used by penniless foreigners, and little hotels specialized in putting up trekkers and hippies.

So in Afghanistan you were by no means the only European?

No, not in Kabul at least, but I wasn't there for the same reasons as other trekkers. I had images from comic books in my head, memories of travel narratives from earlier centuries, and childhood dreams. When I was young, I wanted to be an explorer. Later, and especially at that time, I dreamed of being the lone foreigner following a caravan of Pashtun nomads or Moldo-Vlach gypsies, or discovering unknown villages in far off Nuristan.

Starting in Istanbul, I did join a sort of caravan, but a very modern one composed of hippies and trekkers who all met up at the same way stations, rustic inns occupied exclusively by low-budget Westerners. The first stop along the way was the Pudding Shop in Istanbul. There, groups were formed and tips exchanged, including information about con men to be avoided. Sometimes there might be a minibus that someone proposed filling up so long as each person chipped in; but more often there were buses of local operators who were keen on exploiting transient Westerners, and they would fill up with hippies and trekkers who would sleep all the way to Tehran. There they would regroup at the Amir-Kabir Hotel, another hippie hangout that the police allowed to function so long as no one left. From there, everyone went directly to Kabul and then waited for an Indian visa, which was difficult to obtain, to continue on to Kathmandu. The road was still only partially tarred, especially in Iran.

There were of course police stations along this route, but one could also sense a certain postcolonial aura. The most dirty and destitute Scandinavian trekker still had more money than the local poor people, and even if he was slumming it, he remained a white man. It was as though the bubble in which colonials lived still existed but had simply rolled into the gutter.

The police left us alone. It's something that we forget in these times of the global economy, finances, and communication—the world then was entirely open. Jacques Séguéla recounted how he motored around the world in a Citroën 2CV in 1954. It's obvious that one cannot undertake that route today. Mind you, though, it wasn't entirely safe back then. There were murders, rapes, and disappearances that years later I was still being asked to help elucidate.

You set off for the East and found more of the West—so where then was the "authentic"?

Once we'd arrived in Herat, the first Afghan town, I decided there was no way I was going to stay with my fellow travelers, who were all nearly identical anyway. So I set out on my own in a direction no one took—the northern route—a road that was of no interest to the hippies, who were eager to start smoking in their Kabul hotel rooms. I wanted to go to completely lost places where, if possible, no white man had ever set foot. Nuristan, a little region situated near Pakistan, seemed to correspond to my ideal. It had always sparked the imagination of travelers because it was a forbidden place. The inhabitants spoke a very old Indo-European language, they had converted to Islam only three generations earlier, and their civilization, with very low tables and chairs, for example, was very different from that of other ethnic groups. It was said that these mountain people, with their very specific culture, were descendants of Alexander's warriors who had gotten lost in the hilly terrain. It's true that the proportion of blue eyes one observes among them is significantly higher than in other parts of Afghanistan or the Middle East. Of course, this was just one of many variations on the legend of the lost legion or tribe.

Could you go where you wanted with no problems?

To go to Nuristan, one had to get special permission, which was granted only to people who had the right connections, or to rich people, who went there to do high-class hunting. I showed up with my backpack at the Ministry of the Interior dressed in jeans, and at first I was sent from office to office with no success. No one was willing to receive me. I returned several times, and at one moment I fell into talking with an Afghan policeman who had done an internship at a police academy in Kempten, Germany, where it so happens I had also been on a school exchange. We spoke a few words to each other in German, drank a few glasses of tea together, and finally another police officer filled out an authorization for me. It was another lesson in how to get around bureaucracies: use modesty, ingratiate yourself gently, speak their language, and establish a personal rapport.

I took the bus to the last stop, located at the entrance to the valley, and found myself entirely alone, like I'd wanted, but not knowing what to do. Some students from the village of Barg-i Matal who were returning home on foot for vacation let me join their group. After two days of walking, we arrived at the place of my dreams—or beyond my dreams. It was almost the last village, at the base of some mountains, dominated by a small fort controlled by a captain accompanied by a dozen soldiers in rags holding old rifles with bayonets as long as swords. These soldiers fed me and gave me a place to sleep. Then the captain asked me what I wanted to do. In truth, I didn't know, or I no longer knew! I told him I'd like to go as far as the pass that constituted the border. So he arranged that I go with a soldier in civilian clothes, and we set off together into the mountains, sleeping with local inhabitants. I was finally at the end of the world. Except that I was beginning to understand that this could not be an end in itself. What the heck was I doing there besides admiring the beauty of the natural landscape? And frankly, the end of the world doesn't exist—there's always something else beyond the edge. I celebrated my twentieth birthday all alone thinking about what Paul Nizan had written in *Aden, Arabie*,[2] a cult book (as we didn't yet say) at that time: "I was twenty. I will not let anyone say that it's the most wonderful time in one's life." In fact, I had no idea whether I agreed because I was no longer sure I knew what life was.

Did people take you in everywhere, no questions asked, out of pure hospitality?

Hospitality in the Middle East is something extraordinary. I think it's one of the reasons why those who have had this experience can never, ever, despite crises and clashes, adopt the hateful discourse that is developing today in the West. Of course, I also learned the complexity of the rules of hospitality. The Turks received outsiders in the public square, especially if the young man was with a woman. In restaurants, the coffee and bill were often paid by an anonymous person, sometimes even by the hotel. When a Turk picked me up hitchhiking, he always treated me to a meal at a restaurant, but never at his home. In Iran, it was the opposite: people don't really live in public places, and so I slept at the homes of families. In Afghanistan, an extremely poor country, I paid my bills in little village inns, but it cost hardly anything. A meal would cost sixty centimes of a French franc back then, about twelve US cents. The only difficulty was that there weren't many such village inns, only in places where trucks went by. So out in the boondocks, far from any major road, I was taken in by local inhabitants, generally by the village chief—receiving strangers was one of his prerogatives and duties.

So during that summer of 1969 you discovered a deeply traditional country that modernity seemed to have passed over.

Back then when I was twenty, I operated with the romantic dichotomy of perverse modernity versus traditional authenticity. It was conceptually false, but for a time at least quite exhilarating. So yes, Afghanistan back then had something medieval about it, but in the positive sense of the term. Aside from the trucks that passed by only where there were roads, the rifle (the British Lee Enfield of 1916—the Kalashnikov would only come later with the war), and the oil lamp (the German Jena model), the country contained nothing *modern*. But there was always hospitality. When I left Herat to set out on the northern route, barely more than a trail, on an old broken-down brightly painted bus, I spent three days in the company of a group of forty other passengers, including a Kazakh who took me under his wing and paid my whole way. We would stop at inns that had no electricity. In a room lit with oil lamps, sitting with legs crossed, the guests served themselves from a common dish placed on a large cloth. Then a boy would go around with a pitcher and tin basin and allow each guest to wash his hands. Then, in the same room where we had just eaten, we slept on the carpet after rolling up the cloth. As soon as it was light, at around four or five in the morning, we set off again. The bus stopped at the five daily prayer times, and also for breakdowns, of which there were about just as many.

Life was very slow and organized by the rhythms of sun, night, prayers, breakdowns, and meals. We crossed caravans of dromedaries. We always found enough to eat, even in the most remote places. The staple food of these country people was bread dipped in clarified butter and *qrout*, dried casein, that was melted. It was not very appetizing, but toward the end of summer there were different fruits everywhere, and at markets one could find rice and stewed goat meat. In the northeastern mountains that resembled Switzerland at times, especially the pine forests (the Afghans loved painting Swiss landscapes on their trucks, with just a minaret added for good measure, but now the Swiss law of 2009 banning minarets as incompatible with the landscape will force them to be removed), they grew corn with which they made a bread that they ate with goat's milk. But, of course, the rules of getting about and of hospitality varied according to the social structure, in particular according to the ethnic group in question and the division between tribal zones and nontribal zones.

Everyone has heard of the importance of tribes and clans in Afghanistan. How do they work exactly?

I have built up my own personal ethnology that I amend little by little thanks to actual experiences that I've accumulated over time and also from reading academic studies, of course. First of all, though all nomads live in tribes, most tribes are sedentary and have always been so. Secondly, all ethnic groups (for example, the Tajiks and Hazaras) are not tribalized, but everyone belongs to some solidarity group (*qawm*), of which the sociological base may vary considerably (it may be a clan, caste, extended family, territorial entity, religious lineage, city or village neighborhood).

I had, of course, read the French classics (Claude Lévi-Strauss), but I was not yet familiar with American anthropology. A tribe is defined by a lineage, but not every lineage constitutes a tribe. So really, there are many ways to conceive of and put into action your lineage: marriage rules, customs (Pashtunwali for the Pashtuns), territory, the mode for selecting representatives (*malek*), and so on. In general, the reality, as is often the case, was more complex than books accounted for, and when, forty years later, I would teach in the social sciences. I was always bumping up against the methodological dogmatism of certain colleagues. Not having ever actually been in the field (or the mountains or the valleys), fieldwork for them remains entirely metaphorical as they go about making abstract classifications based on the findings of earlier studies.

Can one just plop down like that into a traditional society?

I was nineteen, discovering everything for the first time, and I had a somewhat idyllic vision of social life about which I was seeing only the positive sides. For example, I was oblivious to the violence perpetrated on women who were invisible and totally inaccessible. In villages, they did not customarily wear veils, but they completely avoided strangers. Only the village leaders had guest rooms, and they were situated in a way that prevented the visitor from seeing what took place in the house. To be a leader, one had to have a spare room, and so the poor who did not could not receive visiting strangers. Among the Pashtuns, this extra room communicated directly with the street, and one did not actually enter the house. All the less glorious aspects of daily life, such as land negotiations, the exploitation of sharecroppers, corruption, abusive administrations, et cetera, were things I didn't see. I discovered them later. Unfortunately, it was the war that allowed me to begin to see more of what was going on in the wings and backstage, so to speak.

Even so, a number of things became apparent to me just from being there, such as the way people moved about. When one travels, on foot or horseback, a guide will favor the terrain linked to his own networks over the mere physical geography. Instead of taking the shortest route, he will make a big detour to avoid areas where he has no client or boss, and he'll linger in spots where he's with *his* people. I also learned about the interaction between the state and the tribal system, which mutually support each other, when the officer who was hosting me in Barg-i Matal was required to preside over an improvised tribunal to decide a case of stolen goats (a frequent occurrence in Nuristan). I also learned about enmity and vendetta when I was told it was impossible to leave the home of my host on account of a risk of ambush in the area. I also discovered the local hierarchies through the way guests moved into or, rather, deployed themselves in the guest rooms. I was supposed to *understand* my place within the space where the leader held his salon: postures, positions relative to the door, the language used, choosing to speak, when, and how—all these little things that were unreadable and folkloric my first time there gradually came to have meaning. With time I learned to speak *politely* and to integrate the proper body language and customs (including squatting to pee) as well as the rhythm of the days. I pursued Islamic studies in a very practical manner via the prayers, the sermons, and especially with what people said about religion. The mullahs wanted to convert me, and we would have extensive theological discussions. I examined the books they read. I thus acquired concrete knowledge of "real" Islam as it was thought about and practiced by the local inhabitants. I discovered only later, back in Europe, that Afghanistan was an anthropology paradise and that there were remarkably fine and profound anthropological texts such as those of my friends Micheline and Pierre Centlivres, whose style of writing French has always been a model for me.

All that would become useful later, and I would even say saved my life during the war against the Soviets.

What did you do all day?

During the day I did nothing, except chitchat, I guess. Sometimes the temperatures were near a hundred degrees, and you had to wait three or four days at an inn for a truck to pass. I could move about freely for the simple reason that I represented no one and nothing and therefore was not considered a risk. I got by with my Persian at first, not to have deep conversations, of course, but I could get my point across and understand the basics.

Afghans love talking, asking questions, and demanding answers. During long journeys by truck or while waiting at inns or mosques, people always said to me, *"Ekhtelat kon!"* (Participate [in the conversation]!) And when I didn't say anything, they would nudge me again with *"Khafa shodi?"* (Are you pouting? Are you mad?)

I remember one day when I was hitchhiking on that first trip and barreling down the center of the road was this jeep going in the opposite direction. The driver stopped, I got in, and then he proceeded to take me away from the direction I wanted to go in! Inside the vehicle was a deputy who was doing the first tour of his district because for the first time there were to be free elections. He invited me to get in and explained that there wouldn't be another car for a long time and that the direction we were going in didn't matter—you had to get in the first vehicle that went by, no matter where it was going. It was a metaphor for understanding the march of history perhaps. I lost a day, but I got to be a part of a small local political event.

But eventually you had to return to France, right?

Yes. In all, I look back on it as a marvelously idyllic journey—today one might say I had my head in the clouds. It lasted nearly three months, except that once I had left Nuristan at the end of August and was back in Kabul, I fell into a sort of depression or decompression problem. I realized it was going to take me another month to get back to France, and I didn't know what to do. I had found a letter waiting for me in Kabul that told me I'd passed the written part of the Normale sup' entrance exam and gave me the date (that had already passed) for the oral portion—but really I had already said good-bye to all that. So since I wasn't in a hurry, I decided to take my time going back. I would return to Herat by taking the central route across the high plateaus. They were magnificent, but the feeling wasn't the same—the charm had evaporated. One week later, after seeing the Buddhas of Bamiyan and the lakes of Band-e Amir, I arrived in Chaghcharan. I was already exhausted, even though it would take several more days to reach Herat.

By chance there was an airfield. An innkeeper advised me to wait for the small cargo plane that passed once or twice a week. It was the first time I managed to hitch a ride on a plane. I waited for its arrival at the inn near the airfield. One day there was a *bozkachi* match—imagine soccer on horseback with a decapitated goat as the ball, and where all tactics are permitted and the playing field is undefined. The local police chief, a Pashtun in an elegant uniform, had set up his desk chair to the north of where the action would take place. He invited me to join him. I noticed that he didn't bat an eye when the riders were charging in our direction—Afghans have never had respect for uniforms.

At one moment someone cried out, "The plane!" On the chief's order, the policemen on horseback used belts to clear the playing field, now a runway again, and we all watched as a very modern little aircraft came in for its landing. For reasons that were mysterious to me, the American airline Pan Am had decided to create a regional service here. The plane had twenty seats and a European crew. Thanks to it, I took my first flight ever, lifting off from a dirt runway in central Afghanistan and flying at ten thousand feet until we landed in Herat. Ten years later, I would arrive in Kabul with the Soviet airline Aeroflot, and twenty-five years later with the German Luftwaffe, which was the logistical coordinator of the NATO forces at that time called ISAF (International Security and Assistance Force). The world is unpredictable.

Yes, but then you're still only in Herat . . .

True. But I had a lucky break there too. On the Iranian border where I was getting ready to go on the road with my thumb out, I happened upon the same Frenchman in a VW Bug who had picked me up three months earlier, when he was going to Nepal for his little high-altitude vacation. After a few days cooped up in a camp because of a cholera outbreak, we traversed Iran nonstop, then Turkey, then took the ferry from Trabzon to Istanbul, then crossed Bulgaria and Yugoslavia. For three days straight, I listened to this French wanderer retell me Algerian War stories about his service in a disciplinary battalion. And suddenly, Paris—as gray as ever! And then the international students' campus, Boulevard Jourdan, and an enormous empty feeling. What now?

PART II

FROM LOUIS-LE-GRAND TO
DREUX VIA AFGHANISTAN

Chapter 2

LOUIS-LE-GRAND, THE MAY 1968 REVOLUTION, AND LEARNING PERSIAN

Let's go back to the beginning. From 1967 to 1969, before that first big trip, you were enrolled in the preparatory classes at the Lycée Louis-le-Grand with the idea of getting into the École normale supérieure. What role did the revolutionary events of May 1968 play in your life and how did they influence your travel plans? What did May '68 mean for you?

IN THE BEGINNING, there was really no link among my fascination with traveling, my studies, and May '68. In the first-year preparatory class called *hypokhâgne*, all of us who were boarding at the school were by definition middle-class kids from the provinces. We didn't know a thing about Paris, whereas the day students in our same year were Parisians, and often from a worldly bourgeoisie connected to Paris social life. Bernard-Henri Lévy was two years ahead of me at Louis-le-Grand, for example, and I also knew Alexandre Adler, Christian Jambet, Guy Lardreau, and Olivier Rolin. Of course, we were also all first in our class in the high schools we came from. But when fifty high school stars from the provinces were lumped together in the same Parisian *prépa* program, none of us amounted to a hill of beans. The grades we got were really low because the whole system was geared to push at least half of us to drop out during the first year or, better yet, during the fall semester.

Except sometimes bad grades can trigger good ideas. After our first month of classes, I made a stupid bet (as all true bets are) with a classmate: the one who got the worst grade in "Thème Latin"—translating from French to Latin, our least favorite subject—would have to enroll for a year at Langues orientales (Institut national des langues et civilisations orientales, or INALCO) in a language course chosen by the other. It turned out my grade was 3/20 and his was 3.5/20 (passing was 10/20), so we then went to Langues o', as the school was called, to see the list of bizarre languages on offer, and he put his finger on Tzigane (Romany). So I took a night class in Tzigane for the year and ended up really enjoying it. I have never had occasion to speak Tzigane, which is more a collection of dialects than a unified language, but our professor, Georges Calvet, taught us the logic of the language by having us decrypt and analyze the recordings of personal narratives and stories he had made in camps in Hungary, Alsace, and Wales. It allowed us to do a bit of ethnology while traveling vicariously. Our class of about ten students was naturally a weird bunch. Most of them were half hippy, half egghead and crazy about India and its languages. But there was also Count François de Vaux de Foletier with his cane and signet ring. This archivist, a graduate of the École nationale des chartes and author of a thesis on Galiot de Genouillac (the French artillery commander at the Battle of Marignano in 1515, as everyone knows), was also the president of the 1901 association Friends of the Romany. At age seventy-something, he decided to learn the language of those he had befriended. This was part of the atmosphere at Langues o'—the bizarre and extraordinary became ordinary and familiar. After studying Romany, I met real live Romany in Turkey, and I realized that none of them spoke what I had been learning but instead Turkish like everyone else. After that I changed languages and enrolled in real Persian courses that led to a degree, while taking beginner level classes in Turkish, Chinese, and Arabic.

You enrolled at Louis-le-Grand in September 1967 and so May '68 explodes the following spring of your first year.

Correct. During the May revolution, I was a member of the Gauche prolétarienne (GP, Proletarian Left), whose original name was the

Marxist-Leninist Communist Youth Union. Contrary to popular thinking and some widely circulated images, that month was no party. I remember it as an enormously violent time, though most of it was more symbolic than physical violence. I was at first receptive to the revolutionary madness of the GP, but I quickly realized how, when young, one could become radicalized to an absurd degree under the spell of the group. I was not duped for long by the powerful group dynamic that was deployed in these little radical circles or by the schizophrenia mixed with a little paranoia that they exhibited in their relations with the real society—a cocktail that could very easily lead to terrorism. Those experiences would help me later to understand the logic of the young people joining al-Qaeda.

Terrorism, really? Isn't it a bit anachronistic to use that term in the context of May '68?

True, in May '68, no one is talking about terrorism yet. The magic word is *revolution*, which is sprinkled in everywhere from the image of the sympathetic and supposedly fun-loving Cubans to the mechanical Chinese Red Guards closed within their exalted obedience. In May '68 there were two dominant facets. One was political, inscribed within the long revolutionary history from 1789 to 1917 (all botched by betrayal, of course). What mattered in this way of thinking was sacrifice, fusion into a powerful mass, humiliating mockery of the individualism of the petit bourgeois, and ultimately death. The other facet was the antiauthoritarian model—anarchist and orgiastic—and its leading themes were transgression, *jouissance*, and self-realization. So one figure was the puritan, the other was the libertine. In the case of my May '68, I was more the first than the second. But I think the widening gap between these two dimensions led many young Maoists to have a fascination for violence, seduced by the idea of finally going into action, joining an armed struggle—until the point when this mad project goes suddenly haywire, like an unguided missile, and a few leaders (all students at Normale sup') glimpsed the landslide of their own minds. But many young people never recovered and disappeared.

What exactly did it mean to be a militant within the GP?

You had to get established in the factories, because the leading idea was that the working class would lead the revolution. We were encouraged to go to factories to prepare the workers' insurrection that would be ignited locally by the red base. The revolution was supposed to take hold and expand in waves beyond these red bases. I never went to work in a factory, but in June 1968 I spent ten days on a little island in the Seine with employees of a public construction company that was on strike. Another comrade and I accompanied the strikers who were standing firm (with hot tar and handmade catapults), waiting for an attack by the CRS (Compagnies républicaines de securité) riot police that never materialized. It was then that I realized rather quickly that these workers—as nice as could be and certainly ready to be violent—were hardly revolutionaries. They were striking for more money and there was a definite hierarchy among them: the bosses were French, just below them were the Spanish and Portuguese, and at the bottom were the "Arabs" and Africans. Everyone got along, but make no mistake—it was a white, working-class aristocracy affiliated with the CGT (Confédération générale du travail) that included Spanish and Portuguese collaborators who had only one thing in mind: saving up to build a house back in their native village. As for the Arabs and Africans, their goal was to earn money to send back to their families. No one was talking about revolution—they were just striking as a way to try and make a better living.

They were happy to have the company of us students, however. We gave them the chance to converse, a way to pass the time, to talk about something besides the routine topics of the labor union, perhaps to dream a little. It was sort of Hemingway or *Huckleberry Finn* for the factory set. We chatted while drinking mediocre red wine and passing around ham and butter sandwiches—not remaking the world, but telling personal stories, the funnier the better. They wanted to escape the moment, the strike they were stuck in, and the *taule*, or jail, as they referred to their building division, knowing that they would have to return to work there eventually, until retirement.

Is this an interpretation of the situation that came to you later?

No, mostly right then. I understood that there was no revolutionary class, and that there would be no revolution. That's why the speeches of the GP about the transformation of the working class into revolutionaries struck me early on as deluded incantations. Stuck with this May '68 atmosphere inside a very politicized lycée with people whom I otherwise admired exerting relentless pressure to become militant made me feel rather smothered inside. There were only two doors on offer—join a factory or get into the École normale—but both seemed to lead to the same thing, namely, enormous pressure and, it has to be said, the same guilty feelings about being the little bourgeois achiever who's not able to efface himself and join the masses. It was absolutely essential for me to escape this closed environment, and so I dreamed and later resolved to leave twelve months later at the end of *khâgne*, my second year.

The situation was very paradoxical because my *khâgne* classmates included many brilliant students but most of them were living an uncritical idolatry of Mao Zedong. I think, for example, of Christian Jambet or Olivier Rolin, who were our militant activist leaders. They taught us how we were to attack the offices of the temporary employment agency Manpower and the Hilton Hotel that we attacked during the visit of the newly elected US president Richard Nixon who came to Paris in February 1969 for the inaugural ceremony of a conference on Vietnam. When I think that I later slept in that same Hilton Hotel! I almost feel nostalgic. One day Jambet denounced me before the others in a meeting of our cell because instead of fighting the revolution I was doing my "little Persian," as one did one's "little Latin"—in other words, I was preparing for the oral portion of the exam competition when one would have to translate with no dictionary. Shortly before, I had been caught at midnight studying my Persian textbook. Our dormitory consisted of rows of boxes divided by thin wooden walls, each closed only by a curtain, and we were mostly left to manage by ourselves with little supervision. I was summoned to answer charges of demonstrating antirevolutionary tendencies. A few years later, Jambet had become *the* French specialist in Persian mysticism. I still have no idea where he learned the language, which he speaks better than I do. Perhaps at two in the morning in the same dormitory?

Were you politically active before 1968?

Not in the least! We had arrived from provincial departments outside Paris, and most of us were totally apolitical. In Paris we discovered the "Vietnam committees" that were made up of trained militants who had left the Communist Party and held influential places at Normale sup'. Many of the students who gravitated around Louis Althusser and formed the Gauche prolétarienne had gone through *prépa* at Louis-le-Grand, and so there was a strong continuity between the two schools. The hierarchy of the revolutionary organization reflected the university hierarchy in the sense that the leaders were the Normale sup' students, or *normaliens*, then came the second-year *prépa* students, or *khâgneux*, then the first-years, the *hypokhâgneux*, and finally regular high school students in their final year, called the *terminale*. Each person occupied a place in the hierarchy based on his diploma. One of the many paradoxes of the Proletarian Left was that it practiced meddlesome conviviality with factory workers while at the same time showing complete respect for the hierarchy of the Parisian university system.

One of the enemies was the Communist Party, wasn't it?

Many of those who were over twenty-five were former Communist Party members, and many of them were Jewish. They had become radicalized very young around the question of Algerian independence. In general, they broke with the Communist Party over this issue and became either Trotskyists or Maoists under the influence of the Chinese Cultural Revolution and its extreme radicalness that some found fascinating others repulsive. The Cultural Revolution allowed for a doubling of the Communist Party on its left wing while anchoring itself in a new International. At the same time, those who went in that direction had a complex of sorts with respect to the Resistance generation of World War II, the idea being that Resistance fighters were true heroes, and we, the present generation, should invent our own (belated, exaggerated, imaginary) resistance. People were constantly using metaphors of resistance including calling themselves the Nouvelle Résistance! There were no references to the Holocaust whatsoever; anti-Zionism was the official position, but the weight of the unspoken (the fact that many came from families that included victims of the Shoah) played an important role in the fracturing and then the collapse of the movement in 1973 with the twin events of the kidnapping of the Renault executive Robert Nogrette and the attacks against Israeli athletes at the Munich Olympic Games. If that rupture had not taken place, I believe the GP would have become a terrorist organization along the lines of the Italian Red Brigades.

Did the GP have a charismatic leader or someone who stood out in particular?

One of the key figures, a fascinating guy, was "Comrade Jean," Benny Lévy. He had enormous influence within the group, there's no doubt about it. Because he had no country, he was hiding in the attic at the École normale, probably sensing his future as a great leader as he prepared in his library hideout for the proper moment to seize power. Late at night, young students like me who were having doubts were summoned so that he could convince them of the legitimacy of the political line that had been decided at higher levels; that is, by him. The GP's political grip, or rather the grip of a certain culture of politics, was strong at Normale sup'. We were living in a military ambiance that was rather medieval. The school was perceived as a sort of fortified castle constantly watched and under siege by the police, who were just waiting for the right occasion to arrest the ringleaders (us ordinary comrades didn't count). Benny Lévy directed the GP from his lair, and his safety was protected by each of us taking turns as guards on the roof of the school so that we could look out for the arrival of the first police commandos. I remember being up there with a foghorn and a smoke bomb that I was supposed to use as soon as I saw police cars turning into the rue Gay-Lussac. The line between class warfare and playing at cowboys and Indians was fairly blurry. I liked that.

Was there no opposition?

There were a few right-wing militants who were turned off by this atmosphere at the lycée such as Michel Prigent, the future head of the Presses universitaires de France, and Pascal Gauchon, a brawler who was afraid of nothing and one of the future founders of the Far Right periodical *Défense de l'Occident*. The Catholics, or *talas*, as those who attended mass were known in our school jargon, mostly became fellow travelers of the Maoists out of masochism, I believe. Of course, there were students on the right who were more moderate, and relations with them were fairly good. They stayed immersed in their books and occasionally expressed their consternation at what was happening because it upset the smooth functioning of the *concours*. But indirectly we awakened a calling among some, such as with Guy Pervillé, who became a historian of contemporary Algeria out of exasperation with our Manichaean vision of the colonial wars. When, years later, he had amassed enough scholarly evidence to take apart our discourse of the time, he ended up affirming that we had arrived more or less at the same conclusions but by another path—the practice of revolutionary movements.

Chapter 3

LOUIS-LE-GRAND, NORMALE SUP',
AND THE CRISIS OF
THE HUMANITIES

Normale sup', on the rue d'Ulm, and Louis-le-Grand were all-male schools in 1968, weren't they?

YES. THEY HAD not yet become co-ed. Diversity was still a long way off. I discovered it only at twenty-one at the international students' residence on boulevard Jourdan. Before that, at Louis-le-Grand, where I was a boarding student during my *khâgne* year, we slept in large dormitories, each divided into forty small boxes with bars on the windows. Later, after 1968, we had taken over the lycée and did what we wanted, but we were all guys. The women were at Lycée Fénelon, and every ruse was used to meet them, from working on Latin translation together to being activists together. In first year, we lived in a kind of barracks, and on Saturday you had to check back in at 6 P.M. We only returned to see our parents during vacation and at the time the first vacation was at Christmas, not at Toussaint (All Saints' Day, November 1). It's important to remember that, at the time, for middle-class students from the provinces like me, train and bus travel was long and expensive (six hours to get to La Rochelle in my case), and many students, myself included, would hitchhike.

There was a big difference between the Parisian day students and the boarding students from outside Paris. The spirit of Louis-le-Grand in those days was superbly rendered by Michel Volkovitch in a bloglike diary that is still available today. Volkovitch spent four years at Louis-le-Grand, two more than usual, and ended up never passing the *concours* to get into Normale sup'. Those who redid a year had a special status. They weren't minors anymore and got to have a little room of their own at one end of the dormitory and more freedom. "Volko," as he was known, was always wearing slippers, a nightshirt, or bathrobe. In his diary, he changes the names of the professors, but the portraits are well done, enumerating the strengths and weaknesses of each one. Their limitations were aggravated by the questions and raucousness of the time, an unsettling situation that many professors did not see coming or deliberately ignored. My only quibble with Volko's account is when he claims that at Louis-le-Grand we ate well, whereas I found the food disgusting.

What were the relations like between students and teachers?

The atmosphere was quite tense, but among the students there was more a pervasive feeling of disenchantment than actual political activism. On an intellectual level, we mostly found our professors disappointing. Some of them were very reactionary; others, such as François Châtelet, a philosophy professor who taught me a lot, surfed on the leftist wave. One of the paradoxes of May '68 was that we, the students, all of us top of our class from high schools all over France, had high intellectual expectations. However, when we got settled into our *prépa* classes in Paris, we realized that half of our professors were no good and their courses didn't interest us—except those of Châtelet and René Scherer. This was a shock, because in principle our teachers were supposed to be like us, the cream of the crop, but instead of learning from the elite teaching faculty of France, we felt like we were being served a caricature of outdated humanism. We were still expected to learn poems by Victor Hugo by heart, for example. One day a classmate who was assigned to do a presentation on a Hugo poem[1] comes across this line, "Le pâtre promontoire au chapeau de nuées" (The promontory shepherd with cloudy cap), and claims that one can see in it a phallic symbol. Our French professor replied in an uptight way, made worse by a slight lisp, saying that "the problem with psychoanalysis was that it was always a bit obscene." You could sense the chasm that existed between our interest in psychoanalysis, linguistics, and Marxism on the one hand and

on the other traditional teaching methods that had become entirely scle-
rotic. In short, the level was dropping, but from the top down.

Today it's said that the classical education of yesteryear is on the way out
because Latin is disappearing. In our day, we had six hours of Latin per
week and almost as many class hours of Greek; but my impression was that
the traditional humanities were completely frozen and inert even though
this is what we were highly trained in and supposed to treasure. At the end
of *prépa*, we were capable of translating a Latin text without a dictionary,
all the while persuaded of the absurdity of such performances. For one part
of the *agrégation concours*, I was required to translate into Greek, and with
no dictionary, an extract from Plato's *Meno* and do a commentary. I got a
16/20; that is, an A, and I was proud of myself but also convinced of the
emptiness of the whole thing. This scholastic atmosphere further explains
my generation's fascination with Maoism—the antithesis of culture—
except that the students who were going down the road of the most radical
Maoism were also reading Jacques Lacan at night as well as keeping up
their knowledge of classical culture. All this raised for me a question that I
have never stopped asking: what is culture, and what is *a* culture or *the*
culture? I did all the proper credentialing, and yet I remain convinced that
the decline of the humanities is not due to some leftist plot or the result of
multiculturalism, but is instead the outcome of a deep internal crisis. It's
worth recalling that it was the Right under de Gaulle that started cutting
back on Latin in high schools with the famous Fouchet reforms of 1961;
and a later education minister under Giscard d'Estaing, René Haby, implemented the same middle school curriculum for all, or "*collège unique*." This
is why I find superficial Alain Finkielkraut's tragic rhetoric about French
schooling, since it selectively ignores some of the springs and gears of the
historical process that could be called the disappearance of the humanities.

**Is it accurate to say that the human sciences, which were all the
rage at that time, were not taught in middle school and high
school?**

Absolutely. We found (and stole) books on the human sciences at the Mas-
pero bookshop; we would go listen to Jacques Lacan at the École normale;

Michel Foucault was read but not taught; Jacques Derrida caught on a bit later. There were also specialists in Greece and Rome (Jean-Pierre Vernant, André Mandouze, Paul Veyne) who were transforming the study of antiquity but that we knew nothing about in *khâgne*, and important linguists such as Émile Benveniste and Algirdas Julien Grimas were also underappreciated. Several of these authors had been in the Resistance, some had been Marxists, and so in our eyes they were politically irreproachable, erudite, versed in the human sciences, but also openly opposed to the traditional practice of philosophy of which the emblematic figure at the time was Henri Bergson, a pillar of French philosophy, but a name that provoked smug snickering whenever it came up in class. Obviously, we were incredibly dogmatic—ours was the symmetrically inverted dogmatism of our professors—and it played itself out in a schizophrenic amalgamation between, on the one hand, a very solid classical training and a strong knowledge of psychoanalysis and of the formal rules of logic, and, on the other, elaborate apologies for "the people" according to the most hardened form of Maoism.

The cultural break that occurred then between the humanities and the human sciences coincided with the beginnings of mass education.

True, and we realized quite quickly that we would all start out at least as high school teachers. Personally, I didn't mind that, but you have to remember that Louis-le-Grand and Normale sup' were very elitist institutions, and some of my classmates had plans to become university professors as soon as they could and rise, if possible, to become distinguished philosophers and great writers, which in fact some of them later did. So after noticing that newly minted *agrégés* were being dispatched to high schools outside Amiens in the Somme or to Thionville in Moselle, as was the case for François George,[2] it was tempting to take the plunge: since one could only hope to attain middling status in the bourgeois mediocracy, why not join the revolutionary aristocracy!

Naturally, I am speaking here about reasoning and tendencies that were not shared by everyone. Factions and conflicts were the daily fare of the

Gauche prolétarienne. I remember attending the expulsion of Robert Linhart, convicted of "*déviationnisme*," from the GP's executive political committee in 1968. Benny Lévy was in charge of that purge, which involved people brandishing their copy of the Little Red Book and quoting Mao and Lacan—the Lacanian vocabulary being used to explain that the accused was a class traitor. Linhart had submitted a medical certificate signed by Lacan himself explaining that he suffered from *bouffées délirantes* (bouts of madness). But we were all mad. The battle of egos was strong and violent between figures like Benny Lévy and other ringleaders who were undeniably charismatic but also incredibly narcissistic and theatrical with their staging of Maoist political trials delivered in the idiom of Lacanian diagrams and discourse. I should add that when they changed—generally back to more traditional views or toward religion or toward a new form of humanism—they retained their former reflexes as exclusive and dogmatic authority figures. They claimed to be remaining coherent and true to their former selves across these turning points in their careers, and it's true that when it came to thinking and behaving dogmatically and authoritatively there was a high degree of consistency.

What about Jean-Paul Sartre, whom I think of since you mentioned Benny Lévy? Was Sartre already a guru-type figure back then and a prestigious protector of the GP and other leftist activities?

Sartre played no role whatsoever at that time. He arrived on the scene only after the GP's collapse in 1973. By then I had been out of the group for some time. I had left before it turned to armed radical activities in 1972 with the kidnapping of Robert Nogrette, the assistant director of personnel at Renault-Billancourt, that took place after the murder of Pierre Overney.[3]

Did you stay out of the internal power struggles?

Yes, because for one thing I was an ordinary foot soldier in all that, not a leader, and also, as I've explained, the whole atmosphere just made me feel like I was suffocating. The traditional humanist culture seemed to have run out of gas. The whole GP crowd had an oppressive, violent side to it that was far from the jubilatory May '68 scene of "make love not war" while taking it out on the cops (or so it seemed). We were living in an exclusively masculine environment that wasn't at all festive, while expecting an imminent uprising of the masses. The reaction provoked by the death of Gilles Tautin, for example, in June 1968, is a good example of the fantasies that were in circulation. It was a stupid death, drowning after jumping into the Seine as he was being chased by the CRS riot police. But the funeral had to be celebrated in militant fashion with a giant portrait and fists raised. There was an odd solemnity that probably translated our uneasiness because this was our first encounter with real death, and of a young person like ourselves who probably had not really chosen his fate.

Retrospectively, one has the impression it's a game or revolutionary scenario from the past that must absolutely be replayed.

The leaders acted as though the start of a civil war was unavoidable, but their behavior vacillated between the ridiculous and the tragic. Another incident gave me pause. Students known as *taupins* who were doing the science *prépas* and thought of themselves as anarchists had begun making their own bombs. The Maoist hierarchy decided that it wasn't right to allow some leftist elements to have a monopoly over the bombs; and so, because it somehow got around that at the age of twelve my parents had offered me—rather irresponsibly—a little junior chemist gift one year, I was ordered to join the bomb-making team. The containers of the bombs we had built out of potassium chloride and sugar were either small empty aspirin bottles made of aluminum or else cardboard boxes to keep them from blasting violently and killing someone since the aim was to just make noise with the first kind and smoke with the second. But some—I've always suspected it was students from Normale sup'—said that this wasn't revolutionary enough and that with the same recipe real bombs were to be made, without telling us. The containers were two sizes of empty pressurized gas bottles—a dozen were the classic blue camping-gas canisters the size of jam jars, and one bigger one was the size of a flowerpot—and these could kill people.

They were stored in our dormitory. One day, when the lycée was under attack by the Occident group,[4] one of us lost a hand while manipulating one of the bombs. I remember that we picked up, one by one, his ash-colored fingers, which had been blown to various corners of the courtyard.

The police had circled the building and were preparing to conduct a thorough search of the whole school. We had to get rid of the bombs. Only one boarding student owned a car, an old 2CV, and he quickly jumped a wall, with the plan of waiting for us near the Seine. Only two of us still had short hair and owned a blazer, tie, and gray trousers—I being one of them. So we dressed up to play model students, placed the bombs in a suitcase, went out into the street, and walked directly up to the mobile unit of gendarmes. (A word to the young: always choose gendarmes over the CRS riot police since the former will use their words before cuffing you.) We presented ourselves as good little provincial youngsters appalled by the "*gauchistes*" who had taken power and wishing only to return to the arms of mummy and daddy. The officer in charge opened a path and waved us through with a "good luck, you two" as he did so. And we would need good luck, for how were we going to get rid of a suitcase full of bombs without killing anybody? We couldn't just chuck the whole valise into a garbage bin. We decided we'd throw the bombs in the Seine so they'd sink. But where could we find an inconspicuous place along the Seine? We drove alongside the river for an hour without finding a good spot. Feeling desperate just after going by Gennevilliers, we stopped near a bridge. One of my classmates acted as lookout while I got out of the car with the suitcase. I was tossing the bombs one by one into the water when I heard a whistle. I lifted my head and saw a traffic cop who had been directing traffic on the bridge. He was staring with curiosity at us and our back and forth movements. I was about to calmly get back in the car when I noticed that the bombs had not sunk. Twelve little bombs all in a row were following behind the big bomb, all of them with their detonators in the air like a little tuft of feathers on their heads. It looked like a mother duck leading her twelve ducklings across the water dreaming of the open ocean.

But, meanwhile, as in fairy-tales, the hour of the *concours* was fast approaching, and the clock would soon strike midnight.

Correct. Revolution, even a botched one, was not the only thing on our minds. We were in *khâgne*, and the *concours* to get into Normale sup' was coming up. Everyone was supposed to be preparing for the *concours*, and was preparing for it, openly or silently, including those who were on the barricades. I remember one female comrade who was already enrolled at Normale sup' Sèvres. She was among those calling for a strike and a general refusal to take the *agrégation*, but, having registered for it discreetly, she took it and ended up passing. Always the same contradiction: we talked about revolution and about uniting with the working class; but the students in *khâgne* were cramming for the *concours* while the first-year *hypokhâgne* students were falling headlong into the revolutionary spirit. They didn't study anymore, and most had completely disappeared from school. I don't know what became of them—except Antoine de Gaudemar, who went into journalism and at one time was the editor-in-chief at *Libération*. There was a sort of wave of drifters in the generation that followed my year because they never managed to get their act together at university. And even among my contemporaries, we jumped on the train at the last minute by taking (not boycotting) and passing the Normale sup' entrance exams. In my case, my bag was ready, and the day after the written portion of the *concours*, I left for Afghanistan, in June 1969.

I learned later that I had done well on the written exams, and the oral portion would have been a mere formality if there had been cell phones back then—but, of course, there weren't. The summons was sent to an address I had given in Kabul, but I found out only at the end of August that I was eligible for the oral, which was to have taken place in late July. I also learned that my classmates Stéphane Douailler and Alexandre Adler had taken up a collection to get me back to Paris faster so I'd arrive in time for my oral exam. But even if I'd found out in time, I wouldn't have returned.

Chapter 4

ORIENTAL SCENTS

From Yemen to China

When you got back from that first trip to Afghanistan in September 1969, you decided to enroll at university instead of doing a third year at Louis-le-Grand, assuming you would have been accepted there.

MY FRIENDS HAD almost all gotten into Normale sup', my parents were furious with me and threatened to stop paying for my studies, and generally everyone considered me to be off my rocker. If I'd gone to join some guerilla rebellion in Latin America or been hired at a factory in Sochaux, people would have nodded knowingly. But Afghanistan!

The *prépa* program at Louis-le-Grand readmitted me, but I had no desire to return to the place I had just left. I felt the same way about the École normale, which to me was the headquarters of the GP and therefore not a place where I was ever going to be left alone. The extreme Right journal *Rivarol* (or perhaps it was *Minute*) even published a strange little article in which it was claimed that the GP was luring new recruits with hashish brought back from Afghanistan by one of its members.

So you went to university instead?

I fell into another world at the international student dormitory complex— la Cité universitaire international—where I was placed in a double room with a roommate majoring in science. He informed me that on the strength of having succeeded on the written part of the Normale sup' *concours*, I was eligible to pursue studies in a teacher training program, the Institut de préparation aux enseignements du second degré (IPES), which would give me a stipend for two years, at the end of which I would take another *concours*, the CAPES (*certificat d'aptitude au professorat de l'enseignement du second degré*), and if successful become a high school teacher. To make my decision, I did what I often do: I flipped a coin. It was September 29, and one had to enroll before the thirtieth; I showed up at the enrollment office on October 1. There I happened upon the sort of secretary that has become an endangered species: a large maternal figure who scolded me before letting me know that if I wanted she would let me complete the application form and backdate everything in a way that would bend the rules slightly, but no one would be the wiser. In sum, she offered to let me cheat, and that's what I did since the idea of becoming a high school professor, even if it were somewhere outside Paris, was not unattractive to me. So without further ado, I enrolled at the Sorbonne as a third-year *licence* student, having received credit for my two *prépa* years as was customary, and I was a fourth-year *maîtrise* student the following year.

In the *maîtrise* year, I had to choose a topic for a 100-page thesis. Popular topics at the time were things like "Marxism and Psychoanalysis," "The Formal Logic of the Class Struggle," "Being and Desire," and "Being and Existing in the Work of Nietzsche and Heidegger." I had no idea what to choose. One day a friend had mentioned Leibniz's fascination with China. It stuck in my head, and so in the fall of 1969 I decided to take Chinese in night classes at Paris 3, and I also got serious about learning Persian at Langues o'. Three years later, I got my diploma in Persian but not in Chinese. The Chinese teachers, who were French, certainly not Chinese, were Maoists and class time was not always well used. However, for my philosophy major I needed to choose a *mémoire de maîtrise* topic, so I proposed writing a thesis on "Leibniz and China." Everyone laughed at this idea, but I went to see Yvon Belaval, a famous Sorbonne professor and specialist in Leibniz, and he found the idea amusing and gave me his signature.

Looking back, Belaval was right to let you go forward with that idea. The topic turned out to be interesting with respect to China and useful for your future career path.

True. I hunted down everything Leibniz had written about China. For example, I came across his correspondence with Jesuits in China, and this led me to work on the issues surrounding conversion, acculturation, the relations between religion and culture, and universalism. Leibniz was himself a universalist and a leader of the Enlightenment who did not take account of cultural differences. He read the *Curious and Edifying Letters* written by Jesuits in China, sent by the Church fathers and later published in book form, and kept up a personal correspondence with Jesuits such as Father Joachim Bouvet, for example. He would ask questions, and Bouvet would respond in letters that Leibniz would receive two years later.

Leibniz was eager to receive the answers to his questions because his theory of language was based on the theory of an authentic Chinese grammar and not an imaginary grammar. He considered Chinese writing to be a rational script where the characters expressed concepts, not words. In any case, his study was incomplete without the grammar he was waiting to receive from his Jesuit correspondent. But it may have been that on account of a shipwreck—the reply never came. His correspondence with Italian Jesuits was conducted in French—a language Leibniz wrote and understood perfectly—and sometimes in Latin.

That was the only year of my life that I spent in libraries, including one in Dublin, looking for texts and sometimes translating them. I have very fond memories of that year, including receiving a top grade of *"très bien"* from Belaval for my thesis. This allowed me to go on to prepare the philosophy *agrégation concours* and the added bonus of receiving an offer from Vrin to publish my thesis. Forty years later, my book is still available in the main Vrin bookshop on the Place de la Sorbonne, and they sell about eight copies per year, which might spike to fifteen when Leibniz is among the required authors on the *agrégation* program in a given year. At that rate, their stock might be sold out by 2072, a century after its publication! What's funny is that among that whole generation of *prépa* students and *normaliens*,

I was the first to publish an academic text even though most everyone at the time had me pegged as an adventurer, not a bookworm.

Did you stop traveling?

No. It's true I studied philosophy, Chinese, and especially Persian during the school year, but I traveled every summer. In 1970 I went to Yemen, and during that trip another obsession began to take hold of me: guerilla warfare. I didn't want to be constantly doing the same trip over and over, meeting extraordinary people in magnificent settings. I needed to have some other motivation, some "content"; and that's when I got to know Jean-Pierre Viennot at the international students' Cité universitaire. He was a former student of Maxime Rodinson, a Trotskyist and Internationalist, and was associated with a movement that would soon gain a lot of attention around the notions of minority rights and a people's right to self-determination based on its language and culture. In other words, it was the emergence of the idea of multiculturalism, where the "people" were no longer the working class, but a cultural and linguistic ensemble—something that up until then had been more associated with thinking on the right. It's interesting to see how in the 1970s the Left takes over a series of themes that had formerly been talking points of the Right: the defense of particularisms (languages, locales, the *terroir—Gardarèm lo Larzac*), ecology with René Dumont, but also the concept of geostrategy with the journal *Hérodote* and the books of Gérard Chaliand, and military strategy and security around Alain Joxe, Pierre Dabezies, and General Henri Paris. The Maoists who were always fascinated by violence now finally had the tools to conceptualize it within a university discourse.

In France, the value of regionalism, which had traditionally been defended on the Right, became a cause of the Left, with various liberation fronts springing up in Brittany and the Occitan and Basque regions in the southwest. Attending a Breton *fest-noz* and treading the soil of the Larzac plateau became all-important. The cause of the Irish Republican Army was supported in spirit and in spirits with Irish music, Guinness, and whiskey (I confess to doing my part). Less ruddily celebrated, but sometimes present at a stray table during meetings, were Kurds, and even South Arabians and Baluchi people (three favorites of Viennot, who would be killed in Baluchistan in 1974). The cry of the day was "Long live the just fight of the ____ people!" (and you could fill in the blank with your personal favorite). Viennot spoke fluent Arabic. He had returned from Dhofar, a place I'd never heard of niched between Yemen and the Sultanate of Oman where a Marxist-Leninist guerilla movement was taking place (one that, he claimed, was particularly committed to women's liberation) and where people spoke a mysterious language (studied by Rodinson)—Modern South Arabic. (I wasn't nearly done with my encounters with mysterious languages, the first being my mother tongue, of course.) With two friends, Philippe Roger, the future director of the journal *Critique*, and Jean-Marie Bouissou, who would become the Japan specialist at CERI (Centre de recherches internationales), we decided to go there while pretending that our destination was Yemen.

So you encounter a guerilla group there?

No, but we do have a bizarre experience. France had no diplomatic relations with North Yemen, and with South Yemen relations were tense—France's official representative there being a mere chargé d'affaires. One had to obtain the proper visa in London, which naturally we did by hitch-hiking both ways. But hitch-hiking to Yemen was not possible. A single airline, the Brothers Air Services Co. (BASCO), offered weekly flights between Brussels and Aden with DC-6 propeller planes from the 1950s. Once in Aden, one had to deal with "revolutionary" Yemeni authorities to continue on to Dhofar. It was there that I fabricated my first false papers. We had asked an Algerian friend to compose for us a letter in Arabic that would declare us to be a delegation sent by UNEF (Union nationale des étudiants de France, France's leftist student union) to show the solidarity of the students of France with the democratic revolution of Yemen. We then got our letter signed by the president of UNEF, to whom we said it was a simple statement certifying that we were up to date with our union dues payments. He signed and added several rubber stamps. Ah, so important those stamps!

What we were attempting was obviously a bit dodgy, and I'm not sure the Yemeni officials actually believed our story. After a night in prison and a week of tramping tirelessly from ministry to ministry (I had gotten good at that), we obtained permission to travel to Dhofar thanks to a document signed, who knows why, by the Ministry of Health. Then comes a surprise turn of events: the French embassy invites us to their offices to drink champagne while nudging us to find out how we obtained our letter of transit and also offering us a nice pair of binoculars in case we happen to find ourselves in the vicinity of a mysterious Soviet naval base. We turned down the binoculars, but not the champagne.

Afterward, we left Aden for al-Mukalla with twenty or so other travelers, all seated on the roof of a tanker truck. There was no road, so the truck drove along the beach at low tide, since the wet sand was firm enough to support its weight. At high tide, we slept under the truck until the tide was low enough again. But we were stopped before arriving at the Dhofar border with no possibility of continuing on. It wasn't until ten years later that I discovered why: the British had sent Baluchi commandos serving under SAS officers to the tip of the border, and they had destroyed the convoy that preceded ours and were waiting to ambush the next one—that is, us. Later I met the commanding officer of that battalion, a certain Dennys Galway. In 1980 he was sent by British services to Peshawar to do the same thing as me—support the Mujahideen. We traded stories over drinks.

So in Yemen we were blocked from going on to Dhofar, but we got to visit Hadramaout and on the way passed through the village of Osama bin Laden's father. After returning to Aden, we traveled to North Yemen, where we had other adventures. I should underscore that we were the first French citizens to arrive by that route since the civil war, even though there were other French people living there. No sooner had we crossed the border than the radio announced France's diplomatic recognition of the Yemen Arab Republic. So even with our dusty backpacks, jeans, and twenty-year-old faces, people had taken us for the official French delegation!

We were very well received. We were taken to Sanaa, the capital, and government officials were surprised when we refused to stay at the hotel where they had reserved a room for us—we had no money to pay for it. Instead, we went to a sort of dormitory housing tribal combatants that had just come down from the mountain to test the armistice. Before going to sleep, each fighter placed his grenades and revolver under his pillow, his Kalashnikov at the foot of the bed and daggers at his side. In fact, the next day one of them stabbed a republican soldier in the street right in front of us because the soldier was supposedly looking at him funny. An aesthetic detail: Yemeni daggers hang conspicuously right over the crotch inside ornate silver sheaths. Two days later, an official appeared to escort us to our first meeting with the president of the republic. We had not dropped our pretense of being diplomats, while at the same time playing naïve and innocent. But the president immediately understood what was going on and found it all rather amusing. In fact, he was a good sport in fact and let us borrow his car for three days of tourism that allowed us to visit the palace, where a fallen imam was chewing his khat atop the highest tower, watching the sun set between the droplets of a water fountain. But his wives were no longer there.

But once again you had to return home.

Yes, but when we showed up at the BASCO counter to fly to Brussels, the prices had changed! The only inexpensive airline ticket we found was for Bombay, which would mean a slight detour via India, Pakistan, Afghanistan, Iran, et cetera. Since we only had about fifty dollars each and a bottle of whiskey, which we ended up selling for three times its price in India, we flew to Bombay and took third-class trains and buses from Bombay to Istanbul. So I was back on the hippy highway I knew well. In Istanbul a got swindled out of ten dollars that I was supposed to exchange, and my punishment was to hitchhike back alone—three people hitchhiking together being impossible. I had all of five dollars in my pocket. On the road leaving the city, a young fellow driving a French car pulled over. He told me he was a graduate of HEC (Hautes études commerciales, France's leading business school) and was returning from an internship at a Lebanese bank. What's more, he had decided to blow his pay by eating in restaurants every day, and if possible with a guest. Since those were his conditions for getting a ride, I accepted, and we had a pleasant journey back to France and even picked up Philippe and Jean-Marie along the way in Ljubljana and Trieste. All's well that ends well.

So no stay in Afghanistan that year?

No, just a quick drive-by between Pakistan and Iran. I returned the following year, in 1971, this time with Philippe Roger and a female friend, because I wanted to travel north of Nuristan toward the Pamirs. We trekked across on foot after once again negotiating to obtain the magic letter that allowed us to pass into the forbidden zone. This was trekking before that word and activity became popular. We had two opium-addicted Ishmaels for guides, a burro to carry our backpacks, and got altitude sickness at fourteen thousand feet, where the summer pastures and shepherds' huts of the Nuristani were located. After descending the pass of Diwana Baba (Crazy Grandfather), I arrived again in Barg-i Matal, with its little fortress, its goat thieves, the Kunar River, and the forests of pines and evergreen oaks.

Chapter 5

RETURN TO THE FOLD

So, back to your studies?

YES. IN PARIS I continued my studies to prepare for the *agrégation* in philosophy which I succeeded in passing in 1972, the same year I got my degree in Persian from Langues orientales.[1] I was twenty-two. Unlike a cohort of students in the class just below mine, I agreed to apply myself to passing the *agrégation*, even with the social demotion it would signify by being assigned to teach at a high school—and in the provinces to boot. Some of my classmates looked on that as such a waste. With the exception of a few brilliant individuals, such as Bernard-Henri Lévy or Alexandre Adler, who found other avenues to pursue their careers, most of my peers succeeded in getting out of high school teaching after a year or two and were reassigned to posts as *prépa* teachers in *khâgne* or *hypokhâgne*, or else they went abroad and came back later when they could land a position at a university. Then there were those, like Olivier and Jean Rolin, who established themselves, in their case by writing novels. There were also those who became leaders of missions or secretaries at the National Assembly or the Senate—a demanding but well-paid job that allows one to have several free months off every year. Still others, rather than teach high school, took the *concours* to enter the ENA (École nationale d'administration), France's national school of administration. I encountered some of them later at the Foreign Affairs Ministry. In sum, a new social space was emerging, more fluid and less of a pyramid, but probably based more on meeting so-and-so, networks, and opportunities, and always on the selective *grandes écoles* (France's elite power schools) as launch pad.

After the *agrégation*, you returned to Afghanistan.

No, not Afghanistan. I left this time with a car of my own, a used Renault 4L, and a girlfriend. In Belgrade we noticed that her passport had just expired, so I took out a nice pen and with one sure-handed gesture I changed a two into a three, which instantly gave her an extra year—1973 instead of 1972. We decided to do a big Middle Eastern tour: Iran, Iraq, Jordan—but we got off track in Iraq and ended up in Syria and then in Lebanon. After passing the written portion of the *agrégation*, I left Paris this time after, and not before, taking the oral exams; but I was again on the road when I finally learned from a letter waiting for me in Istanbul that I had succeeded and ranked fairly well at that. When I got back to Paris at the end of September and stopped in at the Cité universitaire, the concierge informed me that the Education Ministry was trying to locate me and had sent several official telegrams (brown instead of blue envelopes) requesting I appear immediately. While wondering what this summons was all about, I did what I was told and went directly to the ministry in my jeans. Today, of course, jeans can be worn on practically any occasion, but at the time it was not considered correct. At the reception desk, I was informed that the general inspector, Madame Dina Dreyfus, wanted to see me immediately.

She was an austere, distinguished woman dressed in black and wearing a pearl necklace. She had been the first wife of Claude Lévi-Strauss. She said to me in effect, "Sir, you deserted your post. You were to begin as teacher-in-training on September 1 in a class under your responsibility at the technical lycée in Puteaux. But as you did not present yourself at your assigned school, you may be barred from l'Éducation nationale and even from the entire civil service. I am calling the director of your school." And as soon as she had him on the line, she continued in the same vein: "Monsieur le proviseur, I have in my office the philosophy professor who did not show up to begin his teaching." The principal replied, "What philosophy professor?" Madame Dreyfus: "The one preassigned to the post?" The principal: "What post?" In fact, he had no idea that philosophy had been added to the curriculum in the last year at technical high schools! Dina Dreyfus hung up in a huff. "Philosophy doesn't exist!" she exclaimed. "Right then, so you'll be pardoned this time, but you start tomorrow."

And that's what I did, finding myself in front of a mixed class the very next day—a discovery for me. Several students were twenty years old, as is often the case in technical high schools, and I was only twenty-three myself. I spent one year at that school.

So now that you were a young professor, you had a salary and could live independently?

Yes, and it was during that year that I finally got to enjoy the festive side of May '68—in a commune. It was more than an apartment share but a real '68-style *communauté* of a dozen people sharing daily life and chores together. In truth, the festive side also came with its share of personality conflicts and a thousand little material problems, but it was an excellent experience. We lived in a large, beautiful, but hardly luxurious house in rue Montbauron in Versailles, not far from the château. We benefited from the real estate speculation going on at that time—owners either left their properties empty or rented to people like us.

Of course, the arrangement ended badly because we didn't cooperate when we were asked to leave. So they cut off the water, broke the locks, removed tiles from the roof and in November we were forced to leave—in the rain. I was able to find refuge in the home of my father's cousin, who lived with his daughters in the house of Monsignor Jean Calvet, their great uncle, who was the dean of the theology faculty of the Institut Catholique de Paris until 1945. Being the only male in the house, I was gently banished to Calvet's private chapel adjoining his library, where I was able to discover Catholic literature that had not been a part of my upbringing. Monsignor Calvet recounts in his memoirs (he died in 1965) that at the beginning of the twentieth century he was one of the first priests authorized by Church officials to pursue a degree in philosophy at a public university—up until then boycotted by the Church. He also mentions that the attending professor for his oral exam at Albi was none other than Jean Jaurès! He wore his soutane to the exam, and all went well it seems. However, fifty pages later, he relates in dispassionate factual language that his secretary, Raoul Villain, assassinated Jean Jaurès on July 31, 1914, "in a fit of madness." I can't help thinking that Monsignor Calvet never got over a slight ache of resentment that started with that secular oral exam in philosophy.

So that was the end of your commune experience?

No, I later had another similar living arrangement because I enjoyed it; but it again finished badly, this time because of an incident involving drugs. It was the early '70s, remember, and the start of hard drugs. Another factor was that I was assigned to Dreux, where a post had become vacant at the technical high school when my predecessor decided to become a sculptor. With two friends I set off to check out the town, and I liked it right away. The school was in the center, and the students were mostly women, which was not unpleasant at all, nor was the fact that it was a technical lycée. In truth, another motive for beginning this self-imposed exile in Dreux was the drug story I mentioned, which the investigative police at the Quai des Orfèvres also got wind of. The officer in charge of questioning us quickly understood that I had almost nothing to do with the matter, but he nevertheless advised me to make myself scarce. I decided to act on his suggestion by accepting this move to the countryside.

And so you settle in Dreux?

I rented a small house from a farmhand in Gironville, a village about ten miles from Dreux. It had no central heating and no telephone (it took two years to get a line installed at that time), but it did have a fireplace, a shower, and a vegetable garden. In short, I'd become the country mouse, just like I'd been told to do, and I soon became acquainted with three other farmhands and some Turkish immigrants who worked a neighboring farm, one of whom would play a decisive role in my life twenty years later. My two female friends whom I'd first gone to Dreux with became my roommates, and we spent a year there. I would go teach my classes at the technical lycée while they went off to the Paris flea markets in the winter and worked locally as additional farmhands in the summer.

Were you in touch with your parents during these years when you entered the working world?

I did not have close relations with my parents at that time. My father was pleased that I had a job, but he was still very upset that I had gone off to Afghanistan and screwed up my chance to get into the École normale. But we didn't break off all communication. I still have some letters—sent or received—that took three months to travel between Kabul and Paris. In fact, my journey from La Rochelle to Louis-le-Grand at age eighteen constituted my break with my family home. I traveled to Paris alone—it was too costly for my parents to make the journey with me. My things were shipped by train in a metal trunk weighing fifty-seven kilos and delivered directly to Louis-le-Grand. I was granted permission to take a taxi from Austerlitz station, which was the end of the line when one arrived from La Rochelle. I arrived on a Sunday afternoon at Louis-le-Grand with my boarding assignment number: 296. I climbed the stairs to the sleeping quarters—a vast, unattractive space with bars on the windows and forty beds, with no partition walls dividing them except for the box of the dorm master situated in the middle. There was another boarder present at the other end of the room. We walked toward each other, and he stuck out his hand and introduced himself: "____, first-place finisher in the general *concours* of translation into Latin." Soon afterward, I was able to move to the dorm of the upperclassmen, where each boarder had his own box.

Chapter 6

POSTCARDS AND AMERICAN POOL

What were you looking for exactly through this compulsion to travel?

IN THE BEGINNING, I bought into the culturalist illusion; I mean the idea that I was entering another world, another society that functioned according to a specific mentality and culture that was unique and exotic. It was a quest for the authentic—to see Afghanistan really and truly, with real nomads in real yurts, meet real tribes, and bring back authentic artefacts. In fact, since I had no money to buy real ones, I brought back plenty of fake stuff. I was a sucker for fake culture: smoking from a hookah in Istanbul above the Golden Horn, crossing a bit of desert on the back of a camel, or drinking burning hot tea while exchanging polite greetings with an elderly turbaned Bedouin. I had swallowed all the clichés from travel narratives and comic books. At bottom, as I've already said, my first trips to Afghanistan were the fulfillment of childhood dreams. But, obviously, at some point either the clichés don't retain their magic or by dint of repetition simply become boring. So it was when, after returning from Yemen, I organized a slide show one evening at the *Cité universitaire*, and my Algerian friend Amina, the one who had written our fake diplomatic mission letter, reacted negatively when she saw the clichés I was projecting on the white wall. "Hey, your show is completely racist!" she blurted out. "Veiled women, armed Bedouins, camels, sailboats—what's next canoes and crocodiles?" In fact, I would have loved canoes and crocodiles, was my first thought—but her remark made me think again. Looking over my slides, I realized she was right—I had been traveling in an imaginary Orient.

Two years later in 1973, arriving in Istanbul in my Renault 4L, I no longer wished to sip tea at the Café Pyerloti (written in Turkish on the sign) while watching the sun set on the Golden Horn. I changed neighborhoods, sat down on a bench, and waited. Two young Turks who were bored too came up and started conversing with me—in English. We went to a drive-in together and ate fried chicken and drank bottles of Coke inside my little car sandwiched between two Mercedes. Then we went to a local fair and rode bumper cars and later played some American pool at a youth club. As it turned out they were left-leaning and manifested easily and often their opposition to the Vietnam War. I also joined them in shouting, "Down with imperialism!" (in Turkish) on the shores of the Bosphorus when an American warship went by. Then they asked if I wanted to go to a bordello with them on Saturday night—something they did once a month, just as, most likely, the students in the generation before mine did in Paris in the 1950s. I had certainly left postcards behind. True life was beginning. It would become a constant preoccupation of my research: to avoid becoming a prisoner of cultural illusions and to better understand a society by paying attention to the banal.

The evolution of your interior thinking is clear enough, but concretely what did those changes amount to?

I found myself confronted in a very concrete way with a fundamental problem that has been the focus of an entire body of writing in the human sciences: What belongs to a universal framework that is common to all of humanity, and what belongs to a particular culture? Marxism was in this sense humanist insofar as, for it, class and not cultural background determines the individual; whereas anthropology, as antiracist and progressive as it may have thought of itself at the time (in the work of Lévi-Strauss, for example), privileged cultural specificities from the start. Put another way, the question is, How might one think of culture beyond cultures?

Everywhere I went, I encountered kindred spirits (young leftist students), and we had common reference points and identical conversations. People were talking about the same things everywhere: in Kabul, with a little group of Marxist-Leninists, we discussed the revolutionary capacities of rural inhabitants, comparing them to those in the working class; and the same discussion occurred in India and Yemen. It turned out I found myself in the same group I was familiar with—the circle of petit bourgeois intellectuals who felt like they no longer fit in and dreamed of revolution. Oddly enough, only literature and Marxism would be deployed in this universalist space—to discuss Mao or Hafiz in Tehran was to go beyond the culturalist boundaries and live in the universal.

In saying that, are you evoking the spirit of a particular time—the mutations of the young students over the 1960s and '70s—or are you making a general claim, namely, that particular cultures are always surpassed by a human universal? And that therefore one ought to be on one's guard against all culturalism?

At that time, I mostly bought into the paradigm of syncretism, which in reality remained always present in the culturalist vision; in other words, I thought Afghans, Turks, and others had integrated elements of Western philosophy and culture, and that we were all moving toward an intermingling of cultures, until after a while I realized that it was absurd to speak of syncretism—the real people on the ground don't live it that way. It's just their life, period. In fact, when I came across it much later, I didn't really like Edward Said's book devoted to a deconstruction of Orientalism—so sure of having the last word, while the native had only revolt.[1] But it's true that I too was stuck between, on the one hand, an abstract universalism (whether it was Marxism or later the social sciences) and, on the other, fake culture (by that I mean reduced to clichés—even if clichés, like caricature, may convey a certain truthiness). The Marxist universalism that totally ignored culture stood alongside phony Orientalism that sought out authentic culture, and the two put together didn't work at all. My question, at bottom, was that of modernity in action, or in the process of happening, and I was interpreting it with old schematic ways of thinking.

Finally, isn't it being on the ground, or an extended presence on the ground, that allows one to see though the mirages and false perceptions of another's culture?

Certainly, my local knowledge changed things considerably. My Persian got much better over time, and so eventually I was able to have "serious conversations" in Afghanistan—about the existence of God, the meaning of life, and so on. I even remember people telling me their dreams and asking me to interpret them. This was rather embarrassing since, as my professor in *khâgne* used to say, psychoanalysis is a little obscene, and so I'd fall back on some Jungian yarns.

I considered myself to be in the humanist tradition: man is the same everywhere, despite the difficulties of communicating together and even if, one-by-one, each person has an imperfect interpretation of another person's body language—the way of sitting, eating, talking, et cetera. These customs and habits probably had an influence on one's thinking, but how? For example, if I can jump ahead a bit, moments of war are always moments of truth. When you share that experience with Afghan mujahideen—when, for example, you find yourself together in an irrigation ditch in the middle of winter after just escaping an ambush—you begin by bursting out laughing. Then you chatter on, and you all feel very close to each other. And yet in my little notebook, I wrote down everything that had preceded the attack and how the military behavior of my companions remained, to my eyes, deeply marked by cultural attitudes (not sending a reconnaissance group and flipping suddenly from a carefree attitude to panic; whereas we, the two Westerners present, felt gradually more afraid, a slow increase of anxiousness that led us to anticipate the worst). But, of course, from their perspective, they were wondering the same thing about us and were noting to themselves what struck them as bizarre and exotic in our reactions. Later we were able to put our two sets of reactions side by side through conversation.

You spoke of a "culture beyond cultures," but is that simply humanism or does it suppose a mastery of particular cultures?

I think that taking an interest in specific cultures sometimes leads to overestimating the "cultural barrier," and to making intercommunication be dependent on mastery of the language and cultural codes such that at some point one may, to use McLuhan's terminology, confuse the message and the medium. One risks losing the content and falling into a fetishism of the code and neglecting the meaning. Later I will speak of the figure of the militant communist and the evangelical missionary for whom there is no problem of cultural codes because one is immediately at the heart of the truth of the other—his class status or his soul. But the relation to art also raises the problem of the necessity (or not) of access codes: are they necessary, or are they *post hoc* social constructions to "reserve" access to the corpus? I don't have the answer. But as often with me, I have a story to tell.

In 1969 I was taking first-year Chinese classes at the Censier campus in Paris, a night class, and I rediscovered the same odd mix of students as at Langues orientales. We were considered dilettantes, and we were given the most recently hired teaching assistant, Mlle Masako, who must have been about twenty-five years old. She was Taiwanese, had a Japanese father, and didn't speak a word of French. So you can imagine class time wasn't very productive, and by 10 P.M. we were usually worn out and chatting among ourselves. The course took place in a building that was already run-down, graffiti-covered, drafty, and poorly lit. There were about fifteen of us gathered at the bottom of a large amphitheater, and only the lights of the first row and one over the podium were turned on. One winter evening, Mlle Masako cracked up—but we didn't even notice at first. She was speaking with her lips pursed in a voice that even in Chinese sounded monotone (Chinese is a tonal language). She was vehemently reproaching us for our disrespect, but we didn't understand her language, her gestures, or her feelings. We didn't see her anger. Then she fell silent, stood up straight on the podium, took a deep breath, and started singing a capella:

Du meine Seele, du mein Herz
Du meine Wonn', O du mein Schmerz
Du meine Welt, in der ich lebe[2]

What we didn't know was that she was a singer, a specialist in Schumann's lieder, and gave Chinese lessons to pay for her studies.

She sang five or six songs one after another. When she stopped singing, we remained stone silent. Suddenly, a round of loud applause erupted behind our backs. We all swung around at once to see at the very top of the dimly lit and deserted amphitheater a line of women. It was the team of cleaning ladies, in fact, women whom one never sees usually because they arrive at night and leave again before the school day begins. They were all black African or Maghrebi women, and they had put down their brooms and mops and stood there standing behind the back row of seats, not daring to sit down. And with deep sincerity they applauded something beautiful.

Chapter 7

PROFESSOR AT DREUX

Leftist, Away from Paris, and Happy

So you continued traveling, but always in the summer because you had to carry out your assignment within France's civil service to teach in Dreux, fifty miles west of Paris, in the years "after the gunpowder," to use the expression of Hamon and Rotman.[1]

IT WAS THE 1970s under President Pompidou but especially marked by his successor, Valéry Giscard d'Estaing. It was a very interesting time. The Left was not officially in power but was culturally dominant. In Dreux, which was my home from 1973 to 2009, there existed a leftist counter-society, with city hall controlled by the Right; a lively secular association (*cercle laïque*); public debates; and peaceful demonstrations. We had teaching salaries that were fairly decent for our convivial and frugal way of life. We lived in subsidized housing, drove the iconic French people's cars—a Renault 4L or Citröen 2CV—preferred camping under the stars to three-star hotels, couscous and Chinese food over restaurants in the Michelin guide, and we had potluck parties among ourselves. By *we* I mean the milieu of professors, association activists, amateur intellectuals, nurses, apprentice union members (though the apparatchiks of the Communist Party and the CGT union didn't belong), and maybe a few additional cultivated types like a young doctor or lawyer before they started taking themselves too seriously.

That was also the time of the beginning of the second wave of immigration that had begun in the 1960s. I began to have *beurs* (slang for North Africans) in my *terminale* classes. At the time, of course, the unquestioned social model was assimilationist. There was no discussion of an overly "visible" Islam or of "Français musulmans" (Muslim-French); the term designated only the *harkis* then.[2] We spoke then of immigrants or Maghrebis, not of Muslims, or even Arabs. I was involved in local associations and the cultural life of the town. Most of us were not, or no longer, Marxists; but we were left-leaning in a way that was less and less politicized and more and more libertarian or rather *soixante-huitard*—the spirit of '68. Of course, we voted for the candidates on the left—no matter what—but with little or no involvement in party activism.

What were the political forces in Dreux?

We encountered Communist Party members at demonstrations and cultural events, or at the lycée, where some teachers were members. But in Dreux it was more primary school teachers who were likely to be Communists than middle school or high school teachers. We had cordial relations with militant activists, partly because some might have personal relations with them as well, but ideological discussions were often very tense. For us, they were Stalinists. We were neither Maoists nor Trotskyists anymore but, as I said, *gaucho*. In concrete terms, that meant we voted Socialist against the senator-mayor[3] of Dreux, Jean Cauchon, a very open and upstanding Christian-Democrat. We operated within the polarizing logic of the time where, grafted onto the division Left-Right, there was the divide between *laïcs* (secularists) and *cathos* (Catholics), something that has disappeared today, or rather morphed into *laïcité* (of the Left and the Right) versus Islam. Like in many cities in the West of France, social life was organized around two networks of socializing: the *cercle laïque* (secular circle) and the Catholic patronage network, in this case emanating from the Centre Saint-Jean. Each network had its vacation camps, sports clubs, cinema, dance and theater groups, and lecture series. There were hardly any mixed marriages. This system or division of the social space began to disappear after May '68, first with the departure of the leftist priests—I think several from Dreux got married in the years that followed—and then with the victory of the Socialists in 1981. But it's likely that May '68 itself did much to shake up the chasm between the "two Frances"—Catholic and *laïque*—and, of course, there was also the Second Vatican Council that revolutionized the Church, especially the clergy.

The National Front, which irrupted onto the political scene in 1983, arrived from outside when Jean-Pierre and Marie-France Stirbois settled in the outskirts of the city. Oddly enough, he never had an activist base in the city itself, only a very versatile voting block. On the other hand, the Gaullist RPR (Rassemblement pour la République) had a solid base but no leadership.

Was your family on the left?

No, my family was not a *famille de gauche*. No one at my house talked about politics. My mother absolutely refused and would not tell us how she voted. The truth is my parents' lives were deeply affected by the Second World War. My mother's father, Augustin Barraud, was the Protestant minister of La Rochelle during the war. He had stood up very courageously, notably during the siege of La Rochelle, one of the pockets along the Atlantic coast held by the Germans right up to the final surrender. For example, even though it was, strictly speaking, forbidden by the Germans, he presided over a special service in honor of the dead mayor, Léonce Vieljeux, himself Protestant, who had been shot by a Nazi firing squad. The funeral homily began with a verse from 2 Samuel 3:38: "Do you not know that a prince and a great man has fallen this day." My grandfather also provided fake baptism certificates, for Jews I suppose, since I don't see how anyone else would need one, and most likely organized escapes into the unoccupied zone in collaboration with the managers of the train station restaurant, who were also Protestants. He never wanted to talk about any of that—true to Matthew 6:3: "Do not let your left hand know what your right hand is doing." He and the local Catholic priest were often called on by the Germans to provide assistance to resisters before they were executed. My grandfather was a friend and colleague of Father Trocmé of Le Chambon-sur-Lignon—they had graduated the same year from the theological seminary at Montauban. He also played a role in the secret negotiations between the FFI (Forces françaises de l'intérieur) and the German garrison. The three main actors—Admiral Meyer for the FFI, Rear Admiral Schirlitz for the Kriegsmarine, and my grandfather—were all Protestants. The purge was very severe after the liberation of La Rochelle. It was the headquarters of the Sidos family, the founders, later on, of the extreme Right group L'Œuvre française—but my grandfather also visited with *collabos* in prison just as he had done with resisters. He placed his moral duty above all politics.

Returning to your teaching, you said you did not dislike teaching philosophy at the high school level, even at a technical lycée.

More than that, I adored it. For twenty-five years, I was pleased to teach philosophy in every type of lycée—technical, general, professional—and to students in every category from A to G. It was an atmosphere that favored close bonding, it should be said, for the simple reason that when I started I was twenty-three and the youngest students I had were seventeen and the oldest twenty. In short, we were very close in age, but our thinking was far apart, as though we were of different generations. My background was fairly puritan, and my schooling was all male. The students, on the other hand, were post–May '68 children, used to coeducation, and in the case of some, mostly girls, used to a sexual freedom that I had never experienced. Therefore, we lived in a sort of state of grace where codes and norms were tossed aside—at least until the emergence of a new set of normative codes arrived, this time from the Left, in the 1980s. The latter gave rise to a vast public debate—exemplified by the heavily mediatized accusations of pedophilia against Daniel Cohn-Bendit[4]—that one could say was a normative anachronism!

I had some sexual experiences with students in my early years. Thanks to a new law, in the *terminale* year of high school, most of the students were no longer minors. Some of them even lived at my house, with the permission of their parents, not as lovers but in the commune spirit that I felt nostalgic about. And since one doesn't change that easily, one June night in 1976, I left for Jerusalem in my 4L with one of my students, Chantal

Labato, a woman I would marry some years later and who would be my companion during the war years in Afghanistan.

May one say, as was often repeated later, that mores changed the law?

It's certain that during that odd time many young people were ahead of their parents, even those on the Left, when it came to liberal mores. Among the adults, there was a hypertheorization of desire—as though it were necessary for theory to make up for what was lacking in practice. Young people were more pragmatic. Paradoxically, I would say the brusque liberalization of mores took place over an underlying discourse of norms, even if it was to transgress those norms. In the following years one saw a return of the norm as normal—it's as though we never managed to make the words and things coincide.

In the world of philosophy teaching, fundamental questions about our role were raised by the group led by Jacques Derrida and others known as GREPH (Groupe de réflexion sur l'enseignement de la philosophie): Should philosophy classes be reserved for an elite, or should there be a people's philosophy taught to all? For my part, I believed, and still do, that philosophy can be taught perfectly well to students in track G, considered the weakest at the time, who were typically oriented toward future careers in stenography and other secretarial work. And I won my bet. I think, for example, that everyone can understand Descartes's *Metaphysical Meditations* or Plato's *Meno*, if one knows how to explain these texts without relying on background information.

Every year, of course, the age gap between me and the students widened—and the mentality gap too. That fusion and bonding of the first years disappeared little by little, and I wound up becoming an adult. I sensed I was repeating myself, and after five years I started looking to do something else, but I didn't know what.

You mentioned Giscard, the president at the time when the Right was in power and yet the Left dominated culturally.

We were living—by *we* I mean the somewhat heterogeneous group I described earlier—in a sort of bubble. True, the Left was not in power, but a moderate and modernizing Right was in power and mostly in sync with the new society that was being born: legalization of the birth control pill and abortion, legally adult at age eighteen, equality of spouses in the marriage, sexual liberalization, and the first manifestations of homosexuals coming out. One too often forgets Giscard's cultural modernizer side. The Left occupied the social and cultural space (and pushed for reforms), but without having political responsibilities—while of course dreaming of an electoral victory that would not come until 1981. Simultaneously the Left was distancing itself from the dark shadows of the Communist Party. We were increasingly receptive to the antitotalitarian critique of Marxism and Communism as articulated by Aleksandr Solzhenitsyn, the philosopher Claude Lefort, or in the pages of journals such as *Esprit* in which I started publishing at that time. The "Maos" had already heavily criticized Stalinism, and since we were against the Communist Party, we were also anti-Soviet. Even if we were on good terms with the local Communist activists (often our primary school colleagues), the mode of functioning of the Communist Party had become the butt of jokes, especially under General Secretary Georges Marchais—a person whose manner was already such a caricature that it was a small step to have him become a ridiculous puppet amusing television audiences. He was literally the Communist tragedy turned into farce.

A select few of my classmates from Louis-le-Grand, including Alexandre Adler, had joined the Communist Party on the idea that under their guiding influence an Italian-like mutation would take place that would marginalize the Socialist Party and actually form a government. At bottom, however, their allegiance was a career move—if one wanted to one day become a minister, one had to join the Communist Party! That's sort of my take on it, with no contempt for Adler intended, but that was the spirit of the time at the beginning of the '70s in relation to the Communist Party: a career choice, and not a revolt, on the part of a small but not miniscule portion of École normale students. Of course, they had made the wrong choice and would leave the party at the end of that decade. The right choice, for anyone who wanted to build a political career on the Left, was the Socialist Party. But it must be said that our activism in the 1970s was characterized by a rather likeable irresponsibility.

Did the very famous "new philosophers" of the day have an impact in Dreux?

The intellectual landscape was the same as in Paris, and we used to go there whenever we got the chance. We were very opposed to those known as the new philosophers, first for intellectual reasons: relating everything to a handful of big concepts (totalitarianism, democracy), filling their discourses with normative injunctions, distributing praise and blame with haughty smugness; and then because we spotted in their mediatized agitation a cynical communication strategy, a modern-day version of the Sophists' tactics denounced by Plato. Perhaps we had the intuition of an emergence into a new era: the end of the relatively homogeneous public space, even if it was the site of sometimes bloody polemics, where the legitimacy of the person speaking came from his or her status—that is, from his relation to the legitimate places of knowledge production, such as the university or important intellectual journals; and the beginning of a different mode of dogmatic and normative utterance where the legitimacy came largely from the media. Or, to be more precise, we were at the intersection of two new modes for producing discourses: on the one hand, networks, the "rhizomes" of Gilles Deleuze and Félix Guattari, where there is no longer a center, no longer any clear disciplinary boundaries, no ranked status, and where anyone can say anything because all speech is deemed valuable (in this sense an Internet culture preceded the actual Internet); and, on the other hand, a new center, which is no longer the state but a place from which the norm is pronounced. It's the beginning of a permanent face-off between acceptable and unacceptable utterances, something much more strict, and with much harsher terms of censorship and repression than with old-fashioned censorship. The latter would only cut, strike out, and blacken—not dictate what to say and think. Today, when it comes to racism, homosexuality, pedophilia, anti-Semitism, and the politically correct, we are in a double space: public speaking is carefully modulated and calibrated, while the Internet lets one say anything one likes. The recent Dieudonné affair is a good example of this double space.[5]

Can you say a bit more about the debate over philosophy?

In the 1970s, so many graduates who had studied philosophy found themselves teaching in secondary schools in the provinces, and this led to the development of an extensive questioning of what we were doing: What is a philosophy professor today? What philosophy should we be teaching? Patrice Vermeren, Stéphane Douailler, myself and some others created a journal with what we considered a beautiful title: *Le Doctrinal de sapience.* Our guiding thinkers were Miguel Abensour, who was an important figure for me; Alain Badiou; Claude Lefort; Étienne Balibar; and Jacques Rancière. Several of these "maîtres" had been close to Louis Althusser. But all of them were already teaching philosophy before 1968, and some of my friends had taken classes with them when they were *prépa* teachers or in the early years of their university careers. These philosophers had all gained in prestige thanks to their posts at the École normale or within universities, but they remained *populaires* in the political sense. They often held positions outside Paris (Abensour taught in Reims, for example) and retained something distinctly concrete—I don't dare say provincial—about them. There was then, in the middle of the '70s, the forceful return of some individuals from an older generation, notably Lefort and Castoriadis, the creators of Socialism or Barbarism in the 1950s, but who were neglected directly after 1968, when they became engaged in theorizing democracy and the antitotalitarian wave. The networks of debates and writings that we built up took inspiration from all these figures and from new journals (besides *Le Doctrinal de sapience*, there was *Les Révoltes logiques,* and *Libre,* under the leadership of Marcel Gauchet). And one mustn't forget Foucault, whose critique of prisons and power was widely read, and also Bourdieu, of course. Curiously (but it was something that occurred to me later), we experienced Bourdieu as a healthy breath of fresh air, whereas his philosophy was really quite suffocating, with its critique of the illusion of freedom.

We were interested in the margins of every genre. First marginal authors, little-known philosophers, utopian thinkers, polymaths, importers and popularizers, popular people's literatures such as the Bibliothèque bleue collection from the nineteenth century, the culture of ordinary people, or more exactly the relation of people to culture. For me, *La Nuit des prolétaires* (*Proletarian Nights*) by Jacques Rancière[6] has always been a model exploration of all these paths, and also all the writings of Michel de Certeau.[7] We dug our fingers into all the cracks and grooves of history and power relations and revealed new and different stories and logics. Thirty years later, one would see American universities elaborating their cultural studies and subaltern studies—work that was often little more than a slightly more pompous version of those earlier explorations. I wrote some short pieces in *Le Doctrinal de sapience* and later in *Esprit*—on Afghanistan, of course, but also about culture—that were a little harsh toward my colleagues.[8]

You mentioned Althusser as being the *maître* of your *Gauche prolétarienne* friends . . .

Personally, I was never all that attracted to Althusser, whose thinking I found very abstract and lacking in skin and bones or the least practical experience. I met him—an extremely pleasant fellow—but with him and some others, Normale sup' had a fishbowl dimension—discussing questions in minute detail, splitting hairs—that was quite the opposite of our outdoor activism, which blended nicely with forms of conviviality and sociability that suited me better. On another front, so to speak, there was the antipsychiatry movement, especially around the teachings of Deleuze and Guattari, with disseminating echoes of what was happening at the La Borde Clinic under the direction of Fernand Deligny.

What disappeared during those years was the learned intellectual, who got replaced by the expert. In the 1960s and '70s, all you had to do was publish an article in *Les Temps modernes* or *Esprit* to get the whole intellectual community talking about it. First, many new journals were founded then, even if some were ephemeral. I mentioned a few earlier, but there were many others. In addition, it should be remembered that the dissemination of the so-called new philosophers, who should not all be lumped together, as labels tend to do, was performed to a large extent by the audiovisual media of television and radio. The hegemony of grand intellectual publications was over. The changes in knowledge-power relations did not take place in our libertarian vision of emancipation and transparency but in this passage from the intellectual to the expert, including in the way of doing things by the "true intellectuals." I was stunned when in the early '70s I learned from Laurent Dispot that the CERFI (Centre d'études de recherche et de formation institutionnelles), a research group founded by Félix Guattari and others and that collaborated with Foucault, had just signed a research contract with the Ministère de l'équipement (Ministry of Infrastructure).

Why the mistrust?

For us, the state was more or less the enemy that could only instrumentalize all intellectual research to consolidate and extend its own power. This was our vision of things: the Giscardian state was on one side, and autonomous countersocieties (universities, neighborhoods, etc.) were on the other. The idea that one could collaborate positively with the state on matters of technical rationality to advance the management of societies was simply anathema. But it took place nevertheless right under our eyes, and the victory of the Socialists some years later lifted the last inhibitions while rendering the administrative norms more flexible, and this opened up a sort of royal road for the implementation of a new political economy of research dominated by consultancies and experts. These changes contributed to a breakdown of university hierarchies and permitted young researchers to obtain money and sometimes notoriety by contracting with a power structure to which they felt—sometimes mistakenly—close, even to the point of imagining having an influence over that power's decisions.

It would be worth reexamining, without polemical squabbling, the history of these reconfigurations of relations between power and knowledge that had always existed but were now changed. A new configuration gradually came into being that allowed one to leave the ivory tower of the thinker and the attic of the *anti*militant and instead get one's hands dirty—not through the traditional abstract militancy but through expertise. The point was to no longer work like the university professor who never left the library and instead be a knowledge technocrat of sorts working within a political technocracy. This arrangement raised new questions: should one, or must one, be politically neutral in one's university work? What political use could the state make of university work for its social policymaking and implementation? Or, as in the case of Pierre Bourdieu's work, what repercussions are there on various actors, such as the social workers in contact with those on the ground? What would be the political economy of these new intellectual practices?

So you're suggesting that as early as the 1970s a new relation between intellectuals and the state was emerging, and this would explain the eventual "silence of the intellectuals" that was deplored after the rise to power of the Left in 1981—the problem, really, was no longer about the presence or absence of intellectual support of the Left or of power in general.

True, this was the beginning of the attractiveness of think tanks, even if France never succeeded in mounting the equivalent of the Brookings Institution in Washington and even less of creating something like the Rand Corporation in California. The Popular Front, the Vichy regime, and 1950s France also recruited the aid of knowledge workers, but the few intellectuals who chose to become counselors to the prince, such as Alexandre Kojève (1902–1968), probably thought in Hegelian terms: to incarnate the spirit in the process of becoming conscious of itself. They identified not with the prince but with the state, and therefore with history and with reason. They thought they were making society rational. Thus, for them, their expertise operated within a metaphysical vision of history, not in a technical relation to a ministry. But after those three waves, my generation goes from service to the state to a technical collaboration with a governing team, and eventually to personal relations with specific politicians—dinners with the president become a symbol of influence. This changes things. It doesn't mean that there are no longer public intellectuals; it means that they are no longer in sync with the political leader—decision makers could care less about them. The president dines but he doesn't read.

In the modern consultancy arrangement, the power holder defines the demand. One sees it today with the invention from whole cloth of new disciplines in the human sciences: terrorism studies, security studies, and so forth. The university has some trouble conceptualizing and digesting these new relations between knowledge and power. And the intellectuals concerned have trouble defining a position that is neither a caricature nor shrouded in the unspoken. Once again, I feel very implicated in this debate because of my practice or, rather, practices.

Did you witness the rise of Doctors Without Borders and the humanitarian wave?

There was the episode of the Biafran War (1967–1970) that we followed closely, but I admit not having understood at the time that that famine inaugurated a new humanitarian challenge, precisely because it went from being an unfortunate consequence to being an event in itself. In short, the tragedy was not the outcome of a political event; it was the event. Nonetheless, this problem played an important role because in that type of war there is no longer on one side a "good" anti-imperialist camp and on the other "bad" colonialists. So this and other similar conflicts forced us to abandon our traditional ways of thinking that we had applied to Cuba or the Vietnam War. In fact, the irruption of humanitarianism as a practice (one would go do humanitarian work, just as earlier some joined guerilla forces, or earlier still people became missionaries) and as an ideology coincides with the same turning point that saw the arrival of the new philosophers: value judgments replace political analysis. There is always a good and a bad—like in leftist thinking—but this time the good is no longer that which goes in the direction of history—instead, it's what answers to a system of values. The following decades shape and sharpen this new moralism. Starting in the 1980s, one starts hearing about the right of interference and crimes against humanity, and of international tribunals with global jurisdiction. It gets its start with the political theater of Bertrand Russell, Sartre, and others when they judge the American foreign policy in Vietnam and culminates with the creation of the International Criminal

Court.[9] But the downside will be the abandonment of all political understanding of a conflict. For example, the Western intervention in Afghanistan in 2001 is sold as an action to liberate Afghan women from the burka. And as a result, the humanitarianism quickly ends up a failure, because, of course, women are not liberated by a military intervention—things are much more complicated. But such moves fit within a system or normative morality that ranges from sensitivity training or political correctness to the humanitarian right to intervene, as well as to the simultaneous rejection of women in veils and prostitution—those women are not allowed to speak for themselves because they are declared alienated and are then corralled within a normative discourse that brooks no criticism or pluralism.

Returning to the situation in Dreux, what were your impressions of the Left gaining power and of the municipal elections that preceded the presidential election?

At the end of the 1970s, the spirit of '68 was fading, and there was the rise of the Left and the hope that it would take power—with the idea that it would change everything via state control and massive nationalizations. In the municipal elections in Dreux in 1978, we all backed Françoise Gaspard to defeat the incumbent mayor Jean Cauchon. But when the Left came to power in the cities, the Socialist Party went about municipalizing everything. The cost—though it was not perceived immediately—was that a large swath of informal conviviality was siphoned off by the Socialists in power through the hiring of leftist activists into the local, regional, and national public service—activists who then started behaving (without always being aware of it) like perfect little technocrats, even apparatchiks. The informal spaces I evoked earlier began to wither, and there was no one from the younger generation willing to take the baton. In 2013 the Cercle Laïque de Dreux was led by the same team that was in place in the 1970s, in other words a handful of individuals who had always refused to be turned into an institution such as my friends Jean-Pierre Dubreuil and Louis Papillon. If renewal has happened, it's been elsewhere in offbeat places. For example, young Maghrebis in certain neighborhoods have become educators, but in a different context and sometimes with a religious dimension. These mutations would, of course, be interesting to study further.

So you were disappointed by the Left in power?

I saw several of my former high school students join the Socialist party, pass into the ranks of power, and become professional politicians. The Socialist Party will never recover from that—the thirst for promotions and social climbing, the faster the better. Money was not yet the principal motivator, but it would be soon. Most came back to earth fairly quickly, but at the time there was a strong spirit of revenge for the political defeat suffered in May 1968. There, in the spring of 1981, we held the power—finally! In small cities, everyone knows everyone else, and personal relations easily become clientelism and are obviously a key to political action. Some young party members became parliament aides, project leaders, city hall employees, and so on. They hitched their wagon to state power and entered the bureaucracy. Françoise Gaspard, for example, who would be much talked about later, when the National Front became her adversary in a face-off with national implications, thought (and she was not the only one) that culture should not remain in the camp of the opposition. Consequently, there occurred the municipal takeover of cultural life and a drying up of the civil society at the very moment that this term was becoming fashionable. At the time, I wrote an essay published by *Esprit* demonstrating how the *notabilisation* (upgrading) of the managers of the Socialist Party led inevitably to the desiccation of the civil society.[10] The piece led Françoise Gaspard to threaten the journal's director, Olivier Mongin, with a lawsuit for defamation—a fact that nicely confirmed the misguided direction that my piece was underlining. The oppositional Left had become the establishment Left and was single-mindedly preoccupied with managing the state. And by taking itself seriously, it ended up obsessed with seriousness.

Françoise Gaspard was, I think, an *énarque* (graduate of France's École nationale d'administration) and had passed the *agrégation* in history. How did she end up in Dreux?

She did not end up in Dreux. It's where she was from! She grew up in a well-to-do Dreux family of leftists and Freemasons. Therefore, she could live her arrival in power as revenge after a parenthesis among the Christian-Democrats. Except for the Communist Party, the Left in Dreux was never very far to the left, but it had a strong Masonic tradition, and this Freemasonry still exists in fact. As I said earlier, Dreux was a typical city in western France, divided between two networks of social life: the *laïque* (secular) and the *catho* (Catholic). But the border got blurred even though the incantatory discourse around *laïcité* remained strong, and the concept of *laïcité* gradually became shorthand for opposition to the rise of Islam.

Private education in Dreux was represented by the Lycée Saint-Pierre-Saint-Paul—pretty clearly in the Catholic camp—but the actual Catholic content became diluted and the school simply stood for *le privé* (the private) in opposition to the public schools that were allegedly going to hell because of violence and the *baisse de niveau* (lower level) of scholastic achievement. At the end of the 1990s, there was an effort mounted on the right to revive a "Cathosphere," where one wouldn't have to take off one's cross and put it in a pocket. A handful of parents with traditional tendencies, or worse, requested that the teaching at that school become once again truly Catholic, but demographically they were never able to find enough people to support such a revival.

So if I understand you correctly, on religious matters Dreux also played an important role in forming your thinking in this area that you would go on to develop later?

It would require examining stratifications older than the nineteenth century and the Third Republic to understand the religious sociology of the city. Dreux played an important role at the time of the religious wars. It was a center of the Ligue catholique. The city was besieged by Henry IV, and the population fought against the royal power. Later there was a complete change of paradigm that has been studied by Emmanuel Todd: the devout Île-de-France of 1600 turns atheist by 1800, and the decline of the Church in Dreux during the nineteenth and twentieth centuries is very striking. The decreasing number of priests after 1968 explains perhaps the absence of the Catholic Church in this city in the 1970s and '80s on the question of immigration, and the strong presence of the *cercle laïque* (secular circle). Today, Ali Bouharb, an assistant Muslim military chaplain, puts on his CV that he was trained by the Cercle Laïque de Dreux. The Catholic Church regained visibility starting in the 1990s, when the generation of Lustiger priests arrived.[11] But for twenty years, there was a Catholic chasm—only one full-time priest, no doubt doing his best, rather leftish, open to everyone, but with no significant influence either socially or religiously.

As for Protestantism, it was present in a village near Dreux, Marsauceaux, that had survived all the oppressive measures imposed by Catholics during the Wars of Religion and the Revocation of the Edict of Nantes; but the situation was a bit like with the Catholics: the church was empty until the arrival ten or so years ago of evangelicals who recruit largely among immigrants from Africa and the Antilles. What's bizarre is that there is also in this region a tradition of Protestant sects such as Seventh-day Adventists and Jehovah's Witnesses whose regional headquarters are in Dreux. There is also a Pentecostal church that predates this recent multiplication of churches. Today Dreux is also home to a center of Tabligh, a pietist Muslim movement. In truth, given its rich historical past and its gradual integration into the greater Parisian metropolitan area, the city was a good observation deck from which to view French society.

You alluded to the second wave of immigration in the 1960s. In the '80s, Dreux becomes a leading city for the implantation of the National Front, the high point being the tension resulting from the election in September 1983 of the Gaullist RPR candidate Jean Hieaux, who had allied with the National Front, beating out Françoise Gaspard by a few votes.

Dreux and the surrounding area specialized in emerging industries and subcontracting (furnaces, auto parts, televisions, electronics). There was a need for highly qualified technicians and an unspecialized array of ordinary workers. At the start of the 1960s, the immigration to Dreux was massively working class, especially of Moroccan origin, and already included many families. High-rise apartment buildings were built to house the families, something that was considered a luxury at the time. When I moved out of my little country house, I myself lived in one such subsidized housing development, or HLM (*habitation à loyer modéré*, or moderate rent housing). It was undeniably a step up, with central heating, a bathroom, and overall better hygiene. This new housing made possible the integration of the wave of immigrants of the 1970s that would see the population of Dreux go from twenty-one thousand inhabitants in 1962 to thirty-three thousand in 1976—an increase that would, of course, affect everything else. While there was a true mix of ethnicities in the 1970s, the high-rise buildings—in particular the Chamard towers—came to be occupied exclusively by immigrants. Like everywhere else, the middle-class "white" population left them and then left the neighborhood. The buildings and accompanying services became run-down, juvenile delinquency increased, and feelings of insecurity increased as well. One of my friends, who ran a bar in the city center, was predicting already in the late '70s that the Left would get knocked out over the question of insecurity. Dreux encapsulated the entire history that's now become the standard tale of immigration since the 1960s. Whereas the 1960s generation was strongly integrated, the following generation would find itself in serious difficulty and react with an array of strategies. But starting in 2000, one could witness a new phase beginning: a bourgeoisie of immigrant origin moves into the city center. Doctors, journalists, lawyers, engineers, and professors with a certain mixture of backgrounds and lifestyles begin to take center stage. The weddings announced in the newspaper testify to a stable number of mixed marriages (around 20 percent), but unlike in the 1980s, young women of Maghrebi origin are marrying native Frenchmen.

Chapter 8

OUT OF SCHOOL

How did the experience of a May '68 lifestyle, even if somewhat displaced, tie in with your thinking about questions of culture?

WHAT I TOOK from that experience was more a reflection on the norm than about culture. Or more precisely, the relation that culture maintains with norms and codes. Later I saw clearly why culturalism had attracted me in the early years of my traveling: for a culturalist, alterity is all the more fascinating as it seems comprehensible—more decodable at any rate than other alterities such as *the woman*, for example. At that time, I'd also decided to undergo psychoanalysis. I remember that my analyst was surprised by my desire to go to Afghanistan. He asked me what I was going to do there. I replied, "Over there, codes can be described in an explicit way. One learns a culture like one learns a grammar. I eventually know what the gestures and body language mean, whereas in France I don't know them and I can't figure them out. Everything is random here." It should be recalled that at the time it was a period when everything seemed possible, but as a result that liberty blurred or destroyed the codes. Even though they existed of course—no one could do just anything.

Sexual freedom, for example, did not open up a general permissiveness as much as simply the possibility or not of sleeping together—and thus introduced an uncertainty. Today this liberty exists, but in code, or with reinvented codes that did not exist in the 1970s. Naturally, I don't rule out that other uncertainties cropped up, like the less clear blurrier role of fathers, for example. Back then it was freedom—or its limits—that had to be endlessly reinvented. In our community, as in many others, the question arose about whether it was necessary to establish a set of rules about doing the dishes, and so forth. Not far from us there was a community of Trotskyists whom we loved to mock because in their entryway they had hung a sign that read, "Comrade, remember your chores!" We had always refused this type of law. Except, look what happened—our community fell apart! The lack of a norm and rules made it so that we were forced to constantly invent new forms of relations. This required interminable discussions—we'd spend the whole night talking and bickering.

Did you feel the demand for recognition from homosexuals?

It was the time when homosexuality was just beginning to be publicly affirmed. But this recognition merely enshrined homosexuals within the category of human beings like any other, by including their sexuality within the norm of all sexuality (a banalization that would end logically with the recognition of marriage for all). What struck me more was the emergence of a diffuse tolerance—in the name of the desiring nature of the child—of what would later be called "pedophilia." It should be remembered that, at the time, few people saw clearly what the problem was, even among those opposed to open and predatory pedophilia practiced by adults with authority over children (teachers, priests, or other educators). There were communities with children and although, of course, their mothers did not allow them to become targets of predatory pedophilia; they did tolerate a precocious sexualization of their behavior, their nudity in the house, the absolute refusal of all discipline, having sex in front of the children, etc. There was a constant call to lift prohibitions and *taboos*—a word frequently repeated with a sharply negative connotation of course. One was supposed to refuse the law that orchestrates sexual repression by maintaining an atmosphere of peace and love underwritten by the theories of Wilhelm Reich that everyone knew chapter and verse. In the letters to the editor of *Libération*, people would wax poetic about the "desiring child." Later, the childhood stories of the children of '68 recalling such goings on would appear—but to denounce them. I have in mind, for example, the fine account given by Virginie Linhart.[1] What people didn't see was that this libertarian atmosphere could be a favorable terrain for real pedophiles, all the more since the line between predators and adepts of free love was not exactly clear to say the least. What was overlooked was the reaction these children would have as grownups. People had adopted a very idealistic vision, a transparent vision, of sexuality, but one that corresponded more with our fantasies than with any reality. I would add that there's probably a link between the imaginary construction of a liberated sexuality and a certain puritan (or simply conservative) reminiscence that is quite strong today.

What's your conclusion then?

It led me to think about the speed with which a paradigm (an ensemble of representations and norms about a specific object, in this case sexuality) can completely change within a single short generation. Many things associated with the post–May '68 era are today incomprehensible and come in for moral judgments—as does the machismo of the 1950s or the racism of the 1930s. How can one speak of cultural continuity when one is confronted with such wide qualitative leaps? How can one think of it in terms of an immutable or immobile ethics? Ought one to revert to an ideology of progress, even though that ideology has been seriously put into question by all the crimes committed in the name of that alleged progress? One sees the problem each time some old story resurfaces, like, for example, the one that was talked about in the spring of 2014: an assassination that happened forty years earlier in which the IRA leader Gerry Adams was supposedly involved, the same Gerry Adams who later plays an important role in negotiating the peace accords in Northern Ireland. The question that always arises with crimes against humanity is that of transitional justice, which oscillates between the very Christian notion of pardon in exchange for a confession, and the legal notion of imposing—or not—a statute of limitations, with, in between, the pathetic but sincere and for me very significant declaration, "I didn't know (that X was wrong or X was happening), but you cannot understand what I am saying because you cannot understand those times." How does one conceive of an ethics without moralism, and how does one think in political terms about that which derives from ethics?

And the teaching of philosophy in all this?

By the end of the 1970s, I had the feeling that I'd just about covered it. Inevitably, the teaching had become rather repetitive after a number of years. I'd had my fill of the communitarian and convivial leftist bubble. It burst, as I said, with the arrival in power of the Left, first with the municipal elections and then in 1981 with Mitterrand's arrival at the Élysée Palace. It was necessary to finally get out of the cozy, low-rent utopia I'd built for myself and confront the reality of power. Each of us remembers how very quickly the constraints of the real were decisive.

Were you a conformist professor with no past?

I believe I was generally considered a good professor who respected the philosophy curriculum as it was laid out and who assiduously prepared high school students for their baccalaureate exams. I was certainly thought of as something of an anarchist, including in school matters. I sometimes held class in cafés, I would take my students to Paris, and I did things that rattled the administration. But I was also untouchable because at that technical lycée I was the youngest professor and the only one to have the *agrégation*. My relations with the principal were, it's true, somewhat ambivalent. She herself was a nonconformist with a strong personality, and she had a slightly maternal attitude toward me. The tension between my generation of teachers and the administration centered around the inspection process. One can be a responsible teacher who respects the exigencies of l'Éducation nationale (following the curriculum, prepare the *bac*, etc.) and yet balk at some of the bureaucratic rituals. How and how far may one contest those rituals? At the time, the battle zone was inspections. Ought one to refuse to have one's teaching inspected? If so, was one going to cease all evaluation of the professors? What about grading the students? I always hated assigning grades.

It so happens that Monsieur Lechat, my first inspector, an old man near retirement age, told me the exact day and hour he would be coming a full week in advance, and everything went fine. He practically treated me like his colleague. How could one resist such amiable treatment? But my anti-inspection cohort criticized me for allowing myself to be taken in! The next time around my inspector was none other than Madame Dina Dreyfus, whom I spoke of earlier and whom I considered to be a grand personage that everyone respected. She also told me ahead of time when she would be coming. When she entered my classroom, she addressed the students, telling them that "your professor and I are peers."[2] It was priceless! This second inspection also went very well.

My third inspection happened the year after my first contact with the mujahideen, which took place in July and August of 1980. A rather unlikeable character arrived late without greeting anyone and sat down in the front row without a word. Therefore, I asked him to leave. He rose, blank-faced, and went immediately to the principal's office to send off a telegram demanding my immediate dismissal. I was immediately informed of this by the principal and in turn prepared my counterattack: a letter to the head of the inspection bureau, Jacques Muglioni, in which I told him that I had just ejected Monsieur l'Inspecteur so-and-so from my classroom and explained why I had done so. I went on about how I had been a philosophy professor for seven years; that a good philosopher must never identify with his social role, nor take himself too seriously, which is what this particular inspector had done; and therefore, he was, in my eyes, not qualified to hold the title of philosopher and even less qualified to judge a philosophy class. I rounded this out with a little more blah-blah and a quote from Montaigne, and, hop, I mailed the letter off.

I was immediately summoned to Paris by Monsieur Muglioni, who said to me with some discomfort, "It's rather a sticky wicket, your affair, but we're going to try and work something out." I learned later that the inspector who had entered my classroom was a hard-ass member of the Gaullist RPR, someone imposed by L'Éducation nationale to restore order to the inspection system, but who was detested by his colleagues, and notably by Monsieur Muglioni, who entirely shared my dim view of this person's philosophical competency. In short, my revolt suited his purposes. He explained to me that he was going to annul his colleague's report but that I had to be evaluated, and then he proposed to come inspect me himself on such and such day and time, promising to arrive on time and sit quietly at the back of the room. Obviously, his visit went very well, so well in fact that he invited me back to his office and offered me a job teaching a *prépa* class of *hypophâgne* in a school worthy of my talents. I declined the offer, explaining that I was leaving for Afghanistan.

"But it's just a holiday, right?"

"No, I'm taking a leave of absence and plan on staying in the country for some time, I don't know how long."

"But you're not going to do like Lévi-Strauss? Not ethnology? You, a philosopher!" and he raised his arms to the ceiling as he said this.

He promised to hold my place for me and said upon my return that he would reclassify me within the corps of "*professeurs de lettres supérieures.*"

But I never returned.

PART III

THE AFGHAN DECADE

Chapter 9

ONCE AGAIN, AND FOR REAL, AFGHANISTAN

In 1980 you decide to return to Afghanistan.

AS I'VE SAID, for some time I had been wanting to make a change in my life without really knowing what direction to take. I had begun a doctoral dissertation under the direction of Miguel Abensour on the notion of culture because this was an important problem for me: popular culture, literary culture, exotic culture, the culture of a group, era, or generation. Everywhere I turned, I bumped up against the idea that there were certain keys to understanding, a code, a hidden truth, or simply some meaning, and I couldn't find it. I saw life as an enigma. At thirteen I had seen the Orson Welles adaptation of Kafka's *The Trial*. As a prologue, there was a short film that retold a chapter from the book, "Before the Law." A man waits his whole life for a porter to open a door, the door to the law, but he refuses, and when the man is about to die, the porter says to him, "No one else but you could ever have obtained admittance. No one else could enter this door. This door was intended only for you. And now I am going to close it." I wanted to force my way through that door.

When the Russians invaded Afghanistan on December 27, 1979, I understood that the door had opened a bit and that my life was going to change. I knew right away that this invasion was a major event. No matter what their intentions or politics were, Western countries would need to pay attention and understand the situation. However, few people knew the country, and few of those who were already working there would stay there. Experts were needed and I would be one of them.

What's more, now I could finally join a true guerilla movement and therefore pass to the other side of the curtain—away from exoticism, Orientalism, culture, and appearances and come in contact with "real life." I had the odd idea that war was the real life because artifice was no longer possible—no decorum, no pretending (of course, I was mistaken), and I thought I was going to be at the heart of the true society. I thought it was my moment of truth, and that it happens only once.

A rather odd way of thinking, no?

Yes, odd it was, I admit, but war seemed to me to be the way to penetrate into a society that was refusing my admittance. The ten previous years, which included the failure in Dhofar and my repeated trips to Afghanistan, where I always had the impression I was missing something, now seemed like a prelude, a sort of dress rehearsal in preparation for the real opening act. There in Afghanistan, I felt, was an opportunity to find the entrance. I knew that I was changing lives, that I would never again be a high school teacher. But I was also not at all thinking that this path would lead me to one day get into higher education and that I would become a university professor. On the other hand, I was completely convinced that I was going to write *the* book about the war in Afghanistan—because, of course, I intended to write a book. I spoke the language (my Persian had become fairly decent), I already knew the country quite well from all the trips I had made there, and I had accumulated empirical knowledge about the society. I immersed myself in the scholarly literature, I pored over every relevant item in libraries and other document collections—I even took courses in Pashto. As for the future, I said to myself, whatever will be, will be. Perhaps I'd be an arms merchant like Rimbaud or a spy like John le Carré, or a researcher, consultant, novelist, diplomat, warlord, or prisoner—anything was possible. The only thing that I did not envision was dying. And about that I guess my premonition was correct, even if looking back I wonder how I survived when so many others died.

So I made my first real trip in the summer of 1980 and returned in time for the start of school; but my head was elsewhere, and in June 1981 I applied for a sabbatical and left for Peshawar.

Was it an unpaid leave of absence?

Yes, and so there remained the problem of how to pay for what I planned on doing (I had saved enough to last one year) and where my entrance into Afghanistan would be. I could go to Kabul with a visa, but once there, how would I join the other side? Was I going to jump off a bus and walk straight until I bumped into a guerilla unit? Not easy. It made more sense to go to Pakistan, to Peshawar, and make contact with representatives of the resistance. But to tell them what? What reason would they have to take me into their organization? In fact, they didn't give a damn and were willing to take in anybody, but I didn't know that. As usual, I wanted to have a reason for being where I was. There were only two possible gateways: humanitarian work or the military—in this case, arms merchant. On the humanitarian side, my old circle of acquaintances from Louis-le-Grand played a role. Bernard-Henri Lévy had just founded a hunger relief organization, AICF (Action internationale contre la faim), in collaboration with Françoise Giroud, Jacques Attali, Guy Sorman, and others. Afghanistan was a terrain to further their antitotalitarian combat. Moreover, Bernard-Henri Lévy had put forward a lucid diagnosis: Afghanistan was going to be a long-term problem, and the presence of the Soviet Union made this a just cause, all the more so since the guerilla movement itself was not Marxist.

He had imagined organizing a caravan of camels and horses that would travel to Afghanistan with food and medical supplies—no doubt with the idea of making a great film out of the whole thing. The leader was supposed to be Jean-Christophe Victor, an ethnologist who spoke Persian and had lived in Kabul. Meanwhile, the AICF had rented advertising space in the Paris metro for the last week in August—a time when rates were cheaper. The poster announced that the maiden voyage of the humanitarian caravan was ready—except there was no caravan. For complicated reasons, nothing had been concretely settled in Peshawar. The announcement of the event preceded the event—a foul-up that was quite typical of the times. And yet, a caravan needed to pass through before August 15.

Bernard-Henri Lévy contacted his former codisciple, Philippe Roger, who then got in touch with me, and we went together to the headquarters of the AICF. We were given a sack of $10,000 in small bills and were promised a wire transfer at a later date along with our plane tickets. There were only two hotels in Peshawar, we were told, by which was meant hotels that were up to Parisian standards, for I knew that in fact there were hundreds of hotels—but it was explained to us that humanitarian organizations were not supposed to fall into roughing it in misery. Nevertheless, the Hotel InterContinental was too luxurious for our brand image, and so we were to stay at the Dean's Hotel that had become the mythical waystation of adventurers of every stripe who were looking to pass to the other side, all the while guzzling the beer and gin that was reserved for foreign non-Muslims. So we arrived in Peshawar in early July with our boots, jeans, and dollars and the aim of mounting a caravan in only two weeks. And we managed to do it. The caravan, which transported shoes and clothes and included more journalists and humanitarian workers than Afghans, finally passed to the other side with only a little doctoring of the dates—it was announced that it had happened before we had even set off. I therefore had to nudge the real date to something more compatible with the announcement that had been made, but also in time to launch the advertising campaign. The grand humanitarian adventure, from the country hospital to TV talk shows, was launched.

But in the photographs that accompanied the advertising campaign, one could not see a single image of a caravan that had actually traversed the border—mine. The photos had all been taken elsewhere, far from the front, in Pakistan. When I expressed some surprise at this, the person in charge replied, "Come on, take a good look at the film footage you brought back! It looks like a jaunt in the Swiss Alps. There's no war, no suffering, no desert. Think of the public we're trying to reach! We need to show emotion, willpower, and hardship, my friend. Look at the final shot in your video!" And as he said this, he threw onto the table, with a certain contempt, a photo of a splendid edelweiss in bloom on the slope of one of the

Pamir Mountains. He would probably have preferred a palm tree, or better yet a cactus with a vulture on top of it looking wide-eyed and content.

For me, the essential thing had finally been attained: I was in the loop. I knew where to present myself in Peshawar, and I had passed my initiation test. And as fate would have it, if I can say that, this expedition took place in Nuristan, thus taking up again one of the multiple incomplete stories that endlessly return in my life.

But you returned to France after this expedition.

Yes, I spent another year at the lycée in Dreux, but my decision to ship out for good had been made. I wanted to return to Afghanistan no matter what. But although the humanitarian groups were willing to pay my traveling expenses, they had no intention of giving me a steady salary. It was then that I was contacted by a Belgian arms merchant, a Colonel Patou, perhaps his real name, which means "blanket" in Persian. He informed me that he was an arms merchant, which was fortuitous since the Americans had decided to arm the Afghan resistance. Except the CIA did not want to go in itself—they thought it was a lost cause, that the terrain was too poorly known, and so forth, and so they preferred to subcontract with private actors, an obsession that would be the source of no end of high costs for the American taxpayer in particular, and in general for all the people involved. Patou tells me he knows nothing about Afghanistan, is getting on in years, and is more than willing to hire me. I would be living in Peshawar and be responsible for dispatching arms to Afghanistan. My pay would be $5,000 per month plus life insurance. Of course, the arms would be delivered at no charge to the Afghan resistance fighters, and I was supposed to sort out the good ones from the fanatics, fakes, hotheads, and corrupt. It was a position with "managerial responsibilities," as they say in the want ads.

It was an ideal arrangement for me, but in the end the project collapsed because the CIA finally decided not to let clowns like this Belgian and me do the work and they did it themselves. And it has to be said that they were true professionals—I mean they were bureaucrats, not cowboys, even if I'm not sure they made the right choices. I didn't give up trying, however, since I needed to find some source of support for the periods between my trips, because once in Afghanistan I hardly had any expenses. Luckily, the Left came to power in May 1981, and Mitterrand was an old anti-Soviet. He decided it was important to at least try and discreetly help the Afghan resistance, so he gave a sort of yellow light to go ahead. But at the same time, he was suspicious of the army and intelligence services. He thought, not incorrectly perhaps, that they were against him. In addition, he owed some favors to retired officers on the left who had never been promoted to general or who lacked a star or two because of their affinity for the Socialist Party—yes, there really were leftist military personnel, at least there used to be! So these officers were put in charge of research institutes. The Institut de polémologie, devoted to the study of war, was put under the direction of Colonel Paucot, a former officer of the Second Tank Division.[1] He was a decent man who agreed to hire young researchers of my generation such as André Brigot and Dominique David, who thought, as I did, that one ought not leave questions of geostrategy entirely up to the Right. They received some funds to work with, and Brigot, who had heard about me from Abensour, called to offer me a job. This is how I came to sign a contract with the Institut de polémologie, but really it was with the Ministry of Defense, and so for two years I was paid a research stipend that allowed me to continue making trips to Afghanistan.

So you traveled in an Afghanistan that had been invaded by the Soviets?

I went there clandestinely, dressed in Afghan clothes. Those were extraordinary years. I finally penetrated into the real country—a country of mountain trails, paths through the desert, tiny secluded villages, passes at ten thousand feet, lost valleys that led nowhere but that allowed one to avoid the zones controlled by the Soviets. We traveled on foot, on horseback, or by camel for days, sometimes weeks. I got lost, ruined my feet, was detained for days for reasons that were often impossible to decipher by petty commandants who were either wonderfully hospitable or completely paranoid. I bought horses, learned how to take care of them, crossed enemy lines at night, was taken for a Soviet spy, abandoned by my guides, handed over by them to shady characters, saved by total strangers, fed and lodged by poor folks, or sometimes hosted like a pasha by strange local bigwigs whose allegiance in the conflict was not entirely clear. I was bombarded by planes and helicopters, pinned down by barrages of artillery fire, escaped from ambushes (most often organized by other mujahideen), exchanged blows with young Algerian jihadists, made friends with their Turkish colleagues, rode a motorcycle, and learned to shoot. It was one adventure after another.

Everything began each time in Peshawar—going to meet the various mujahideen representatives so as to have the greatest number of favorable recommendations from different parties; choosing the right smuggler, who would get you across the Afghan-Pakistan border and then pass you from front to front, each time handed on from one guide to the next in exchange for a "receipt." Often the guides would sacrifice their lives for us, but sometimes they would abandon us, and I would have to make my way alone from village to village, not knowing whom I was going to come upon, friends or foes or what.

Do you recall your itineraries and your destinations?

The first year I went to Nuristan. The second time I was supposed to go to Panjshir, where there were some doctors and Jean-José Puig, a Centrale[2] graduate who had kept up the hobby of fly-fishing for trout in Afghanistan, with or without Soviets invading his streams.[3] Puig was the first person who spoke to me about Commander Massoud. The following years, I went to fantastically beautiful places that no one knew anything about: the central route, Herat, the Sistan, Faryab, Kandahar, and the village of Mullah Omar were some of them. To get to Panjshir, one had to get over five passes at elevations of around ten thousand feet. We walked, camels carried our bags, and, of course, there was snow. In 1982 I traversed all of Afghanistan, from the eastern border to the Iranian border. From there I descended to Pakistan, passing from one nomad camp to another on foot, motorcycle, or boat, before rejoining a caravan of Baluchis (who, by the way, spoke Brahui), and finally, with a guide and camels, I crossed the desert of Registan. But since it took me a month to do all that, instead of the four days that had been announced when I was near the Iranian border, in Peshawar I was declared missing, a situation further complicated by the fact that the chain of transmission of receipts had broken down because the nomads I had met were illiterate. Chantal, my companion, was back in France and had lost track of my whereabouts after Herat. I wasn't able to send news from the desert region that we crossed on camelback while also trying to avoid Russian ambushes that sent helicopters with instructions to shoot at every camel and motorcycle that moved. So we traveled at night. During the day, we would lie down among low scrubby bushes after taking care to disperse the camels so that the Russians didn't identify them as part of a caravan. At dusk we had to gather them together again before traveling on. We crossed the Helmand River on camelback in broad daylight, which was quite risky.

I also remember a region of lakes and marshes that we crossed during this same trip in October 1982. In this place, called Hamun-i-Helmand, people traveled in open boats made from braiding together dried reeds very much like the ones I'd seen in encyclopedias of Lake Titicaca. The boats were maneuvered by poles among reeds ten feet high as well as around some placid cows that the local inhabitants, Persian-speaking Shiites moved from island to island in search of a little pasture for grazing. These people were called *gawdar*, which translates roughly as "cowboys." I spent ten days on an island that was about a thousand square feet welcomed by a group of mujahideen. They had taken refuge there because they were safe from Russian tanks on account of the water, and the helicopters couldn't see us because we'd quickly hide in the reeds as soon as we heard them coming. Our principal source of food was migrating birds that we killed with muskets that shot little lead pellets. It was early November, the period of migration for woodcocks, ducks, curlews, ortolans, and lapwings. Two young boys would leave very early in the morning to get bread from the nearest Iranian village, which was about twelve miles away, and they'd get back around six at night when the birds had nicely finished cooking in the pot.

How were you perceived?

It depended on the person. For activists, I was an eyewitness who was going to spread the word about their cause, and that mattered. But that was hardly everyone's view. On the trip I was describing, there was a dangerous area to get through—a narrow deserted corridor of twenty or twenty-five miles between Shindand and the Iranian border that was regularly patrolled by Soviet armed vehicles and helicopters with the aim of cutting the supply lines coming from the south and destined for Ismail Khan in Herat. The closer we approached from the north, the more I encountered men designated by Ismail Khan to pass me along. And there was no way to protest against their services. The driver of a jeep handed me over to a man on a motorcycle who passed me to a second motorcyclist who, in the last village before reaching the corridor, cracked up. A meeting took place in a little mosque with a dirt floor. The very young mullah calls together all the young men, my guide offers to lend his motorcycle, and the mullah pronounces a fervent prayer: "It is more praiseworthy to get this stranger, who will be our witness, safely through than to kill ten Russians!" I am finally being valued properly. A young man raises his hand without saying anything. We jump on the motorcycle, tear off, we start seeing the fresh tire tracks of the last convoy to pass, and arrive in the first winter village on the other side. The youth then turned around without a word and rode back. I never learned what became of him, and I feel some remorse about that. But in this new setting, everything's different. The people don't know who I am, they're afraid, they can't read and don't understand the letters of transit that I show them. They feed me, but are also eager to conduct me on foot to the next village, where the people react the same way. And in everyone's eyes, I see the same fear: the fear of reprisals, fear that I'm a Soviet spy, fear of a stranger. I have contempt for cowardice, but I respect fear. It was a fear that increased more and more from village to village until the last where, by night, the inhabitants said they were going to turn me over to the Russians. Out of fear. And yet in that situation I had no language problem. They were Noorzai people, so Pashtuns, but Persian-speaking. The problem was that what I was saying made no sense to them. They made me their prisoner (the longest night of my life) and eventually turned me over to a group of mujahideen, and the chief knew how to read.

So your presence was considered a bit odd, in fact.

I was the only European to have set foot there since the start of the war, perhaps since long before the war. I had the most extraordinary experiences during the month that I was declared missing. But at the end of each trip, I had to clandestinely recross the Pakistan border to avoid being arrested, first by Russians, but later also by the Pakistanis, because the border zones were off limits and in any case my visa would have expired.

I finished that trip with a guide and a camel whose wool became covered with frost each night because in November in the desert the temperature dropped below freezing. After a bit of uncertain wandering, we crossed the border in secret north of Dalbandin in the zone of the Baluchi tribe the Mamassani. In Pakistani territory I was received by the tribal chief, a grand lord with a touch of condescension. He was holding court, and I was made to sit at his side when suddenly a Pakistani police officer entered the room to greet him. I started to panic and wanted to explain to the chief that I was a foreigner with no papers whom he ought to hide from view of the officer. Then, in front of the deferential officer, he said to me out loud, "Don't you worry. Here there is no state. *Injâ hokumat nist.* There is only the kingdom of you and me. *Mamlakat-e man o shomâ.*" This is a good definition of Afghan political culture.

The Pakistanis, of course, often closed one eye, but not both, when it came to clandestine travelers like myself. The game was to get back to the French embassy in Islamabad without being arrested and there a specialized diplomat (from the intelligence services, of course) would negotiate for us an exit visa.

Chapter 10

ON FOOT, ON HORSEBACK, AND WEARING A BURKA IN WARTIME AFGHANISTAN

Chantal, your companion at the time, did not come with you on this trip in 1982.

NO, BUT WHEN I got back from this second trip where I had gone missing, she told me I had to choose between her and Afghanistan. But I suggested a third possibility: that she come with me. So we returned together in 1983 and did a trip that was very memorable for us. By the usual method, we arrived in Hazarajat in the center of the country, and our Pashtun guides departed. But the Hazaras, who are Shiite and, luckily for me, Persian speakers, have very different interpersonal relations compared to others. Being much more individualistic, they simply invited us to make our way on our own. So we bought two horses, and we crossed half of Afghanistan, just the two of us and with no problems, right up to the Soviet border at Meymaneh. Of course, people asked who we were and what we were doing there, but without making any trouble for us. Not far from the border, near Meymaneh, we spent a week in a madrassa (for Sunnis and Naqshbandi Sufis[1]) turned into a military installation. We encountered some very nice people but there was absolutely nothing happening. Chantal said to me, "I thought there was a war going on, but there is no war." So I went to the chief to relay the message. "My wife's complaining that there's no war! We send you arms, but we don't see you doing anything. We can't take any pictures!" The chief replied, "Tomorrow we'll go on a mission."

True to his word, the next day we left in a column on horseback and then on foot and penetrated into a Communist zone to attack a governmental post (i.e., non-Soviet) after nightfall. After some exchanges of gunfire, the Russian base that was situated farther back began shelling the area to liberate the post under attack. A retreat was wisely decided on with no capture of the post, of course. So we took refuge in a mausoleum-mosque of a local saint (*pir*). We were instructed to make ourselves comfortable there and rest—while keeping our shoes on just in case. We were informed that our hosts were preparing a real meal (in other words, that would include meat). The young mujahideen were particularly excited by this news—coming from poor families and living in an isolated madrassa, they rarely had the chance to feast. At that moment, shells started falling near the mosque, but no one budged. I asked the chief if he planned on giving the signal to depart since the Russians, it seemed, were in the process of adjusting their aim to good effect. He answered, "No, we'll stay here. We have eaten nothing since this morning." Since I insisted on the dangerousness of the situation, he added, "There's no risk. Here we're protected by the *pir*'s *barakat* (the saint's blessing)." That was when I realized that religion is not merely a matter of opinion or theology. Eventually, food was brought in, and while we were eating, no mortar shells fell on the mosque. Later the chief said to me, "We're going to have to wait here a bit. There are no horses for you." I told him that we could ride on donkeys. He said it was out of the question. But then a shell fell a few meters away, the shock lessened somewhat by the earthen walls. As soon as the horses arrived, we left as quickly as possible. Of course, all the photos were blurry, and luckily the operation resulted in only four wounded on our side. However, among the young *moudj*, as they were called, the skirmish gave rise to days and days of heroic stories being traded and ended up being turned into a grand battle.

You then descended through Afghanistan toward Pakistan?

Yes, and we faced a new problem then: how to get across the border, especially with Chantal. They proposed that she put on a burka and that I present myself as an Afghan refugee. They made fake papers for me—Madame didn't need any. I was given a mujahideen card that turned me into an

Afghan refugee: Daoud Safdar. As a Sunni joke, I was declared a Shiite. We crossed the border and the customs and police checkpoints with a group of Afghan refugees—Chantal in her burka and me as an Afghan, with instructions to not speak any French. In short, we had completely gone through the looking glass. We weren't just supposed to pretend; we had to interiorize the rules of behavior, attitudes, a way of looking, walking, bending over, remaining impassive, eyes on the ground. The route back was complicated. We were treated very well, but we needed bribes for the slightly corrupt Pakistani police, which was nothing new, in fact. We traveled in crowded trucks and slept at inns. But for Chantal in her burka, it wasn't just a problem of toilets and keeping clean, but also a challenge at mealtime that required her to face a wall that allowed her to lift her burka. These were the ordinary things of life that one doesn't understand until one is inside and that inscribe one in a world of codes and gestures that one ends up interiorizing.

Once again I became aware of the importance of body language. The problem wasn't the regular language—there are so many different Persian accents that ours did not stand out. The foreigners were identifiable mostly from their body language. That fact led me to do true ethnology, you might say, because it wasn't so much that we were forced to speak the language as we had to dissolve into the landscape and mold our bodies into new shapes and movements. It was as though, in these circumstances, our clothes really did make us into what we were.

Could you list again the exact dates and number of these trips?

My first war trip took place in 1980 with the humanitarian caravan of Bernard-Henri Lévy, and for the next eight years, including 1988, I went every year, except in 1986 after the Seurat affair.[2] I made seven big trips—four with Chantal—to Panjshir, Hazarajat, in the north, and to Kandahar, in war zones where aerial bombing was at times common. In Kandahar, for example, in 1984, we came upon a Soviet offensive. We spent a week in an oasis that was bombed every day, hiding in little bunkers or amid the irrigation canals that served as trenches. Eventually, we were able to escape on camelback through the desert in the middle of the night. When we arrived in Panjshir in 1985, a Soviet offensive had just taken place and we could still see corpses of Russians decomposing in the middle of ruined villages. We were really in the middle of the war, and in a way it was as though I were fulfilling a certain necessary life chapter. My two grandfathers had served in World War I. My father experienced war in 1939–1940. But us, what was our war? The Gauche prolétarienne would have liked to live May '68 as a remake of the Resistance. You only have to read what they wrote—we were facing the "CRS-SS" in an occupation of our universities by the cops, and there was the popular resistance and identification with the Manouchian Group. There was war mythology that was transmitted from generation to generation, always ambivalent and hesitating between pacifism (as with my two grandfathers after 1914) and an eagerness to be on the side of the just (the Resistance, people fighting against imperialism, then against totalitarianism and dictatorships). At bottom, our generation would have liked to have had its own war, but since there wasn't any, it went to war via proxies.

You've described some very dangerous situations, but overall you give the impression that these trips were mostly pretty easy.

We may simply have been lucky, because despite all the risks we took we stayed alive. Looking back, I believe we may have underestimated the dangers. It's worth remembering that, besides the facts of war (essentially the bombs and the ambushes), there was the constant risk of having an accident: falling off a horse or a bus falling into a ravine. In Nuristan, Chantal almost fell off a precipice with her horse, which had slipped on some ice. She very nearly died right there. There was also the chance of meeting hostile people and being assassinated because we were not loved by all Afghans, and we knew it. We witnessed some violent altercations between Afghans that ended in death. A great friend, Bahauddin Majrooh, a poet and philosopher, was assassinated in Peshawar in 1988. Many of my European companions also died—killed in battles against the Russians or assassinated by other Afghans: Thierry Niquet, for example, and Andy Skrzypkowiak, who was killed in October 1987 in Kantiwar, Nuristan, some days after we had traveled through the same village. Others committed suicide after coming out of the interior. Four people, who had just gotten married, killed themselves when their child turned one year old. To me, it was a mystery of the human soul and of statistics.

Chantal and you were always on the side of the mujahideen. Was this fieldwork or your political preference?

Both. My trips were adventures and also fantastic study opportunities because I was in direct contact with mujahideen. And I was not only able to converse with them but also understand and jot down their lifestyles and choices. My first research project consisted in systematically asking them, "When and why did you first take up arms?" This question enabled me to tabulate the pure, hardened Islamists who entered the resistance between 1968 and 1975; those whom I called the traditionalists, who were revolted by the Communist coup d'état and who felt nervous about agrarian and educational reforms and the census taking, which was an important spur to mobilization; and finally the nationalists, who took up arms at the time of the Soviet invasion. Traveling on foot through certain regions allowed me to determine village by village the zones of influence of resistance parties, but also of the Communist forces. I was able to observe up close how and to what extent the mujahideen administrated in rural zones, the complex relations with traditional area leaders, the changes of local leadership, the disturbing role of arms distribution, the recomposition of ethnic and tribal groups, and also the force and complexity of Sufi networks, and finally the phenomenon of the rural madrassa, which is very specific to Afghanistan, and their slow transformation into a Taliban front. I also witnessed how the mujahideen administered justice (or shoved it aside), relations of violence and domination, but also of friendship, devotion, and sacrifice. I insist once again on how moving about on foot or on horseback and avoiding the most traveled routes, while also lodging with local people, allowed me to gain intimate knowledge of an Afghanistan that few knew about. And I was acquiring that knowledge at the very time when that deep Afghanistan was being turned upside down little by little because of the war.

I also investigated the knowledge of the ulema and their way of connecting religion and culture.[3] On this point, the war allowed me to meet people in Kabul that I would otherwise never have seen. In the Panjshir, where I was in 1981, I met Mawlawi (the title of the ulema of the Indian subcontinent) Mirajuddin, a man from the village of Astana who was very proud of his library, which included ancient manuscripts and nineteenth-century lithographs. Here's where one gets a glimpse of not a cultural Islam, but an Islam rooted in a culture, in this case Persian culture. He was also the local schoolteacher. The language, poetry, the wisdom of nations, cosmogony, and the rudiments of Islam were taught from a book, the *Tchar Kitab*, composed in verse and rhythmic prose. It's a book that I would also come upon in Central Asia. Of course, there were texts devoted to *fiqh* (Islamic jurisprudence) and *ilahiyât* (theology), but he taught and practiced medicine with a manual of Galen (Jâlinos) published in Arabic and geometry with a manual attributed to Euclid, which was also in Arabic. In short, for him religion was not opposed to a profane culture, but there was the world, knowledge, and simply wisdom. And yet his favorite book was a manual on alchemy. He took me aside to let me know that he was preparing the recipe for a liquid that would melt the Soviet tanks, but it was important to keep it a secret because the mujahideen didn't take him seriously. All he was missing was some silver sulfate, which, thanks to my memory of the inventory of my little chemist's kit from childhood, I was able to deliver to him the following year.

In 1985, during a Russian offensive, his library was destroyed by Russian tanks. The recipe seems not to have worked. I came upon him a short time later, fleeing into exile in a mountain refuge in Nuristan at the Paprok pass. We shivered together outside because the hut was reserved for a flock of goats whose owner had just recovered his beasts from a sly thief in the neighboring village who had made off with them. Why they spent their time stealing each other's goats, I don't know. Mawlawi Mirajuddin had lost everything except his dignity. He murmured, "I saved the most important thing," and then pulled out from beneath his blanket the little book of alchemy!

With these local experiences as your foundation, you constructed the theoretical analyses that you later developed in your teaching and publications?

Yes. Within the university discourse, I contributed to the development of the concepts of Islamism, of rural guerilla activity, of tribalism and ethnic groups, and especially the reconstitutions that resulted from the war. This began with the publication entitled *Afghanistan: Islam et modernité politique* (1985), a work whose subtitle announces straightaway a decisive intuition that will traverse my unexpected vocation as a "political Islam specialist." But *L'Échec de l'islam politique* (1992) and *La nouvelle Asie centrale; ou, La fabrication des nations* (1998) continue to deepen—with new readings and new territories—the initial experience that I had in Afghanistan.[4]

But I want to stress that I did not simply see up close one "traditional" or "backward" country among others, but a country at war that was undergoing the pressures of extraordinary changes. I witnessed first-hand the arrival of the first volunteer foreigners (especially Arabs but also Turks) starting in 1985. I observed their ambiguous relations with the locals, but also what was then not yet called Salafism—in other words, their visceral hostility toward any cultural Islam. In sum, I gathered empirical data and analyses that would form the basis of my writings for a long time to come. I want to underline especially that I avoided starting from a conceptual model and a methodology defined in advance by the social sciences and instead privileged direct contact. Today in universities, the opposite happens: a theoretical model gets defined, and one proceeds to verify, as briefly as possible, how this model coheres or not (but it's better that it coheres if one wants to succeed institutionally) with the theory defined by one's professors.

We will return to this lesson that your career path taught you, but if you don't mind, let's go back to your first book, a real groundbreaking study entitled *Afghanistan: Islam et modernité politique*. What do you make of that book when you reread it today?

That book brought together and theorized the observations I had made in Afghanistan. The title was the focus of a discussion with Olivier Mongin, who was the director of the Esprit collection of the French publisher Seuil. The question was whether we ought to stress what I perceived as the modernity of the Islamists? The title chosen for the English translation was *Islam and Resistance in Afghanistan* (1986). Before being picked up by commercial and university presses, the book was immediately translated into English by the CIA but also into Russian by the KGB to train the

Soviet civilian and military leaders—with no royalties for the author, of course. The book focused on the social transformations caused by the war, but also on the strong influence exerted on military or political modernities by the traditional grammars of social relations. Admittedly, this book had some weaknesses—for example, it was too optimistic about the emergence of a political order (I was expecting more individuals like Massoud). I had accurately noted phenomena that were not retraditionalization but a return to a traditional grammar of social relations (solidarity groups), while thinking that they would somehow be subsumed by a political approach that would rely on a military rationality. However, this turned out not to be the case. But the men that I identified as the principal figures (Massoud, Ismail Khan, and Gulbuddin Hekmatyar, for example) did turn out to be the important actors—for good or ill. The major trends I identified (ethnic polarization, the prevalence of infrapolitical loyalties, and the success and crisis of the Islamist model) were confirmed. And if I didn't clearly identify the Taliban phenomenon (which didn't yet exist at the time), I did notice and report on the militarization of the madrassas of Kandahar that would turn into a Taliban front.

In any case, it was the first work that proposed a synthesis and analysis derived from actual inside experience of guerilla activity.

You spoke earlier of expertise. These are the years when you start becoming recognized publicly for your specific knowledge of the Afghan territory.

Yes. Here too 1985 marked a turning point. It's the year I joined the CNRS and thus entered academia. Jean-François Bayart and Jean-Luc Domenach, who were members of the research group CERI (Centre d'études et de recherches internationales) affiliated with Sciences Po, invited me to get involved back in 1983. Domenach advised me to try for a post within the CNRS, something I had not really thought about until then. I had studied philosophy, I was an intellectual, if you like, but I had not thought about going for a full-time university post as a teacher-researcher. I applied for a position in 1984 but was unsuccessful. The following year, after the publication of my book, I was immediately recruited. In the meantime, I had come to the attention of people in the Foreign Ministry at the Quai d'Orsay, in particular by the CAP (Centre d'analyse et de prévision) and its director, Jean-Louis Gergorin, who offered me a contract shortly before he resigned in 1984. As for the Defense Ministry, which had bankrolled me for two years, I think some of them disliked the idea of a leftist civilian explaining the war to them. You have to remember that, since the end of the Algerian War in 1962, and if one doesn't count Kolwezi[5], the French army had no combat experience. There was a generation of younger officers who had not been in Algeria and had never experienced a mortar shell exploding next to them. The generals who, as lieutenants, had experienced the Second World War and Indochina, and the colonels who had served in Algeria, also as lieutenants, were all retiring.

It's in that context that I was asked to give some introductory lectures at Saint-Cyr, the French military academy, that would explain the war in Afghanistan. There I encountered young officers who wanted to assert that the Soviet army was in the process of winning the war against Muslim insurgents who were using guerrilla tactics. To summarize, on the one hand, they were remaking the Algerian conflict and identifying with the Soviets, but at the same time they were animated by anti-Sovietism and supporting the mujahideen against the Bolsheviks—all the while convinced that it was a lost cause, because for them the Soviet world had turned into a military empire entirely devoted to war. "Pacifism is in the West and the Euromissiles are in the East," François Mitterrand used to say. At the beginning of the 1980s, with the affair of the missiles stationed in Germany, attention was focused on the Soviet military threat. At the time, the Red Army was considered a formidable war machine. But I was telling them, "No, the Soviets aren't capable of conducting war in the way you imagine. The soldiers aren't motivated—their military machine has broken down. The Red Army is a paper tiger." So in the early going, my relations with military personnel were rather complicated.

And what about later?

I met a man who at the time was a lieutenant-colonel, a certain Bruno Élie. He worked at the SGDN (Secrétariat général de la défense nationale) and was responsible for analyzing the Soviet military system. While reading in Russian certain specialized documents on the Soviet military, he came across some rather cryptic articles that mentioned ambush experiences in an unnamed country X. It was expressed rather abstractly, but he conjectured that they might be happening in Afghanistan. And, indeed, I was able to specify the places where the ambushes and counterattacks being described had taken place. It was in fact in Afghanistan. The technical literature of the Soviet military academies was factually correct, which is normal enough—one can only train officers based on reality, even if it contradicts the official discourse. Thus, in most of the cases described by the Russians themselves, the behavior of the officers and troops was aberrational and the operations particularly ineffective. The conclusion to be drawn was simple enough: the Soviet army was far from being the all-powerful bulldozer described in Western military reports, even if its firepower could and did inflict a lot of damage on civilian populations.

In the 1980s, the West's leading enemy was still Soviet Communism, which was said to have the best army in the world. Because the Soviet system was unreformable and militarized, the only solution was war. This presented an interesting convergence between the official NATO doctrine and the philosophical analyses that now considered totalitarianism as the quintessential existential threat, defined as an abstract paradigm, detached from its historic context and from all sociology of a given society, and thus replacing the good old American imperialism discourse that circulated in my younger days. It was at that time, for example, that Cornelius Castoriadis proposed his theory of the Soviet system as a *stratocratie*.[6] We were living in panic with the idea that Western armies would be powerless against the deployment of Soviet tanks. In that context, what I had to say made a rather heretical splash: "The Soviet army doesn't fight; it massacres." But this officer had come to the same conclusions as I had by reading Soviet military journals. And here we have a recurring problem when it comes to expert testimony: what recommendations ought to follow from our analysis? Kill the weakened bull with a sword between the shoulder blades by arming the mujahideen or, on the contrary, allow the Russians to flounder slowly but surely in their own quagmire without lifting a finger?

I presented Élie to the specialist on Soviet Islam, Alexandre Bennigsen, an old White Russian, whose ancestor fought to take Paris in 1814 and who had himself been a French officer in the *"drôle de guerre"* of 1939, then in the Resistance. He took a liking to Élie, and at the end of our meeting he uttered this sentence rolling each *r*: "You know, Olivier, there are only two good types of soldier: the intellectuals and the killers."

But the political class didn't see things that way!

The upper administration was very divided. At the Foreign Ministry, the CAP was highly anti-Soviet and thought it was necessary to aid the Afghan resistance; but the minister himself, Claude Cheysson, refused to allow France to go down that path because he was against all forms of Islamism. This is a problem that one still encounters today: how does one define the leading enemy? At that time, with the Iranian Islamic revolution going full tilt, it was a choice between communism or Islam. Everything turned on how one measured the Islamic threat: an epiphenomenon, only the expression of the frustration within the Muslim world, something with a murky foundation, a new planetary tectonic shift, troubling but potentially useful allies against Communism, or on the contrary the avatar of a radical anti-Western movement? These questions are still being asked. In any case, back then I was making arguments to Denis Delbourg, a graduate of Normale sup' and the ENA and a member of Cheysson's cabinet, to persuade the minister to take an interest in Afghanistan.

It was in that context, I suppose, that I invented the concept of "moderate Islam." Burhanuddin Rabbani, the leader of the Islamic party Jamiat-e Islami, whom I knew well, arrived in Rabat in 1984, at the summit meeting of the Islamic Conference, as the president of the Afghan resistance. I knew that he would be passing through Paris to catch a connecting flight back home. I pressed Delbourg to tell the minister that he should absolutely meet with him. But Cheysson was an ardent *laïque*, and his secular bent made him want to avoid receiving any turban-headed individuals. So I presented Rabbani as a moderate Islamist and said that, since the phenomenon was in any case unavoidable, it was necessary to speak to those with whom we could find common ground. Indeed, this is still my position, for example, when it comes to the Ennahda in Tunisia or the AKP in Turkey. The minister ended up meeting with Rabbani.

You also got interested in Iran, and you were one of the first to write on the Khomeini revolution.

True. I first got to know Iran at Langues o' because my Persian language and civilization classes focused on Iran. Our professors, both the French ones and the Iranians, didn't care for the Afghanophile spirit of students of Persian in those days, and our Afghan accents sounded rather country bumpkin to them. What's more, to get to Afghanistan one naturally had to pass through Iran, and I made stops there for various lengths of time during each of my trips. Those who were in love with Afghanistan didn't like Iran, which they considered too Western. At the Cité univesitaire in Paris, I was acquainted with members of the Iranian opposition, those on the left of course, but also the Islamic leftists who read Ali Shariati. When the revolution started, I followed it closely while in France. I remember that Khomeini had settled in Neauphle-le-Château, just a mile or two from Dreux.

But in 1979, on my way back from a trip to Afghanistan with Chantal (a touristic journey before the Soviet invasion), we spent a full month in Iran just at the moment when the revolution was tilting toward Khomeinism. We witnessed it as spectators, but the events themselves were fascinating, all the more so since we had crossed the country to get to Kurdistan, after having stopped over in central Iran at Kerman and Yazd, and on the shores of the Caspian Sea. Like in all revolutions, including the collapse of the Soviet Union, it was that period when anything and everything seems like it could still happen, when the reinvention of a new order can be glimpsed but without yet appearing definitive—where pockets of resistance, or even indifference, still existed. The regime did not yet have control over the whole territory, the administration had not yet been purged, and people believed they could speak without fear. And then everything shut down. During that moment, when everything was in suspension, we could go everywhere without being stopped. It was fascinating to us to see how codes and rules disappeared all at once. For example, the police didn't know whether they were supposed to arrest us or let us pass through a given checkpoint. So finally, they let us pass through. In that way, we got to see, from a certain angle and not for long, it's true, the new disposition take shape. It was very exciting, especially since everyone was discussing and arguing over what was happening. But little by little, the Khomeinist order took hold: arrests, executions, purges, and fear—even if a modicum of freedom and autonomy was always maintained in private, within families and in the irreverence of ordinary folks like taxi drivers, truckers, students, booksellers, and old scholars who were always ready to badmouth the regime and take refuge in literature or philosophy. The regime had a true revolutionary logic, a coherent political and cultural project it pursued—but one that was taking place in an ancient society, Iran, that had seen previous revolutions come and go.

After the death of Khomeini in 1988, the intellectual space opened up somewhat, and I was able to enter a bookshop across from Tehran University and buy books of new critical thinkers such as Abdolkarim Soroush and Mohsen Kadivar.[7] The bookseller stocked all those books, and with each title I read off to him he would climb up his ladder and pull it off the shelf. When he had placed the tenth book on top of my pile, he looked me straight in the eye and said, "You, you're looking for trouble!" Booksellers are wise.

Chapter 11

BLUE HELMETS AND RUSSIAN BOMBS

Did the kidnapping of Michel Seurat in Lebanon in 1985 play a role in your dealings with Afghanistan? At that time, the tragic end was not yet known, but it was a major event as I recall.

I RAN INTO him several times in the 1980s. We attended some of the same lectures and conferences together. He was kidnapped on May 22, 1985, in Beirut. The day before, I attended a CERI conference with him. We had dinner together that night and launched into a big discussion—the only one I ever had with him one on one—about our respective experiences in Syria and Afghanistan. We discovered we had many things in common: our relation to war, to politics, to languages, our way of living in various societies, our interest in Islamic movements, and our political commitments and involvement. And for me there was my relationship to the USSR, and for him to Syria itself, a country whose political system he had analyzed remarkably well. At one point, we brought up the question of the possible dangers linked to our involvement, mentioning the people we knew who had been kidnapped, taken hostage, or killed. We came to the conclusion that nothing would happen to us, that we were untouchable because we spoke the local languages; we were close to the local people; had been introduced into the political movements, and so on. He told me that the next day he was returning to southern Lebanon. A week later we learned that he had been kidnapped and died in captivity after a few months.

We were not untouchable.

But did it change anything for you?

The 1985 trip had already been arranged. It was tough, not so much because of the danger, but because we arrived in Panjshir, as I said, in the days just following some bloody fighting. It was afterward that I reflected on the possibility of meeting the same fate as Seurat. Nineteen eighty-six was the only year in that decade when I did not go to Afghanistan, even though Chantal was motivated to go. However, we did travel to Peshawar, but instead of taking the route through Afghanistan, we took the Chinese route to Xinjiang. China had opened its borders in 1984, though it would not last. A new road had been built that linked Pakistan to Xinjiang. This was another amazing trip through Central Asia because the itinerary passed through the mountains of Pakistan and then through the high plateaus on the Chinese side that are home to the Uighurs. Once again I played the amateur ethnologist, especially since it had been decades since any Western researcher had traveled through there. We went to the markets, we had discussions at inns in a mix of Turkish and Persian. I felt like I was living a sort of remake of my first trip to Afghanistan, an experience I would have yet again when the Soviet portion of Central Asia opened up a few years later. The impact and progress of Chinese colonialism was very evident, but the resistance of this Turkish-Persian culture was also striking. No Persian power had ever reigned across Xianjiang, and yet the Uighur language was filled with Persian words. And before the Chinese bulldozer could destroy everything, there were traces of the past; for example, the British consulate in Kashgar with its Victorian architecture that had been turned into a hotel for tourists on the road. I spent a bit of time there with hippies I'd traveled with fifteen years earlier and who this time were looking for the road to Lhasa, which had replaced Kathmandu in the popular imagination as the world center for levitation.

What did you take away from that discovery of China?

My trip had a purpose. I wanted to meet with the Chinese officials who were following the Afghanistan situation. China's political stance in this area intrigued me. They were very present in the territory and had provided arms, but they kept a very low profile politically. Also, tensions between

Afghans were increasing, and the fact that the principal beneficiaries of foreign aid were not the groups most active against the Soviets but in fact were among the most radical of Sunni fundamentalists, this was increasingly bothersome to our little group of backers.

We decided informally to conduct some lobbying efforts in favor of a more pragmatic approach to the Afghan resistance and one also oriented more toward the future. The dominant view in the West was that the mujahideen's combat was doomed to fail, and, therefore, among the most concession-minded, it was important not to antagonize the Soviets, while the most hawkish wanted to bloody them as much as possible. For my part, I was more and more convinced that the Soviets would be required to negotiate a settlement and that it was therefore important to take a longer, postwar view; and for this I recommended supporting the mujahideen, who demonstrated the most political approach, and the most "constructivist," let's say, when it came to the future play of alliances.

So it was with this in mind that I sought to question and understand the Chinese view of the whole matter. Naturally, this was preceded by an extensive feast during which I took a definitive dislike of "100-year-old eggs," which I just couldn't swallow, even with the help of several glasses of local vodka. But it turned out not to be very helpful as I started to realize that the Chinese were not really interested in the religious or ideological dimensions of the conflict. They were waiting to see who would win, convinced that geostrategic factors would outweigh everything else in the end. They believed that the time would come when, after the other powers had become fed up with their interventions, they could advance their economic interests in the region.

This trip was part of a larger project. Between 1986 and 1987, I was making many trips to the United States, where I made the rounds among Congress, the State Department, the Pentagon, think tanks, universities, and the media. The alarm bell I was ringing said essentially this: *Wake up! You have to plan for the postwar situation and make better choices about who your aid recipients are going to be.* I was given a cordial welcome, but not many listened to me. A sentimental Frenchman spreading propaganda for his buddy Massoud—that was how most perceived me.

And you go back to Afghanistan two more times.

Personally, I didn't want to return to Afghanistan, at least not clandestinely. Going every year, as I had been doing, was really tempting fate. But in 1987 we did go back with Alain Guillo, a freelance photographer-journalist friend. We crossed the border together with a sixty-vehicle convoy of arms to be delivered to resistance fighters. It was the high-water mark of the flow of arms then. We traversed half the country sitting on crates of weapons and ammunition that could have been blown up any minute with a mine, a rocket launched from a helicopter, or from simple stupidity since whenever they were bored, young mujahideen loved playing with ammo. It was obviously a bad idea, including from a political standpoint. We separated from Alain in the mountains. A few days later, he was captured by the Soviets and was later transferred to the sinister Pul-e-Charkhi prison in Kabul. The sword of Damocles had fallen right beside us. The night he was captured, we were sleeping hidden in a cave near Salang Tunnel, and Chantal woke up in the middle of the night and cried out, "Something's happened to Alain!" When we went back through Nuristan, the journalist Andy Skrzypkowiak had just been assassinated a few days before, and the caravan of Solidarité Afghanistan had also been pillaged. Things were definitely heating up and becoming more and more corrupt.

I didn't want to continue with this routine, doing another trip year after year. The situation was changing, and I thought I needed to find a new way to be present in Afghanistan. It was then that on December 31, 1987, just before the clock struck midnight, a call came through to me in my half-drunken state from an American diplomat friend who informed me that the Russians were soon going to leave Afghanistan. Why was he telling me this? Who was his source? I never found out. A bit shook up by this news, I went to see Jacques Amalric a few days later. Amalric was the head of foreign coverage for *Le Monde* and an expert on the USSR. He told me, "It's not possible, because if the Russians leave, it's the end of the Soviet Union." He was both wrong, since it was possible, and right, since it would indeed be the end of the Soviet Union.

In February 1988, Gorbachev announced, just as my informant had predicted, the withdrawal of Soviet troops, and so then preparing for the aftermath was all the more necessary. The UN named a coordinator for Afghan affairs, Prince Sadruddin Aga Khan, the uncle of *the* Aga Khan, and the prince contacted me and Chantal and asked us to join his staff. We received special UN passports and worked with the coordinator with the idea of creating conditions for a post-Soviet peace.

So with this new post your status changed. Did the job also change you?

Yes, this job was my first experience in the official world of international relations. I was no longer a consultant but in charge of a negotiation process. Of course, I didn't participate in the upper-level discussions; instead, I was given the responsibility of making more discreet, unofficial contact with various individuals. This was more suited to my background—being a sort of free floating particle whose existence was easily deniable. Specifically, I was chosen to negotiate with the Iranians and get them to permit the UN to open an access corridor through Iranian territory to the west of Afghanistan. This meant negotiating with Ismail Khan, the leader of the resistance in that region and therefore the obligatory interlocutor, so that our delegation could pass through the area even though it was proceeding under the authority of Iran, which he hated at the time. I was not the only one conducting these negotiations—there was also the representative of the High Commission on Refugees in Tehran—but the advantage for me was to get myself for once on the official side of the room. Since I knew the Afghans, I was particularly adept at playing the role of local facilitator. After four months of negotiations, we obtained from the Iranians the right to pass through Iran, on condition that we bring along with us Iranian officials who, of course, were affiliated with their foreign service and secret police. I became reacquainted with revolutionary Iran, but this time observing backstage the various services, the border guards, the internal rivalries, the distrust, and all of it covered with a most exquisite icing of politeness. We were housed in Iranian military barracks and entered Afghanistan in UN vehicles equipped with blue flags and radios, after having alerted the Russians beforehand of our arrival. Since I had already spent time in Herat in 1982, I knew Ismail Khan well. The goal now was to negotiate a local agreement so that the withdrawal of the Russians proceeded in orderly fashion. They were to leave Afghanistan by February 1989, and it was then December 1988.

So this UN delegation was of course very international?

True, the UN delegation included three Turks, someone from Quebec, a Muslim Indian, and the two of us, Chantal and myself. No one except us had ever spent time in Afghanistan or spoke Persian. Once we crossed into "Afgha," I came upon my former contacts from 1982; but things were enormously tense because the Iranians preferred to deal with the local Shiites, whereas Ismail Khan was a committed Sunni, very anti-Shiite, and insisted that everything go through his authority. We established a file with all the petty local chiefs of the resistance but accorded Ismail Khan preeminent status, while also forcing him to allow the Shiites to participate in the discussions. We also had to tread carefully with the Russians, who, officially, were still the representatives of the Communist government and refused officially to conduct discussions with the mujahideen. Together with the local government, the Russians still controlled Herat, and they had installed a line of defense around the city and forbade all attempts to approach this security perimeter. We were situated at the intersection of this power face-off among, on one side, Russians; on another, Iranians, who had the clear intention of bringing Herat within their sphere of influence; and on yet another, Ismail Khan, who insisted on having a monopoly on representing the resistance. In addition, there were the rivalries among UN agencies that disputed who was in charge of this or that operation and who didn't hesitate to exploit local rivalries and found themselves in turn being exploited by those local rivalries. Understanding and untangling—that was my mission.

When we decided to go around the Russian blockade and get closer to Herat, we had to leave our vehicles because they couldn't get through, as well as the protection of the blue flags, and proceed on horseback, even though our steeds would not have diplomatic license plates. Ismail Khan wanted us to see that he alone controlled access to the city, and I wanted my colleagues to see that this was indeed the case. A skilled communicator, he had prepared a welcome committee composed of his troops. In a large field he had assembled fifteen hundred of his mujahideen fighters who stood at attention in a U-shaped formation. He then suggested or, rather, nudged us, to make a speech. The Turkish head of our delegation, a very secular, Kemalist diplomat who on principle wanted to remain neutral, let himself get carried away in this atmosphere and made a rousing pronounce- ment—which he asked that I translate at the top of my lungs and with no microphone—about the just fight against the oppressor. May I say I consider that translation to have been the most shameful moment of my life. Whipped into a lyrical lather that was no longer really secular, he cried out, "And may God keep your martyrs under his very holy protection," which I ren- dered as, "And may God keep your martyrs in good health" all the while being immediately aware of my slip-up. Solemn speeches are really not my thing!

Obviously, the Russians did not look kindly on this violation of the tacit accord, and the next day, as we were getting ready to saddle up, they attacked us with two fighter planes that bore down and shot at us with machine guns. We were about fifteen, entirely exposed in a soccer field–sized area, but by extraordinary good fortune no one was injured. I saw the impact of bullets on the ground in front of me as one sees happen in car- toons. We ran to shelter ourselves in the irrigation ditches, which were full since it was winter. After it was over, we climbed out wet but alive, and we hurried to contact Geneva as quickly as possible and get the UN to tell the Russians to stop their attack. To do that, someone had to get the radio and its antenna going and make contact. This was not easy to do since at the time telecommunications were not what they are today. We still relied on antennae that needed to be deployed and relay vehicles that were back at the Iranian border to send short-wave messages. Despite all that we accom- plished, our mission went more or less as we'd planned, but right up to the last minute the reality of the war was there and therefore the risks.

And so was that your final exit from Afghanistan?

When we returned to Geneva, I thought it was over for me in Afghanistan— or in any case that it was not wise to return because we had really cut it too close. One day the crazy luck that we had benefited from would not be there, and we'd all be killed because even though we were on an official mission we had almost died out there. And besides, there was nothing left to do since the diplomatic machine was now turning its wheels, as were the wheels of internal war, and therefore the expertise we'd acquired could serve only to establish relations to help with a decision that would arrive too late or end up being beside the point. But Chantal did not share my view. She preferred to stay. The UN took her on as part of the staff that was to consolidate the peace. She settled in Kabul, and it was the beginning of a gradual separation between the two of us.

Chapter 12

THE FAILURE OF POLITICAL ISLAM

It's the end of the '80s, you've been on the road for years, but you're also a CNRS member. How did you get your foot back in the stirrup of theory?

I RETURNED TO France in January 1989. I should have mentioned that as a member of the CNRS I didn't have the right to enter Afghanistan, not even on behalf of the UN. But I had built up a sort of double life: on the one hand I was covered by the French Foreign Ministry, which was issuing mission papers to me as a consultant; and on the other the CNRS, which was paying my salary and looked the other way when I went to Afghanistan because in fact they had authorized me to do this consulting work for the Foreign Ministry, part-time of course. The CNRS always renewed this authorization, even if belatedly a low-level bureaucrat who held the position of high functionary of defense at the CNRS did all he could to block researchers from doing research by declaring half of the globe a prohibited zone. Consulting had even become a CV enhancer—thanks to the rubric "valorization of research"—for those wishing to burnish their careers at the CNRS. In my view, it was a good thing since, when confronting practical issues, you are forced to do true political science and you avoid the jargon-filled and abstract bloviating that has today become the norm in political science, especially in the American context, where it's common to no longer confront the test of reality. I spent twenty-five years as a consultant at the CAP, and I left when in the spring of 2009 Bernard Kouchner, who had become the minister of foreign affairs, kindly offered me the post of director. Now that changed everything! I developed a solid network for myself at the ministry, but also among journalists, the military, foreign diplomats, and, I'll admit it, the secret services, all the while remaining in the background as a simple observer or small-time operator carrying out more or less unofficial missions. That discretion suited me because it left me free and I never really wanted to climb any higher.

The end of the annual travel ritual in 1988 left me with more time for other things. I resumed my research on Iran. The first Gulf War, the start of the Algerian crisis, and the recurring theme of an Islamic threat mobilized an entire team of young diplomats and researchers within the CAP. Together they churned out reports, conducted meetings, led debates, did field work, etc. I learned a great deal from this work and the research on countries I hardly knew at all even though I was also beginning to make trips again to the Middle East.

I brought all that together in *L'Échec de l'islam politique*, which was published in 1992 but written in 1990–1991.[1] In it I articulate the lessons I learned from my many experiences over the previous years in Iran, Afghanistan, and Pakistan. I also take up the Algerian affair, especially the electoral victory of the FIS (Front islamique du salut) that was violently overturned by the army in 1991. I had plenty of material to work from.

The title of the book was misunderstood.

Yes, many thought I was announcing the end of all references to Islam in politics or that I considered it impossible for Islamists to take power—both are absurd misunderstandings. In fact, what the book really explains is the structural failure of Islamist ideology for two reasons: either the religion destroys the state, or else the state destroys the religion. If one defines an Islamic state (and the same is true for a religious state of any denomination) as one in which the state recognizes only the sovereignty of God and implements only religious law, well, then the state has renounced its own sovereignty and there no longer is a state—everyone simply appeals to what he defines as religious law.

This was the spontaneous tendency of the *qadi*—those who made judgments according to sharia. They refused all codification and all intervention of the state. But it was an unsustainable situation: first for the state, which could not accept being stripped of all law, and second for the society, because there was no place and time for a final, supreme decision—a situation reminiscent of the society depicted in the Borges allegory "The Lottery in Babylon."[2] Moreover, claiming that state law is religious law supposes that there is *someone* who can say what the religious law is—because God is silent—and that's the big problem for theocracies. In this situation one may defer perhaps to a group of doctors of law, for example Iran's Council of Guardians or Saudi Arabia's Council of Ulema. But what happens when there is a contradiction between state law, be it voted into law by parliament or decreed by the sovereign, and the religious norm decreed by the ulema? The latter have no means to require the politician or politicians to yield except for anathema or the excommunication of kings, as was practiced by popes in the Middle Ages with very limited success. Therefore, it's always the state that decides, either by annulling decisions, putting the ulema in prison, naming more docile ulema, and so on. The politician or politicians are the obvious deciders of the place of religion, and not the reverse. The Iranian solution, a possibility in Shiism but not in Sunnism, is to affirm that a "doctor of the law," the guide, can occupy both functions and be the highest political authority as well as the highest religious authority. But who decides who will be the highest religious authority, and who installs that individual in power? Once again, it's the politician or politicians. Officially, in Iran the guide is chosen by a council of experts that itself is elected by the nation. And any and all compromises of principle by the guide, in business or in purely political affairs, automatically destroys his status as the man who is held to be the most virtuous—and such a downfall occurs immediately, either by his own hand or by his children. It's one of the few good arguments in favor of the celibacy of priests! The truly virtuous man is one who avoids getting involved in politics and who speaks as little as possible. The Iraqi ayatollah Ali al-Sistani understood this, and so does the Dalai Lama. One always encounters the same tension: in a religious state, only the state remains standing.

In 1995 I gave a talk in Qom, the holy city of Iran. My audience was composed of mullahs who, like you, demanded that I explain my title, *The Failure of Political Islam*. Their reply to the aporia I presented was to say that, unlike with Sunnism, Shiism had the concept of the Grand Ayatollah, which solved the problem of the two powers. Then I asked them, "But who decides who will be the guide?" Silence. Then a young mullah stood in the back of the room and shouted out, "The Kalashnikov!" Half the room burst out laughing, and the other half started protesting. That said it all.

But the very concept of Islamism or political Islam was controversial, no?

Yes, I was criticized for having invented not just the concept but also and especially the very category in question. The journal *Esprit* organized a debate on the subject in which I defend the specificity of the concept and its object: a modern political movement that considers Islam as a political ideology with a view toward state building (putting in place an Islamic state) and not simply as a juridical framework based on the implementation of sharia.[3] Of course, there is always a bit of arbitrariness when one tries to define an object and distinguish it from something else with which it could be considered to be in continuity. The Muslim Brotherhood is a religious collective, and it also wants to implement sharia, but the concept of Islamism can claim a heuristic value. One can easily see today that it's indispensable to understand the specific nature of the Muslim Brotherhood in relation to other religious movements, such as the Salafists, for example. Otherwise, one can't understand anything about what's going on in Egypt. What's more, the interested parties, who in the 1980s rejected the concept of Islamism that was attributed to them, later often took it up themselves, and I was invited by them to Iran but also to Turkey to debate what I had called their failure. What's interesting is that here again there is an interaction between research and its object, because this object is also a subject that reads, thinks, and acts—and is therefore interested in what is said about it or them. And inversely, the researcher who is accused of Orientalism or of being a neocolonial agent is obliged to think through the positing, value, and evaluation of his or her ideas. Here's an example of how the social sciences can influence the subjects they treat as objects of study: in Turkey the young managers who were going to build the AKP (Justice and Development Party) in the 1980s touted their modernity and compared themselves to Protestants with a work ethic similar to that of the Calvinists that is also to be found in Islamist entrepreneurs. One day I asked a leader in this organization (TÜSIAD, Turkish Industry and Business Association) if he had ever read Luther or Calvin. He looked at me, surprised. "No, of course not." So where had he come up with his concept of work ethic? "You know," he answered, "in the writings of Western sociologists like Max Weber!"

This interactive dimension between researchers and social actors is either unacknowledged or rejected by that which gets put forward under the name of deontology or research ethics—discourses which don't manage to scientifically define what objectivity would mean, and therefore give it a moral or moralizing meaning.

Why has political Islam lasted so long?

What do you consider long? It hasn't lasted as long as communism did. In truth, political Islam can prosper in the future only as part of some opposition; but it's doomed to fail as soon as it takes power, as the examples of Tunisia and Egypt demonstrate all too well. Put another way, the exercise of power marks the failure not only of the Islamist ideology but of the very idea that religion offers a program for governing. The fact is, exercising power ends up secularizing the religion because, as I've said, the politicians decide what place religion will have, and not the reverse, including and even especially in the case of so-called theocracies. Ennahda came to power after the Tunisian Revolution ended up voting in favor of the most secular constitution in the Arab world—it's a document that not only refrains from Islamizing anything but defends the principle of freedom of conscience; in other words, the right to change religions or to be atheist. True, it took three years to obtain that result, but that's nothing when looked at against the long timeline of history. As for Egypt, one can easily see that the secular liberals never really had strong democratic convictions, so instead of letting Islamists pursue their (bad) management of power, they offered them a dose of opposition. In the case of Iran, the mullahs are the archetype of failure: it's the Islamic Revolution that's managed to produce the most secularized society in the entire Muslim world, where the practice of religion has consistently declined!

At any rate, I remain pleased with this book and its title. I remember we talked about it at the time, and you had some reservations, preferring something more along the lines of "Is There an Islamic Threat?"

True, as a publisher I was worried about the ambiguity of the title. You seemed to be announcing the imminent failure of political Islam or its disappearance, whereas in fact you demonstrate that given the structure of political Islam, or its conception of the political and the religious, or the nature of the political, that it is bound to fail.

Correct. And twenty years later, I believe that Morsi in Egypt and Ennahda in Tunisia prove I was right. It's a little bit like the case of Emmanuel Todd, who predicted in 1976 that the Soviet Union was going to collapse. In the 1980s, everyone mocked him, and then we saw what happened.[4]

And yet this book lacks an account of al-Qaeda.

Obviously, because in the picture I paint in 1992 al-Qaeda wasn't yet part of the landscape. And yet in Afghanistan I had met militants who would later turn into al-Qaeda. Looking back, I have the feeling that my book was not really read and people simply fixated on the title; but I don't mind that and I stand 100 percent behind that title.

The book underlines an unavoidable choice that has to be made. The failure of political Islam automatically entails considering two possible alternatives: either (1) the normalization of Islamist parties into law-abiding institutional parties that are conservative—not necessarily liberal, but accepting of the rotation of governance and the preeminence of institutions (AKP and Ennahda would be examples); or (2) the development of a neofundamentalism focused on the strict application of sharia, with no political vision and no global conception of society (here Salafism would be an example). To me, the radicalization of a small jihadist fringe results less from the failure of political Islam than from the globalization and deterritorialization of Islam. This is what I examine in *L'Islam mondialisé* (*Globalized Islam*).

In 1999 you coauthored, with Farhad Khosrokhavar, *Iran: Comment sortir d'une révolution religieuse* (Iran: How to exit a religious revolution). Was this an extension of the thesis contained in *The Failure of Political Islam*?

Yes, but it's also an effort to broach what is very specific to Iran, a country that many wanted to see as the archetype of the Islamic state, when in fact it's an exceptional case due to three very particular features: Shiism (and therefore a clerical institution that took shape over a period of many centuries), Persian nationalism, and virulent anti-imperialism originating on the left that made a significant contribution to building the ideology of a regime that always preferred Fidel Castro over the king of Saudi Arabia, sharia notwithstanding. In the 1990s, I traveled there often, and that's how I was able to write that book with Farhad Khosrokhavar about finding an exit to revolution—an exit, it should be underlined, that has already been passed through by Iranian society but barely initiated at the level of the regime.

In fact, Iran illustrates my thesis at several levels. First, the state is secular because the very existence of the state has a secularizing effect, especially when it's a theocratic state, since, as I said, it's the state that decides on the place of the religious and not the reverse. Second, the transformation of religion into an official ideology empties it of all spirituality and displaces religiosity toward other forms of religious life (Suffiism, syncretism, or conversion to other religions) or away from religion entirely. Religion then builds itself outside, or even against, the state. That's a phenomenon that one can also witness in the papal states of the nineteenth century, where authentic Catholics were able to rise up against the pope as temporal authority without fearing excommunication. I have in mind, for example, the Perugia uprising in 1859, where the monks fought against papal troops. One cannot understand how Catholic Italy converts to republicanism in 1870 if one doesn't see how religion can become independent of politics while at the same time not going over to secularism.

There remains the mystery of the religious moment of the Iranian Revolution. In 2004 *Vacarme*, a journal animated by young Foucault enthusiasts, asked if I would contribute a text on Foucault and Iran.[5] So I set about reading everything Foucault ever said about Iran, and I was struck by the totally erroneous interpretation that one had made of his writings. He had been categorized as a sort of fellow traveler of the Khomeini revolution, which is absolute nonsense. Foucault in fact loses interest in the postrevolution—he doesn't believe in joyous future days of song (*"les lendemains qui chantent"*) or in the virtues of Islamism. He is really the total opposite of a philosopher of history because history has no meaning or direction for him. Foucault perfectly understood the religious dimension of this revolution. Not in the sense of it giving rise to a new political order, but on the contrary of enacting a "strike against politics," a massive and profound, and therefore unbearable, *retreat* from politics. The religious can be only a moment and never a state, and even less a State. Foucault understood that this religious dimension would be killed by the very dynamic of the revolution. Consequently, the religious can maintain itself only through death (but Foucault stops before that step), through suicide, which, far from being a means to realize a political goal, remains the only way of staying pure, of exiting the aporia of political Islam . . . through death. Martyrdom, as Farhad Khosrokhavar has shown, is the proof of failure of political Islam.[6] When certain Iranian revolutionaries understood that revolution ends in corruption, they went to the Iraqi border to get themselves killed. I repeat, though: one must not see in this any sort of invariable Muslim fate. There exist in this example elements that can also be identified in the French Revolution. Marat, for example, is constantly representing his own death until finally it actually takes place and makes of him a real martyr and object of cultish veneration: *"I shall die because the revolution is not living up to my expectations."* A religious revolution destroys itself.

Chapter 13

WAR EXPERIENCE

Prisoners and Bandits

So we're at the end of your time in Afghanistan, but if we could just stick with that a bit longer, what would you say you learned from those years?

IF I WERE to sum it up, I would say I learned most about the experience of war, specifically about guerilla war, ambushes, and faked identities. I also witnessed the games people play, tragedies, death, and adventure.

Contrary to a widely held belief, Afghanistan is also a country where people are often laughing—the tragic and the comic, the sublime and the sordid, hospitality and cruelty are constantly intermixed. And let me say once again that one cannot understand that complexity and richness within a framework of what is defined today as the politically correct. It's a vain pursuit to always be looking for the just norm, distinguishing between the good guys and the bad guys, always siding, of course, with the good guys, keeping one's hands clean, even if that means washing one's hands by pulling out. There's one area where tragedy, comedy, ambiguity, and absurdity were all tangled together, namely, with the fate of prisoners.

Consider what happened in late August 1983, for example. The Sufi front at Meymaneh that I mentioned earlier was located in a very poor region. When we started our operation, the obsession of the little group of mujahideen we were living with was to improve day-to-day living conditions. The hillsides situated in front of the post that we were supposed to attack were covered with melon fields, and the fruit was just about ripe. Each family of owners had installed a little lookout post in the middle of his field to guard against thieves. As we were marching through the area at dusk, our conversation became exclusively about the melons. The leader of our line of troops repeated our orders: not to touch private property and therefore to leave the melons alone. But after an hour of marching, a young fellow was unable to resist. He put down his rucksack, slipped into a field, and brought back an enormous melon; but right on his heels was a grandmother, shrieking and hitting him with a stick, entirely unafraid of the man's Kalashnikov. The leader stepped in to solve the problem and pleaded that the presence of two foreigners in their group was the reason for helping themselves to this melon. Seeing that this argument was not working, he added, "Plus one of them is a woman." The old woman finally piped down, walked over to Chantal, looked her up and down, and spat out, "They'll come with anything to steal my melons!" But she let us have the melon, and so the chief announced a melon break. The attack could wait.

Then we started marching again. The man in front of me turned and asked me, "Do you know why the Soviets invaded Afghanistan?" Despite feeling rather exhausted, I started mumbling through my geostrategic analysis of the situation, but he was clearly unimpressed and interjected, "I think it's on account of the melons, because really I don't see what else they could be interested in here." Two days after the attack, the commander tells me that he's taken two prisoners. I had already had one difficult experience with prisoners, which I discussed earlier, so I decide that I will see how they are treated though without trying to interview them. Several times when I was in the presence of these prisoners their guards encouraged me to ask them questions, but that of course raised an ethical problem. The CICR (Comité international de la Croix-Rouge) is very clear on the matter: even if one is supposedly neutral, one must never ask to interrogate prisoners. It's one of the principles of war in the Geneva Convention: a prisoner is "bound to give only his surname, first names and rank, date of birth, and army, regimental, personal or serial number" (article 17, section 1). It's a good rule because anything else he might say can be turned against him either during his captivity or after his eventual release. While snooping around the corridors of the madrassa, I come across a padlocked door guarded by a man who's clearly armed. I deduced that this was the prison. But the next day, while passing through another corridor, I come upon a small group having a lively debate, and suddenly I am presented to the two prisoners. They're standing in the middle of the group drinking tea—the only difference is they're not carrying weapons. And even though it's an animated discussion, there's no animosity because they're all from the same village. So what then was in the padlocked room? I return there as soon as I can and ask the soldier what he's guarding. He looks at me, a bit surprised, and says, "Why, melons, of course!"

I suppose that your stay was not that droll every day . . .

On my second time in the Afghan war zone in 1981, I found myself in Tora Bora—the place that would later become Bin Laden's hideout and head-quarters. At the time, it was the base camp of Pashtun mujahideen on the side of Yunus Khalis—a tough bunch probably, but not hostile to foreigners, and they had turned the camp into a little village. We occupied high ground above Jalalabad, and the mujahideen would go down to carry out operations against the city and the government army and then retreat to the camp where I was.

The place was constantly blasted by the wind and covered with dusty sand. It got so bad that at the end of one day I asked the commander, "Isn't there a place out of the wind?" He looked at me a bit surprised and replied, "Sure, there's a place with no wind." I asked him if I could go there and rest a bit. "Rest a bit?" He then tells a soldier to take me there. They spoke to each other in Pashtun, and I didn't catch what they said. The soldier ends up taking me to the jail that was dug into the ground. It's true there was no wind down there. The soldier informed me that, of course, I could get back out whenever I wanted—that I just needed to knock on the door and he would open it. He then closed the door, which was guarded by two armed men. So there I was in jail with half a dozen men who wondered what I was doing there. I tried starting a conversation with them, but most clearly they didn't want to talk because, of course, they took me for some sort of double agent. But then one of them started speaking off to the side with me.

He explained that a prisoner ended up there for violations against group mores: apparently, he had sold his granddaughter because he was out of money, and someone had denounced him. Two others, both peasants, had got into a fight over their property lines, and they'd been thrown into jail to get them to calm down. But two others were political prisoners, policemen in fact who had been taken prisoner during an attack against a police station. One pleaded his innocence: he came from Kabul and had killed no one. He would be liberated after a plea was entered by his family. The other one remained completely silent. Every evening when the chief returned, there was a reeducation session. The prisoners were gathered into a room, and I was included. They were supposed to pray and show they were good Muslims. But the second policeman refused. Apparently, he was a hardcore Communist. The first one seemed to know all his prayers by heart and spoke them all as clear as a bell. Since the second one seemed to be standing firm about his ideas and his actions, the camp chief decided he would be executed.

I asked him why, since he was, after all, a prisoner of war, and I added that the mujahideen would do well to respect the Geneva Convention, and so on. The chief heard me out and answered, "He tortured and killed a lot of people. He was in charge of a unit of the political police—the much feared KHAD—in Jalalabad. He's a killer. And besides that, he refuses to say his prayers and repent." He had no doubt, given the context, that the prisoner had blood on his hands. In Peshawar I had heard a number of reports about the atrocities of the regime, especially during the first two years after the Communists took power. The policeman was taken outside and shot in the head, and I watched the whole thing. I had not spoken with the prisoner—he didn't want to speak—but I found myself faced with the same dilemma that war photographers go through: observing without interfering.

I can't say I understand the moral of the story.

There's a story, but it's true there's not necessarily any moral to it. And that's the problem—today we're constantly searching for a moral everywhere. It would be absurd in those circumstances to play the part of the indignant witness. We were in the middle of a war, both a civil war (the worst kind) and a patriotic war against an invader. The question arises again in 2001, when a human rights organizations wants to exclude the warlords from the peace process because they have blood on their hands. But one only makes peace with those who have up until then been making war. So then, if experiences like those I've described leave a bitter taste and a mix of uneasy feelings, including that of powerlessness (which goes far in explaining why so many combat veterans don't speak of their experiences), you can see why I wasn't inclined to defend a systematic and formalist approach to human rights that would ultimately lead to a denial of any political logic to the violence. Violence is at the heart of politics, but to domesticate that violence one cannot simply cast it aside as a crime or barbarism. One has to transform it into a political process. That's why I have always defended professional diplomats against accusations of hypocrisy or laxness when they're negotiating with killers. That's also why I have great respect for the CICR, which knows how to be deeply political even while its mission is to protect people like those that I saw executed.

Another somewhat unexpected problem also arises: who or what exactly is a prisoner? Strictly speaking, prisons were not very common among the mujahideen, for obvious reasons that have to do with guerilla warfare. A prison is a static locale that immobilizes a significant number of fighters around it. As such, it's an ideal target and therefore raises logistical problems. So the tendency is to either kill the prisoners or exchange them—on condition that one shares with their families a common code of good manners—or else integrate them into the local society. In the Panjshir valley in 1985, I met an eighteen-year-old Soviet soldier, Leonid, who had been captured only weeks after being sent to Afghanistan. He was Moldavian and spoke French. He was dressed like an Afghan, circulated apparently at will throughout the valley, spoke with local people, and took meals with families. He had learned Persian and converted to Islam—and with total sincerity because he would remain Muslim even after his return home ten years later. He had become a sort of mascot in the valley, but he didn't have the right to leave it. His status intrigued me since it derived from a kind of logic that I didn't understand at the time. I saw him again in 1987, still in the Panjshir. In 1989, when the Russians departed, I expected that he would have been liberated, but that wasn't the case. In 1992, when Massoud took over Kabul, he was still not freed.

I and others pleaded his case. Why were they detaining him? I finally began to figure out the real reason. He probably knew too many stories about families in the valley. In 1994 he was finally handed over to the Russian consulate in Kabul, where he was told, "Sorry, the Soviet Union no longer exists. You're Moldavian, so you should go to the nearest consulate of your country." The nearest was in Moscow, but a Russian diplomat took pity on the poor guy and got him on a plane to Moscow with some sort of letter of transit. To me that story is emblematic of the mental tragedy that occurs with the fall of the Soviet Union. There were very few deaths, but millions of people wake up one day with an identity and nationality that didn't necessarily mean that much to them before, and then, by inertia, weariness, choice, or simple twist of fate in a history without history makers, it becomes real. In the years that followed, the dragon that is history regularly spit out pieces of the past that no one wanted to inherit.

Fifteen years after our first meeting, the Moldavian showed up on my doorstep in Dreux around midnight, seeking my help to get political refugee status in France—and he ended up getting it.

It's not easy to understand the role of religion in all this. You give examples that speak of a deep human feeling, of fanaticism, a sense of humor, and intense religiosity.

Religious practice was and remains today very strong throughout Afghanistan, but that's not the point. The problem was the switchover to politics. There were some people for whom Islam had become a militant ideology and others who simply kept on as very good Muslims without becoming ideologues for Islam. So the religious person could have quite a few different faces. A confirmed crook could very well never miss a prayer session, just as an Italian mafia member might never miss a week at mass. To call that hypocrisy is to accord a logic to their religiousness that they simply don't have. There's a tendency to overestimate the religious factor when it comes to the decisions and behavior of Muslims. A Westerner who lives in a secular environment and for whom religious signs appear exotic or fanatical may obviously be struck by the large place held by religious signs in a more traditional society, and he transforms that visible presence into an explanatory factor, whereas it may often be just a manner of speaking. The city of Florence during the Renaissance lived with that preponderance of religious signs, but only Savonarola believed that one could put religion at the center of political life . . . and he ended up being burned at the stake. As soon as one gets into the real inside of a Muslim family or society, one sees clearly that religion is never an explanatory factor, even if it's recruited to lend legitimacy or weight to other considerations, for example, the honor of the family.

In Kandahar, for example, in 1984, Chantal and I found ourselves in Taliban territory. We spent a week at the Panjwai oasis south of Kandahar, where there's the village of Mullah Omar, still a little tyke at the time. No sooner did we arrive than we were told at the first checkpoint by mujahideen that we'd really come at a bad moment: "The Russians are going to launch an offensive tonight." I asked them how we could flee the area, and they replied, "Impossible. They're deploying their men in the desert and circling the oasis. Go as far as you can in the oasis and shelter yourselves in the safest place you can find." We left, on foot of course, and after a while we stopped to sleep in a barn used for drying grapes. Just as they said, at two in the morning the bombing started. We stayed put until morning and then set off again. And that's how we ended up at Mullah Omar's village.

We went up to the madrassa, which had been transformed, like all of them, into a mujahideen military camp, and knocked on the door. Someone opened the door, and we were confronted by the two or three men guarding the place. They didn't let us in. "Who are you? Who sent you?" It was a very chilly reception.

Perhaps it was because there was a woman present?

I'm not so sure. When we said who had told us to come there, the leader of them reacted strongly and said he wasn't surprised. The person who sent us there was, he said, a "son of a bitch," and he added many other cuss words for good measure. I asked why he was so furious. His answer: "Instead of killing you himself over there, he sends you here so that the dishonor falls on us! No way are you going to get yourselves killed here! Leave!" And so that's what we did, and there we were alone with only our backpacks for company. Curiously, the man's argument was not at all religious, but instead based on a tribal sense of honor. But then a little bit farther on, shots rang out and sounded like they were coming from every direction. We were in a little ruined village that seemed as though it had already been bombed several times. That's when we met up with a friendly group of mujahideen. They were half crazy, shady characters smoking hashish, but they said we were welcome to join them. They told us not to worry—the shooting would last a week and then it would stop, they said, as they led us to their base camp.

The camp was a little farm built on a flat area of cleared ground in the middle of vineyards. In this region, where water is scarce, people build ditches one or two meters deep between each row of grapes so that the water circulates down there without evaporating. As a result, fields with twenty or so ditches of this kind constituted an excellent antitank defense and also offered military cover for soldiers to literally lie low and also install the few rare machine guns that the resistance fighters had. (The prestige of the machine gunner, and therefore his age, increased with the caliber of the gun. The 12.7 DShK, or Dushka, was the most common.) So we were relatively well protected from aerial bombardments—if the bomb, or shell, or tank didn't fall directly on top of us—especially since the Russian foot soldiers rarely roamed far from their tanks. On the other hand, we were vulnerable to attacks from "Stalin's organs," the multiple rocket launchers that were shot off in high concentration to saturate a limited area. It was the neighboring village that got the worst of it that time, with ten or so civilian casualties. Things calmed down at night until about 5:30 in the morning, when aerial bombing around the refuge would begin while we were dispersed in between the rows of grape vines. We would return when it was over. It went on like that for about a week. Then on the last day it was like the finale in a fireworks show. Apparently, the Russians were dumping their last weapons (shells, rockets, bombs) before returning to their base—then suddenly it stopped and there was complete silence. The mujahideen leader stood up and declared, "It's over." We were stupefied and skeptical, but he then took us to where the Soviets had been only shortly before. He told me to pick up whatever I wanted. I remember finding and keeping a three-ruble voucher—to buy vodka at a military store—lying in the middle of blood-stained clothes, bandages, helmets, and military fatigues. The commander, whose name was Daro Khan, then took care of getting us back to Pakistan, first by motorcycle and then by dromedary. One of his men accompanied us right to the Pakistan border and a place he assured us was safe—because we still had the usual visa problem. After the war, this commander became a petty local warlord and punk—in fact, he already was one, it was clear to see. Without knowing it, we had stumbled upon the small-time local mafia. Mullah Omar began his own career by assassinating this commander in 1994, for thievery.

But in the end this thief was pretty kind to you!

Absolutely. And the "safe place" in question, Quetta in Pakistan, happened to be the office of a certain Hamid Karzai. The man who guided us to the border was in fact a sharecropper for the Karzai family. We explained to him our situation, especially that we no longer had a valid visa and therefore could not go to a hotel. We were well received by Karzai, and he took us to the only Chinese restaurant in Peshawar, thinking he was giving us a special treat. Well, I can tell you, halal Chinese food is not exactly haute cuisine!

We got out of a country at war unharmed—and from a battle that killed many people. What I mean to say is that we mostly saw peasants burying the dead, because, like always, the mujahideen were armed and knew how to protect themselves. They had dug bunkers and were mobile. On the other side, the Russians bombed territories with no precise targets, and so the victims were most often civilians. I think between two hundred and three hundred people died in the zone where we had taken refuge.

So the Russians behaved like modern technological armies—they bombed enemy targets without scrimping on the number of bombs dropped so that they'd avoid victims on their own side by avoiding face-to-face combat?

Most of the time, yes, but not always, as was proved to us by another war experience that we had the following year, in 1985. We reached Panjshir via the mountains some days after one of the most violent Soviet offensives. There had only been two of that intensity in the valley. It had been decided on after Massoud had taken control in May of a series of government outposts that surrounded the valley. Massoud had begun to reconquer Panjshir, and in so doing had taken hundreds of prisoners. Afterward, he released the ordinary ones, but he had kept the officers to conduct Afghan-style exchanges—in other words, negotiations with the families so that they would achieve the liberation of captured mujahideen. The Afghans had dug a sort of open-air prison at the end of the valley, near Paryan, as far as possible from the Russians. When the Russians learned that government forces were negotiating the liberation of prisoners with Massoud, they decided it was unacceptable and mounted a commando operation to free the prisoners themselves. Of course, it failed. The guards simply killed all the prisoners as soon as they heard the helicopters coming over the crest of the mountains. Nevertheless, the combat was violent, literally face-to-face. The Russians had sent elite troops who were dropped by helicopter near Massoud's camps. We arrived a short time later. Dead bodies could still be seen here and there. I went to see the prison in question. There the bodies had been evacuated, but I was able to speak to the guards. They had killed the prisoners with grenades. Feeling traumatized, they were taking lots of tranquilizers or other drugs—a rather rare occurrence. All the villages had been destroyed, and the houses where we had stayed in the past were nothing but piles of rubble.

And what about women in the war?

For the Afghans, there were three sexes: men, women, and foreign women. The foreign women had to choose between staying with the women and dressing like them or going with the men and doing what they did. In general, they preferred staying with the men because the atmosphere with the women was suffocating. That was the case with Chantal, who wore a headscarf and otherwise dressed like a man.

The Afghan women, as I've already said, were often invisible to us foreigners. I never saw a woman among the Pashtuns even at the time of the
king. Among the Tajiks, the women wore large scarves on their heads. One
would see them in gardens or passing from one room to another but with
no chance of speaking with them. It would have been very impolite to
speak to any of them with the exception of the old grandmother. On the
other hand, among the Aimaqs, seminomadic Persian speakers who live in
central Afghanistan, the men spend the summer at high-elevation pastures
(*aylaq*), and the women guard the village. When we arrived in one of these
winter villages (*kishlaq*), we were therefore received by the women who
prepared food for us and spent some time talking with us until the men
descended from those pastures. These women in the Afghan interior were
the freest women I met. Our scant knowledge of the world of Afghan women
is based too often on the idea that if I don't see them, they don't exist.
However, the testimonies of female doctors, nurses, or anthropologists
who have worked alongside Afghan women reveal that they are not simply
the passive victims of a fate that they're forced to accept but in fact exert a
form of resistance and action. To put it simply, the Soviets and Westerners
had a very similar discourse in 1979 and 2001: Afghan women must be
freed from oppression—described as feudal by the Soviets and fundamentalist by Westerners. But one forgets that the women are part of the same
society as the men—their men, fathers, sons, and husbands. And that no
one gets liberated through an intervention from outside. What's more, neither Westerners nor the Soviets ever understood or wanted to understand
the relationship that women might have with religion. That relation is
always perceived as one of alienation, all the more so since the religions in
question (Christianity, Judaism, Islam) are anthropologically, if not theo-
logically, patriarchal. This was the discourse practiced by the anticlerical
contingent in the nineteenth century (the Left in France refused to give
women the right to vote in the belief that they were overly influenced by
their clergymen), and it's the discourse of those opposed to headscarves in
2004: a veiled woman, it is said, has no autonomous freedom of speech.
The problem is all the more important since secularization paradoxically
increases the influence women have in faith-based communities. The sexual dimorphism, that is, the fact that the proportion of women surpasses

that of men among regular religious practitioners and among the lay leaders of a religious group, emerges in France at the start of the nineteenth
century in the Catholic church and becomes only more pronounced—and
I see the same thing starting to happen among Muslims. The number of
militant women in the most radical groups is on the rise (among Salafists,
Orthodox Jews, not to mention al-Qaeda). Few writers have studied the
matter—one interesting exception is Saba Mahmood at Berkeley.[1]

**A lot has been said about drugs, but especially starting in 1990, I
think, in other words, after the war.**

During the war years, in other words, from 1980 to 1988, the year of our
last trip, we had witnessed the rise of drugs, but in an indirect way. It was
in fact the consequence of a sort of generalized banditry among a portion
of the society and of petty warlords, but not a deliberate policy decision by
the major Afghan commanders. In concrete terms, on my first trips to
Afghanistan, everything was free. I didn't spend a cent. I was offered the
use of horses and camels, given food, and people took considerable risks
helping me get across borders or through government zones. Afghans who
helped foreigners cross borders were systematically tortured if they got
caught. In spite of that, I also found guides to volunteer to help me cross
deserts or mountain passes or cross roads shortly after the passage of Russian convoys—except that they also had to go back the same way and so
risked being captured a second time! It was far more dangerous for them
than for me. But when one had got through these danger zones, the country
was safe and welcoming. The spread of banditry became apparent in 1985
with the emergence of groups of armed delinquents who stole indifferently
from local merchants as well as from foreign humanitarian workers. The
groups obviously developed in marginal areas where no major commander
controlled the territory, and they sprouted like mushrooms as the general
situation deteriorated.

Chapter 14

JIHAD

Did you meet foreign jihadists who went to fight in Afghanistan?

YES. THEY WERE both Salafists (partisans of a normative and literalist Islam) and jihadists (people for whom jihad was an individual religious duty, something that is refuted by the doctors of law). They were mostly Arabs, but one also saw Turks, Kurds, a few African Americans, and other converted Westerners. They had the honesty of real fanatics—they weren't interested in seizing money, but rather tombs, which were accused of being part of a mortuary cult contrary to Islam, and foreigners.

We met our first "Arabs" in 1985. Generally, I walked a bit in front of the mujahideen group with which we were traveling. It was easy for me since my bag was usually being carried by a horse or by a young person in the group. As we were coming back from Panjshir via Nuristan, I came to the top of a pass from where I could see barreling toward us from the other direction a column of about four hundred men wearing Afghan berets, boots and military fatigues, and baggy beige pants. Each also had a brand-new Kalashnikov and a sleeping bag of a surprising blue color. They marched toward us in a column, each with the regulation space between the one in front and behind, like a real military unit—in other words, not all like Afghans who in general march in disorderly fashion. They filed past me without saying a word when all of a sudden one of them who saw me go by turned around and called out in French, "Hey, what are you doing here? Go back home, you *kafir* (infidel)!" He was Algerian. Relations were and would remain afterward very tense between the Westerners and the "Arabs" (who in some cases could be converted Westerners). In fact, they ordered the local Afghans to choose between them and us. Every precaution was thus taken to avoid meeting up with them.

But that story had an epilogue twenty years later in 2006 in London. At a conference about deradicalization, I found myself on a panel next to a tall, bearded, muscular Algerian. He said to me in Persian (he had forgotten his French), "I know you. We met somewhere in Afghanistan." We tried to piece together our itineraries, but we weren't absolutely certain we'd met before because I just couldn't recall his face. But he swore he cussed out a Frenchman on a mountain pass while he was heading north in 1985. His name was Abdullah Anas, and he was the nephew of Abdullah Azzam, the founder of the movement that would become al-Qaeda. When Azzam was killed in 1989, the nephew ought to have become his successor, but he was edged out by Bin Laden. He eventually returned to Algeria and with other militants founded the Front islamique du salut (FIS, or Islamic Salvation Front). When that movement was put down by the army, he returned to Afghanistan to his friend Massoud. He took part in the capture of Kabul in May 1992. On the evening of the victory, he went to sleep thinking, "Mission accomplished—we have won the jihad." But the next day, fighting erupted between different factions of mujahideen, and in a matter of months the city would undergo more damage than it had during the ten years of war against the Soviets. So then he started asking himself, "How did things get so screwed up?"

He had had an intellectual upbringing that was rather similar to that of French militants of the Gauche prolétarienne. He didn't seek to blame foreign conspirators, but was asking, "What did we do? How were we crazy?" He went to London, followed the decay of the situation in Algeria, and even if the FIS cannot be held responsible for the massacres committed by the army and GIA (Groupe islamique armé), he was raising the question of his own responsibility as a jihadist. What's more (and this really sounded familiar to me), he asked why, given that people of his generation had ended up realizing the necessity of negotiation and dialogue (in 1993 his FIS comrades would enter into discussions with the Catholic Community of Sant'Egidio[1]), why did the young people after 1995 take up jihad again, and more radically than before, and at the same age that he was when he went off to Afghanistan, that is, at nineteen . . . like me, and why hadn't he managed to transmit to them his experience, his wisdom, that he hadn't pulled ready-made off a shelf but acquired the hard way?

I suppose there weren't many like him!

I have no idea, because so far no one has studied what becomes of these militants after they join up—if they survive. But I do think we completely underestimate this notion of a political journey among these jihadists, whereas we see it as perfectly acceptable among militants on the far right or the far left in Europe. At any rate, this story brings me back to the question of *universalism*. When I use that term, everyone fires back, "Yes, but the Muslim mind . . . the jihadist way of thinking . . . et cetera." The implication is that Islam has a specific essence, and therefore will never accede to or be contained within a universal. Yet, this practicing Muslim, who never missed his prayers, was reasoning exactly like members of the GP of 1973, who in their case were questioning communism's history and its affiliation with totalitarian regimes. It's simply not normal that a project for people's liberation and social justice end up committing atrocities. What is our share of responsibility for that? It's the same question that all ex-radicals ask themselves. And today, as we ask about the French youths who are going off to Syria, we tend to point a finger at the brain-washing techniques of mysterious Salafist preachers, or else harmful Internet websites, without trying to understand the logic of radicalization that has nothing specifically Muslim about it.

Abdullah became not just a moderate but a deradicalizer who felt a duty to reach out to new generations of young people who were going down the path of radicalization. He would say to these youths, "I was wounded in battle several times. My body is covered with scars. My father-in-law was the leader of the Arab volunteers. While liberating Afghanistan, I was also a founding member of the FIS . . ." His legitimacy or street cred was unassailable when it came to approaching young radicals in mosques in the outskirts of London, preaching to them in Arabic, and explaining to them that if jihad seemed attractive, it led inevitably to a dead end—to "the failure of political Islam," as I have said. He had even read my book! He said it was accurate, and we've remained friends since then. He still lives in London, and we've seen each other on occasion. He told me he wanted to publish a manuscript about his experiences, and in French because he noticed that with the TV station he had created in London his audience was mostly located in France. His public is francophone, they're young people of Maghrebi origin; but he has not really succeeded in reaching London's young Pakistanis, who are very seduced by jihad.

We've mentioned al-Qaeda and Bin Laden several times, but they're not yet present in the 1980s, right?

Bin Laden arrived in Afghanistan in 1986, but his famous battle near Khost (the battle of the so-called Lion's Den) was only a skirmish that got mythicized later. Those referred to as the Arabs already had their headquarters in Peshawar. They were known and one would meet them in the city. The big man at the time was Abdullah Azzam, a Palestinian who is the true founder of what would become al-Qaeda. Some had heard a bit about Bin Laden as the one who was in charge of logistics. He aided in transporting men—all the radical dissidents of the Middle East and the Maghreb—via Jidda, and there they took flights to Karachi thanks to letters of transit furnished by the office in Jidda, and therefore by the Saudis. The Pakistanis were not only completely aware of this, but they collaborated on the logistics. At the airport in Karachi, the new arrivals didn't have to go through border security so long as they were immediately traveling on to Peshawar, where they were given accommodations in houses that benefited from a sort of extraterritorial immunity, and then they finally crossed the border into Afghanistan. Despite widespread rumors that the CIA was managing all that, in fact it was the Saudis and the Pakistani secret service—a service that was advancing its interests for fifteen years before the Americans finely figured out its playbook.

Were there other Europeans around besides you?

Yes. Most notably there were the doctors and nurses of MSF (Médecins Sans Frontières) and AMI (Aide médicale international), male and female doctors with MDM (Médecins du Monde), and also humanitarian workers and former interns with the partnership AFRANE (Amitié franco-afghanes). There were people with Solidarités International, directed by Alain Boinet, and ACTED, founded by Frédéric Roussel and Marie-Pierre Caley. I regularly collaborated with them in the work required to find safe zones, and also in the follow-up work of inspection and verification when problems arose. Of course, there were also journalists, a very particular type of journalist who could go on assignment for two to four weeks. They were therefore most often freelance types of all nationalities. There were also war photographers and video makers. We all intermingled in the hotels in Peshawar while waiting to pass to the other side. I should also mention the non-medical humanitarian workers who worked in the areas of development, supplies, and education. It's in Afghanistan that humanitarian work evolved gradually from amateur to professional status, with all the perverse consequences that come with such a transformation and that would reach its peak during the years 2001–2011.

At the beginning, though, they were a bunch of amateurs, greenhorns, adventurers, volunteer mercenaries, or simply bored youths. Gathered together there in Afghanistan were former leftists who turned toward humanitarianism (like Bernard Kouchner, a founder of Médecins Sans Frontières) after passing through a phase of antitotalitarianism but who remained left-leaning in their lifestyle and ideas and voted Socialist back in France. There were also the *fanas-milis* (military fanatics) who had come to combat Bolshevism, youths more or less all aligned on the far right and fascinated by war and the smell of gunpowder. There were also a few nutcases, wild loners—people sometimes nice enough but often dangerous because of a tendency toward mythomania. The shoes people wore were a telltale sign. The lefties had proper hiking boots; the *fanas-milis* had combat boots. When this varied crowd descended on Peshawar, everyone checked out everyone else rather stiffly, including a furtive glance at footwear. But once in Afghanistan, everyone got acquainted pretty easily because we all had dealings with the same mujahideen, we ate the same food, met the same people, and faced the same dangers. This fraternizing even gave rise to some mixed marriages on occasion.

Over time the humanitarian organizations became more professional—the marginal types were nudged out by people with degrees in logistics or management, and the clueless neocolonialism became more self-conscious and assertive, with four-wheel-drive air-conditioned vehicles, villas with house servants, bilingual chauffeurs recruited at the local universities, night-clubs with daily bouts of heavy drinking and the occasional bomb, development projects that were more or less nonsensical but pursued to win grant money, and the ostentatious display—in the sacrosanct annual report, the thinly disguised sales pitch that assured a certain job stability for this new missionary class—of a society that would always and only be the reflection of what the West dreamed of being but never was: equality between the sexes, microfinance and small-scale development, *empowerment, agency, sustainability.*

How did you get to know the Taliban?

During the episode in the oasis, we were all alone, because the Kandahar region was not covered well by the humanitarian organizations since the people there had few representatives in Peshawar. Kandahar was the big Taliban zone at the time. A certain number of fronts were already referred to as Taliban fronts. They weren't yet anti-Western politically, and in the madrassas, of which there were many in the Arghandab Valley, a Western visitor was received peacefully and properly. All my knowledge of the Taliban started there: I lived and slept in those places, I conversed with them, and examined their books and their teaching methods. The phenomenon of the rural madrassa is very specific to that region—it doesn't exist in Iran or Turkey, nor in most Arab countries. In fact, there was a sort of mushrooming phenomenon. The term in horticulture is *marcottage* (layering), when it comes to these madrassas.

You have to know that in Afghanistan they were traditionally Sufi, and as in confraternities, if the preferred disciple replaces the master (most often by marrying the master's daughter), other disciples would leave with their *ijaza*, that is, the formal authorization to found another madrassa a bit further away. As this process repeats itself, a whole network of madrassas sprang up over time, each one conserving the memory of the genealogy from which it came. But when it was time to do higher studies, one would have to go to Pakistan, to the Deobandi,[2] who came out of an urban tradition (Delhi) that took refuge in the countryside over the years, either by choice to preach more militantly or else to flee the pressure of colonial authorities. Starting in the 1970s, so before the war, these Deobandi were beginning to be infiltrated by the Wahhabites, who, in the 1980s, took definitive control of the major Deobandi schools. From then on, these schools sent a new generation of young Pashtuns into Afghanistan. I said infiltrated, but this phenomenon was more like what I describe in *La Sainte ignorance*; that is, the secularization of the official teaching led, paradoxically, to the disappearance of all profane teaching in religious schools—the latter being unable to keep up in the new disciplines such as advanced math, Western languages, economics. Therefore, one sees a coalescence around the pure religion that contributes to those schools' disconnection from their cultural and social anchors. In short, secularization produces fundamentalism.

In Afghanistan, as I just said, the small, local madrassas were very often old Sufi madrassas. It can seem odd, and it tends to be forgotten, but the Afghan Taliban came from Sufism—it's clearly the case with Mullah Omar! The only thing is that the Sufi spirit disappeared quickly in the 1980s, the loser in the competition with Wahhabism, the latter being more congruent with the ideal of the "Arabs" in al-Qaeda, even if al-Qaeda was never a religious movement, in the sense that it never advanced a particular preaching but always stuck to jihadist activism. Those living in the madrassas were mostly young people uprooted by the war—their families had taken refuge in Pakistan, but they wanted to fight and study at the same time. So either they went to Wahhabite-influenced madrassas in Pakistan and went to fight as a sort of part-time job, so to speak, or they went to Afghan madrassas that had been turned into military bases, in particular in southern Afghanistan. The hierarchy of these madrassas was in fact turned into a military hierarchy—first the emir, then the professors and the students.

So these young people were not all religious?

Of course, but the young secular ones who wanted to get more education left the country because the situation was unbearable for them. They preferred to go to Iran or Pakistan, work for Western NGOs, or go to Europe (to France and other places), to the United States, Canada, and so on. In Pakistan, good secular schools were (and still are) almost nonexistent, and one had to pay to get admitted, and most people didn't have the money for that. The madrassas, on the other hand, were free, and it was boarding school—students had lodgings and three meals a day—hence their success with families that would enroll their sons. Those schools operated with very little overhead: teacher salaries were very low, and starting in the 1970s the Saudis were paying more and more of the bills anyway. In the past, the Deobandi were financed by networks of civic leaders—they were, as in other places, the pious good works of generous rich believers. It's worth noting that in southern Afghanistan, most resistance fronts were religious, and it was precisely the madrassas that supplied the manpower. In the north among the Tajiks, things were different.

Chapter 15

THE AFGHAN CIRCUS

During these years, you also built up relations with the secret service and foreign ministries of various countries . . .

YES, THAT HAPPENED more or less naturally. It wasn't as if I was making it a priority to seek them out. The first time that I went across the border in August 1980 with the caravan organized by Bernard-Henri Lévy—a PR operation as I have said—we didn't get very far, but it turned out OK. The other participants returned to France to organize conferences and publicize the operation more. I went back to the Dean's Hotel. It was a rundown palace that had little bungalows with an enclosed deck in front of each one and greenish or reddish curtains that had not been changed since the departure of the British army. Shortly after my return from Afghanistan, a fellow in an adjoining room out on his balcony greets me in a jovial way and asks where I've come back from. "From Afghanistan," I reply. "Oh, really. Fancy a whiskey?" he asks. "Sure," I say. In fact, he was a British agent who'd gone from the SAS to MI6. He was the man who ten years earlier had destroyed the column of guerrillas who were to have taken us into Dhofar. People obsessed with conspiracy theories would say this encounter was no accident. But I think life is full of accidents, at least mine has been.

Anyway it came at the right time for another reason having nothing to do with *affaires*. Having come back from Afghanistan, we had only one wish: to have some fun. We hadn't had a drop of alcohol for some time and wanted to eat something besides bread dunked in clarified butter. We also wanted to speak French, or, what the heck, English! I already said earlier that in Peshawar there was a real mix of strange characters: career diplomats, journalists looking for a scoop, secret service agents. That's when I realized that in fact these people were really all doing the same job: they all wanted hot information—nothing else really interested them. For me as a researcher, that wasn't my first priority. I was going for the structural account and taking longer views. But, given my circumstances, I often had hot information that, of course, was not going to stay hot for long and twenty-four hours later would no longer be of interest to journalists. So even though I was more interested in resting up and taking it easy once I'd left Afghanistan, I found myself confronted with the maelstrom of those hungry for news, scoops, and big headlines. The center of the universe, at least in Peshawar, was the telex machine (pardon me, I realize young people today have no idea what that piece of technology was) located in the main post office. We would stand in line waiting to send off our stories, and of course, the telex operator, the most well-informed man in Peshawar, worked for the local secret service. One day, I was dictating to him a text for *Le Monde*, and at the end I added my telephone number. Looking over his shoulder, I saw that he had entered another number, and so I said, "Wrong number!" and he replied without turning around, "No, sir, your number has just been changed this morning." He was right, of course. There are spies who know how to live, or at least how to communicate.

Afghanistan was also of interest to charlatans and kooks who also turned up in Peshawar—individuals who pretended to be spies, often linked to Far Right networks but who really were pathological liars. I remember in particular an old man, a Parisian with right-wing tendencies, who put out a newsletter, as one would say today, containing a curious assortment of information, supposedly confidential, that in fact was passed on to him by a nephew (who had brazenly adopted Hadi, "the Guide," as his nom-de-plume), a fellow I had traveled with and who was a good example of the mythomania I'm talking about. He told me he had served as an officer in the French army but been thrown out for his political convictions. But all that was pure invention. In fact, he had been convicted in France for some common-law offense and was sending his uncle made-up stories about Afghanistan.

So you were not exactly alone in Peshawar . . .

By no means! Peshawar in the 1980s was like Beirut, or like Barcelona during the Spanish Civil War. There was a cosmopolitan population that met up in bars, lived in a closed environment, passed on the latest gossip, and, of course, schmoozed with anyone and everyone. A book was recently published by someone who had access to all the former heads of French secret service outposts.[1] One of them, Michel, the head of France's external intelligence agency, the DGSE (Direction générale de la sécurité extérieure), in Islamabad, even became at one point the *"père aubergiste"* (i.e., the head hostel keeper, a term used in the youth hostels at the time of the Popular Front) of all the humanitarian workers. His door was always open, people lodged at his place, and many remained friends with him after he retired and joined him for shrimp fishing expeditions on the Côtes-d'Armor.

It was a fascinating crowd and I was a part of it. As often happens, many had not found their place within French society or were dealing with some feeling of lack. This was also the case among the young humanitarian doctors. I remember one of them saying to me, "Here, I amputate." In France he never would have been able to do it, because a general practitioner in France doesn't amputate. Only a proper surgeon can do that. But on a humanitarian mission, there are allowances made and professional responsibilities given that would be unthinkable back in France. For example, take nurses—absolutely extraordinary women who would have been held back in France and kept in subaltern roles by the omnipotent chief in this or that hospital wing. Over there, they would operate during bomb attacks, built hospitals from scratch, trained local nurses, and, being the only women around a lot of men, were recognized by all, including the bearded contingent, as leaders. A certain nurse had *her* hospital and fought tooth and nail for it to run properly. Taking on ventures or adventures was open to everyone—men and women. Of course, some might at a given point stop everything to pursue a relationship and have children. Years later, one might run into them somewhere in France or in America, now slotted in, literally, but with no regrets, as though the quiet, tranquil life they were leading rendered only more exceptional the earlier years of their Cinderella story when they had had it all. Among the men, things were more complicated because it was harder to revert to a quiet life. There were, as I've said, many suicides, whereas I didn't hear of a single such case among the women. I have in mind one of the most famous cases, my videographer friend Christophe de Ponfilly. After completing his film on Afghanistan and becoming a father to a young child, he put a bullet through his head.[2] There were ten others like him. But tragic stories have their own beauty.

For example?

For example, the young British woman, Juliet, whom I met in London when I was doing a sort of benefit tour for Afghanistan. She was the daughter of a pastor and had grown up in the countryside. She was doing an internship for a humanitarian association focused on Afghanistan. She was in charge of logistics, that is, ordering plane tickets and making coffee. The association had an office in Peshawar that distributed humanitarian aid intended for Afghanistan. They were looking for road warriors, former soldiers, and the like who wanted to go to the country, and Juliet's job was to go through the reply letters and rank the applicants. Only one day they discover they've been taken in by a con artist who in six months in Peshawar embezzles all their money and screws up relations with all their contacts inside Afghanistan. Someone needed to be sent there immediately to put out the fire, so to speak, and Juliet volunteers. She leaves for Peshawar and stays, building a reputation as a solid, indispensable piece of the organization. Then she meets a certain Dominique Vergos, a French freelance photographer fifteen years her senior—a real adventurer, always armed, boastful, smiling, and restless. They got married and had a child. However, a few months later, on Christmas night in 1988 in Peshawar, he comes back home a bit tipsy, starts a fight with her, and goes down to the courtyard. A shot rings out and she finds him with a bullet in his head. Alone with a baby in a city where a new round of violence was heating up due to conflicts arising in the wake of the Russian pullout—what could or should she do? Everyone expected her to go back to England.

But no! She steps into the shoes of her dead husband, takes his gun, buys a horse to ride about in jodhpurs in the streets of Peshawar, becoming the boss in the pure British tradition, with her safari hat and riding crop in hand. She became very respected among the Afghans because that's indeed where she went, and she eventually meets a British war photographer whom she marries and has a second child by him. Later they move to Moscow when he's posted there, and she creates her own agency. But during the failed coup against Gorbachev in August 1991 one Western journalist gets killed, by a bullet—her new husband.

So you were yourself part of this wild bunch in Peshawar, you say . . .

Me? Well, the first time I came back from Afghanistan after the caravan experience with Bernard-Henri Lévy, there was practically a line in front of my hotel door following my meeting with my neighbor, even though I was a nobody at the time, just a secondary school teacher at a high school in Dreux who traveled during the summer, totally unremarkable and on leave with no salary. Thinking I had something to say, I went to the French embassy and didn't even get through the door. I was asked emphatically, "Who are you? Why are you here? Who do you want to see?" When they understood that I wanted to talk about Afghanistan, the first secretary said very openly that it didn't interest him. The embassy was entirely tranquil at the time and appeared to want to stay that way. It was content to organize the routine sorts of diplomatic parties and activities. One day, though, when our embassy in Kabul was forced to shut down, the order came from Paris that they were to wake up about Afghanistan, but that all the personnel would have to be swapped out to become operational—and it was.

So you failed to get through to Paris at that point?

Not completely. While I was waiting in vain in front of the embassy door, and it's 108 degrees in the shade, a tall fellow with a shaved head happens to pass by. After learning that I just returned from Afghanistan, he invites me to his office for a Coke! Compared with the Englishman who offered me whiskey (with ice cubes!), this was not a very classy invitation or not very professional. (An empirical observation confirmed at Sandhurst and Saint-Cyr: British officers are heavy drinkers. French officers are very sober, but I can't speak for the those at lower ranks.) The man serving me my Coke was the head of the DGSE outpost in Peshawar. He offered to hire me as the local correspondent for that organization, but I refused. He then turned to another subject.

The Russians had just deployed a new type of grenade launcher, and every Western secret service obviously wanted to be the first to get their hands on one. So he told me that if I could bring him one of these grenade launchers, the AGS-17, he'd pay me $5,000. The Englishman had made me a similar offer. But a bit later the Englishman invited me to stop by again and quipped, "By the way, if my French colleague wants a grenade launcher, tell him that I have two! If you want one, I'll give it to you." It was the young adventure seeker Hadi, whom I spoke of earlier (wearing combat boots, of course), who had sold them to the Englishman after buying them himself. The Afghans probably bought them from Russian soldiers who were short on vodka or hashish. That was the Afghan circus!

Your tale paints a rather curious portrait of secret services.

One cannot speak of Afghanistan without encountering a whole series of dogmatic and often paranoid theories about the role of secret services, especially about the CIA, and they culminate, of course, with the conspiracy theories surrounding September 11. In particular it was said (and still is) that al-Qaeda was created or at least financed by the CIA, which is false. Viewed from the ground, what is striking, at least at the time, because things have changed, is the amateurism of the secret services (often accompanied by a cast-iron bureaucracy), their prudence combined with trepidation over a possible scandal, and even the incoherence of their actions. One reason, among others, was the gap in each service between, on the one hand, the people on the ground and, on the other, the analysts and deciders back at headquarters who distrust the people familiar with the terrain and who conceptualize things out of prejudices and formal constraints of their house rules rather than from the complexity of the situation in an actual location. Massoud, for example, will suffer from being classified by the operations service of the DGSE as a "fundamentalist close to Iran." Yes, he was a member of a party that emerged out of the Muslim Brotherhood movement, and, yes, he was Persian-speaking (like the Iranians), but there is a profound antagonism between the Muslim Brotherhood and the Iranians.

The problem wasn't so much the intelligence gathering itself but the analysis of it. All the services I was familiar with forbid the analyst to go out into the field. Therefore, he works from secondhand reports and submits his own report to his superior who, in turn, has to fit it within the house *doxa* and be watchful not about the proper comprehension of what's happening in the field but about the coherence of the agency's doctrine, and make sure that the information reported supports the house's presuppositions. The caricature comes, for example, with delusional interpretations such as that of the judge Jean-Louis Brugière, who was always looking to confirm his (highly ideological) public discourse instead of trying to understand what was happening. And yet these services had excellent professionals out in the field. One must also say that some had amazingly difficult personalities, like my friend Robert Baer, the CIA department head in Dushanbe when I was there. One only has to read his books. He was the only American diplomat to live outside of the secure zone of the embassy. One morning, he wakes up feeling really cold; he reaches for his blanket but with no success; then he notices that there's open sky right over his head! A bomb had blown the roof off but he was so drunk he hadn't felt a thing. Two years later, when he was put in charge of the Kurdish area within Iraq, he was arrested by the FBI for having participated in an assassination attempt against a foreign head of state, Saddam Hussein, who would end up being killed by Baer's employers ten years later. A government servant must never be right too early.

There are excellent writings on secret services, but they happen to all be novels—from Graham Greene to John le Carré . . . and one mustn't forget the wonderful works of Percy Kemp. These books should be read before one starts speaking of grand secret strategies!

Do you plan one day to make your own contribution to this literature?

It's still a little too early to say. But I can tell another story, since I like telling stories. Two months after the capture of Alain Guillo in August 1987, the DGSE noticed that the address listed in his passport was my address in Dreux. It so happens that, when Alain wanted to renew his passport, an overzealous minor Parisian functionary argued on the basis of some recently passed circular from Interior Minister Charles Pasqua that Alain, who was born in Haiphong, would have to show proof of his French nationality. That his father was a colonel in the French army, his mother killed in battle by the Japanese army, and himself a ward of the state as a boy was all beside the point—his vaguely Asian-looking eyes raised a suspicion that needed clearing up, supposedly. Alain left and slammed the door behind him. In Dreux, on the other hand, the woman in charge of these matters was more civil, and with a simple certificate from me affirming that Alain was living in my apartment, she agreed to make him a new passport.

I was summoned to offices on the Boulevard Mortier and told that the KGB would be tapping my phone if they hadn't done so already. I wondered why the Russians would take such a risk, and what they could possibly hope to learn from listening to my calls. But the service telling me this was adamant: a Russian does an awful lot of spying, you know! It was decided that a special team would be sent to my place, the kind of team that usually "cleans" French embassies abroad, and this team would make sure that my telephone and home were bug-free. Naturally, I promised to say nothing about the whole matter, especially since I wanted them not to say anything about it either. They were to come on a Monday morning. It was early October. But on Sunday night, my cousin (a sort of avatar of the Tintin character Séraphin Lampion—no footnote please) shows up and turns down all proposals I try to make that would get him out of the house on Monday morning.

As soon as he awakes, I set out coffee for him at the end of the yard behind the house. It was sunny and pleasant out. I tell him that some workers from France Télécom would be coming by to check my line, which had been acting up. At 9 A.M. sharp, the doorbell rings, and in walk four individuals with metal briefcases who all look like the comic book detective Jack Palmer at different ages. They immediately start getting out their equipment and begin working. While I'm preparing more coffee, I detect a familiar odor that's wafting in through the kitchen window. Looking out, I see my cousin taking hits off a huge joint and staring at the open windows. I hurried to bring him his coffee so that he wouldn't budge, but he was already intent on coming in to help out. "Listen, Olivier, these guys here, they don't look like people from France Télécom—I know, I worked at France Télécom." I go back in the house and see that the telephones have been taken apart and one of the four guys is on a ladder tapping the walls with a sort of metal plate, as though he were diagnosing signs of bronchitis. I glanced back at the yard and saw my cousin had lit up a second joint that he was sucking on with all his might. Wafted by the autumn breeze, the suave and delicate exhalations of my cousin had now spread throughout the entire ground floor of my house, and the cloud was softly making its way up the stairs. I was worried about how these four detectives might react. Were they going to be shocked and appalled, or would their behavior undergo some modifications unforeseen by official regulations? I was inclined to go with the second hypothesis when the functionary on the ladder told me he'd found traces of a suspicious metal in the wall of the house. "What do you intend to do?" I asked somewhat nervously. "Well, knock the wall down, of course, but don't worry, we'll fix it before we leave."

I returned to the yard to see if I could put out the fire. My cousin was making all kinds of agitated gestures inviting me to come closer, and he then whispered in my ear, "Olivier, you know, these guys, they don't work for the phone company. I swear it, I'm not paranoid, I promise you. Listen, they're wiretapping your house."

Your Afghan experience threw you into another world, the world of deciders and opinion makers. How does one deal with that if one wants to remain an intellectual and a researcher, which I presume you wanted to do?

There is a mirror myth of the decider on one side and the expert on the other. Whether one sees them as opposites or as associates, one is ducking the fact that, at bottom, the decider does not know what he's deciding, while the expert does not know what deciding means.

Intuitively, I have always been skeptical of the capacity of researchers, or of experts, to influence the making of a decision. My collaboration in that other world, as you call it, allowed me, first and foremost, to finance my trips, to lobby in favor of my Afghan friends, but also, and increasingly, to observe and work on phenomena in relation to the formulation of a political policy at the top level and to decision making. In truth there is a deep interaction among perception, action, and reality on the ground. It's not a matter of observing a phenomenon and then responding to it—a classic way of thinking that gives the starring role to the expert—because the reaction of politicians contributes to a modification of the reality on the ground. For example, the overestimation by the West of Soviet power during the years 1981–1986 rested on an error of analysis, but it contributed to an internal collapse (paradoxically also a pacific one) of the USSR. The American analysis, which concludes with the necessity of invading Iraq in 2003, is totally fantastical, but by working as it does in Iran's favor, it allowed for that nation's return as an international player, as well as the decoupling between the geostrategy in the Middle East and the Israeli-Palestinian conflict, which was an objective of the Bush administration. Another major debate concerned moderate Islamism, that is, the refusal to see Islamic radicalism as the sole logical expression of the conception of political Islam, which is unfortunately the dominant view. Here too, because of the Islamic Revolution in Iran and later with al-Qaeda, the concept [of moderate Islamism] didn't get traction, and therefore the West has never been able to conceive of an alternative politics, besides corrupt dictatorships, of the Muslim world or of a way to reintegrate the religious dimension within a democratic framework.

Here you're discussing theoretical questions. But practically speaking, what does one do, how do you deal with those who approach you?

In fact, independently of any results, being solicited to serve as a consultant, lecturer, or expert has allowed me to make trips within the trip, if that makes sense. I really liked that period from 1981 to 1989 a lot because as soon as I would get back from Afghanistan I would go off to more peaceful destinations—support meetings somewhere outside Paris or abroad, conferences, international meetings, high-level summits like my first invitation to Bilderberg in the Austrian Tyrol in 1988. A bit like in Tintin's *Objectif Lune*, I found myself in a little propeller plane landing in the fog in Innsbruck and then was immediately ushered toward a cavalcade of limousines as black as the suits of the mysterious guests who emerged out of another fog. We slipped into pine forests guarded by special mountain troops who stood like Christmas figurines behind trees covered in snow. I discovered all of Europe and then the United States this way. My Italian translator led me to Genoa, and I was also in Lausanne, London, and Athens, but also smaller places like Udine, Mons, La Chaux-de-Fonds, Orléans, and Blois. Sometimes I spoke to important people, sometimes in the country, in villages, in little community halls, or to support associations. I went from conversing with Kissinger to exchanges with a farmer in the Haute-Saône Department, and I told them all the same thing. I gave a talk to the Sixth Mountain Infantry Regiment of Valais, the last military group in a Western country to use mules, because they wanted to know how the Afghans used their mules to transport ammunition in the mountains. Answer: they actually preferred horses, which goes to show that the rational actor theory is an invention of lazy economists. And the answer within the answer: I also prefer horses, even if at fifteen thousand feet one is no longer sure who is transporting whom. I spent almost a week with the Twenty-Second Royal Regiment of Quebec speaking to them about how the Russians fought in snowy conditions. Answer: they never fought in winter—they weren't crazy! I also gave many talks in provincial cities around France to help support and finance humanitarian interventions.

Given the context of those years, it was understandably the Americans who reached out to you the most?

At first the debate in the United States was kept internal, and so the lobbying was very political. The primary goal was to persuade the administration to increase military aid (at the time the weapon of choice was the

Stinger missile). Back then I met people whom I never would have spent time with in my earlier years. For example, I had contact with tough, right-wing purists within the Republican Party—people to the right of Ronald Reagan. They were half-crazy and proud of it, anticommunist cowboys and brash bigmouths like the Democratic senator from Texas, Charlie Wilson. But I also met people in the left wing of the Democratic Party with sympathy for Third World countries. Fifteen years later, I rediscovered some of my American contacts, who by then had become important figures in the neoconservative movement and were still on the warpath. In France the new Far Right, the right of the National Front, was on the contrary quite anti-Afghan because they still preferred to see white-skinned people, albeit Communists, fight against Muslims. At any rate, this communism was soon going to turn from red to brown, notably in the Balkans in the 1990s, and there the Far Right would find again its preferred opposition with authoritarian nationalist regimes doing battle against supposed Muslims. But in France we were working as much with the traditional Right as with the antitotalitarian Left. They were people like Jean-François Deniau, a lovely man but sometimes also a bit full of himself. I remember he used to walk around Paris with a revolver in his pants, carrying it a bit like a Yemeni dagger, because he believed he was threatened by the KGB. It made him feel younger. And then of course there was Bernard-Henri Lévy. We needed these stars because they could open doors and get us access to the media. On the other hand, they would build up adventurous images of themselves that were a touch too Indiana Jones.

Did they annoy you?

No, not really. We, the people on the ground, preferred to let them tell their stories. We had sort of made a deal with these public personalities: we needed them, but we also got to see what was really going on. Bernard-Henri Lévy never met with Massoud during the war, but he let it be thought that he had—and he really did meet him later in Afghanistan. We let him chatter on, and we even fed him some of the talking points he'd use in his stories. I also saw television crews pull some fast ones with war footage because they didn't have the patience to wait around for a real attack (that, moreover, no local mujahideen wished for), or because the attack had taken place at night and so the lighting wasn't any good. I confess I myself participated in this "editing" process in the way I would translate (or not translate) certain statements. After all, if it's true that the Soviets are attacking, why wait for the improbable alignment of a given attack with the momentary presence of a TV crew that can stay in the area only for two days and demands, as I did in Maymana, to be shown the war, in other words, some real blood and dead bodies? In August 1981, near the Sarobi gorges, when I was translating for a small British team that demanded to film the attack on a fort before 5 P.M. (for the light), I forgot to tell them the next day that the attack (which had really happened but failed) was entirely fake and had been staged with the complicity of troops stationed at the fort. All this took place alongside a subtle arrangement whereby the Communist troops shared its stock of weapons and ammunition with the mujahideen, who, in turn, supplied them with fresh fruit and perhaps other things.

Think tanks and deciders nevertheless did seriously ask for your opinions and analyses, no?

The problem is how to define the domain of the serious. Think tanks are part of a more global landscape of political decision making. But it's true their involvement became much more extensive at that time, or more exactly starting in the 1970s.

This growth was linked to changes in the figure of the intellectual (and the creation of the expert) and to changes in the production and transmission of knowledge. It started in the United States at the time of the Second World War. How was one to make practical use of academic knowledge? At the time, the question was asked in the context of a fight (against Nazism) that most intellectuals supported. As a consequence, two things get conflated: the legitimacy of the war being waged and the pertinence of university personnel participating in national politics. Isn't collaboration with a government entity legitimate only if the intellectual puts his knowledge in the service of a politically just cause—but who shall define what's politically just if not the individual concerned? Or is it more proper to remain distant from all compromised positions linking university research and politics, which, by definition, is ideologically or politically driven? In France at least, there exists a long tradition of militancy within the intellectual class (especially on the left, but not exclusively), but the question remains: when the intellectual is recast as the expert and he ceases to concern himself with defining the end of a course of action and instead concentrates only on the means employed, does he not betray his function as "cleric," as Julien Benda once put it? Therefore, the question is not about avoiding politics—all intellectuals are engaged in politics—but whether to leave the decision about the finality of an action to the politicians. And secondly, it's about deciding on the modes of intervention of the intellectual into politics.

I learned to write think tank papers for politicians—analyses in a few pages that come to conclusions or propose immediate recommendations. In other words, I did what most academics don't know how to do. They can provide excellent political science analyses of this or that situation, but they're incapable of making recommendations about what to do over the next six months. Curiously, they produce material for politicians that is normative and full of will and sometimes much affect, but deciders can't do much with it right away, and time counts. Consider this statement, for example: "We must resolve the Israeli-Palestinian conflict to keep radicalization in disadvantaged neighborhoods from spreading." Therein lies the whole problem of how one transforms university expertise into government action. In my case, I had relations with the Foreign Affairs Ministry and the Defense Ministry, but it's no different when it comes to the municipal government decisions about the crisis in outlying neighborhoods: what concrete policy should be pursued now and over the short term? My work consisted of producing short working papers in the form of rather short notes (I wrote about two hundred over twenty years for the CAP) and attending various meetings. Of course, today it would be an interesting research project to evaluate the pertinence of these notes I prepared, to see if I was mistaken, where, and in what context.

At base, there are three possible attitudes one can have when confronted with a request for expertise: (1) avoidance (remain pure), (2) go with the flow (do what you think is expected of you), and (3) management at a distance (master the use of the information that's made available, which means, paradoxically, involving oneself further in the political decision).

Since I don't see you in the purity camp or in the go with the flow camp, give me an example of management at a distance.

It's the experience that let me hit on what I'll later call the golden rule. It looks like an ordinary anecdote, but it underscores the fundamental problems. In October 1985, when I was just barely starting to be recognized as an expert on Afghanistan, I was invited to a big conference on Islamism by Professor Nadav Safran, the director the Middle Eastern Studies Center at Harvard. He asked me to present the case of Afghanistan along with my mentor in the United States, Louis Dupree, a much older colleague, and alongside Arab specialists on Islamism in Egypt, Iraq, Iran, and so forth. It was important for me because it was the first time I had been invited to the United States to speak at a university, and at Harvard! It was obviously the dream come true for any aspiring academic. And what's more, my airfare was paid for by the conference, a significant sum at the time, but I received no other remuneration. Before my departure, I took advantage of that one invitation to arrange other meetings and other speaking engagements at a number of American universities. I had just been accepted into the CNRS, and so it was normal enough that I get started down the path of my university career!

I was supposed to leave on Sunday, but on Saturday at midnight I get a call from Safran, who informs me that many of my Arab colleagues have canceled their plans to attend after learning that the conference was in part financed by the CIA. He wanted to let me know I was also free to not come if I wished. I asked if the whole conference was canceled. "Not at all!" he replied. "But I'm legally required to inform you of this financing arrangement, and therefore you have the right not to come." I was tempted to cancel, as I thought about the negative image that might be pasted on me on account of my being there. And yet Louis Dupree—a man who signed up at age seventeen to be a part of a parachute division in the Pacific campaign in 1944, a man who used a GI Bill scholarship to go to Princeton in 1946 (and who it's said chose his studies—Afghanistan, anthropology, and archaeology—because they were the first listed in an alphabetically organized course catalog (which was about as solid a deliberation process as the way I ended up studying Tzigane), a man who eventually became a seasoned itinerant professor in Afghanistan, and later a tenured university professor in the United States—that man, Louis Dupree, had not pulled out! Therefore, I decided to go and to put my trust in him—the old wise man. As soon as I arrived, we met up at the standard meet-and-greet session with our paper cups filled with tongue-burning bad coffee. He was quite furious at the situation created by the CIA's participation, which had also provoked student demonstrations, but he decided to attend anyway, he told me, precisely so he could speak out on the whole matter. He suggested I accompany him. He would speak into the mic and I was to remain silent (which was fine since my English was very weak at the time). So he improvised a little press conference right there, and I stood at his side—I was simply supposed to nod my head with conviction each time he advanced his arm in emphasis. He said that he had not known that the CIA was to be a cosponsor of the conference but also that he could totally care less since the event was open to the public. He also added that he was delighted the spooks from the CIA would be in the room, since for once they would have a chance to hear people "who know what they're talking about" and who therefore could contribute to making the CIA do sane and intelligent things instead of simply cranking out ideology and paranoia. So welcome to the CIA! "I'm now going to tell you what I think of the American policy in Afghanistan!" I nodded frequently since I was quite in agreement with him. He was a wise man. He knew that no matter what we would say or whom we might try to avoid, we would always be suspected, no matter where we went, of working for some secret service. So the heck with useless precautions was his message. There was only the golden rule that one need follow: speak with everyone and tell everyone the same thing, write and publish everything we think—in short, go public with one's opinions without looking to meet some standard of purity when it comes to the company one keeps (because one's never in control of that). And go all out. That simple rule has served as my compass throughout my career.

Because, of course, he was right. When one is always under suspicion, one might as well just go all out, no matter what. At the end of the 1980s, I was supposed to go to Iran with a French colleague, a big specialist in Persian language and literature, a truly erudite man detached from politics. I got my visa and he didn't. He asked me to look into the reasons for this refusal. At the Iranian Foreign Affairs Ministry, the diplomat in charge of cultural cooperation questions me, and then asks me to go knock at the little door at the end of the hall. It was, of course, the office of the secret service. I ask my question forthrightly, defending the intellectual integrity of my colleague and even conceding that it would have made more sense if they had refused me my visa. And when I had finished, my interlocutor replied, "Yes, but, *you*, we know who you work for. *Him*, we don't know."

PART IV
THE CENTRAL ASIA DECADE

Chapter 16

A SOVIET INVITATION TO CENTRAL ASIA

You've spoken little about the Soviets in Afghanistan except in your descriptions of some bombings that you witnessed.

SO LONG AS the Soviets were at war, they officially ignored me. There was, however, an article in *L'Humanité*[1] one day that mocked the "pseudo–Afghanistan expert Olivier Roy." It was naturally out of the question for me to travel to the Soviet Union or in the Eastern Bloc countries during that period. Indeed, I have no idea if I would have obtained a visa even if I had wanted to try. But in 1989, things suddenly changed after the Soviets left Afghanistan. In February 1990, I was invited to a reception at the Iranian embassy in Paris, and there a Russian diplomat who spoke French perfectly came up to me. He said he had a colleague, Professor Vitaly Naumkin, of the Institute of Oriental Studies, who would very much like to meet me. "He's coming to Paris next week, and I would be happy to receive you at our embassy, because I would like to introduce you to him." I went and I met Vitaly Naumkin, and we soon became good friends.

He proposed, since I already knew Afghanistan, that I broaden my horizons and consider traveling through Central Asia. I was surprised by his invitation after all that I had written on Afghanistan and the Soviet intervention there. "But we've left Afghanistan, and we know very well that you're the best specialist on that country! Your book was translated, and all our experts were supposed to have read it, and all of your articles as well. For the KGB, if one wanted to know Afghanistan, one had to read Roy!" He said they were told to denounce me publicly as a pseudoexpert but that in fact everyone was reading me in private. So now a little group of Russian experts, who had all worked for the KGB or the army but who were all now pursuing a career change, wanted to meet me.

And so you went?

Of course—as soon as a door is ajar, I push it open. I set off in June 1990 at a time when the whole Soviet system was teetering. But its increasingly rapid erosion had an unexpected consequence: the sudden pauperization of state institutions and of many functionaries who formerly had been living the high life as members of the state's elite. Naumkin therefore suggested that I pay my own way to Moscow, and from there his institute would finance my trip to Central Asia. I ended up traveling with the aid of a mission order from the French Foreign Affairs ministry. But in Moscow—surprise!—I'm told that they've bought my tickets for the Central Asia tour, but Aeroflot tells them there's no room left on the plane. This was new, since during the time of the Soviet Union there was always room for members of state institutions. Now the airline was stubbornly refusing to accommodate us. My host was losing face—how were we going to resolve this situation? It happened that the same institute was organizing the first visit of Saudi ulema of Wahhabite persuasion, who were to be accompanied by Jordanian and Lebanese Salafists. They were to be received by the grand mufti of Tashkent. (What was the purpose of the operation? Money? Propaganda? I have no idea, but during this chaotic period all sorts of crazy stuff was happening.) These people had reserved seats on the plane because they were paying in dollars and not in devalued rubles. The institute was providing Russian-Arabic interpreters. So my host contrived that I be put on the list of ulema, and my accompanier, Alexis Koudriavtseva, who spoke Arabic and French perfectly without ever having set foot in France, was listed among the interpreters.

If the Soviet system no longer functioned efficiently, it nevertheless continued out of inertia since objects in motion tend to stay in motion. As soon as we landed in Tashkent, the local man in charge of our tour was at the foot of the stairs below the plane with a checklist of the ulema and interpreters, and we were on it and were thus invited to remain with the delegation. For three days I found myself being constantly referred to officially as a "Saudi ulema." I was reminded of the story told by Tynyanov about Lieutenant Kijé, whose name appears on the list of cadets promoted by the czar after a writing mistake by an official scribe, and this phantom follows a normal career in the army even though he never existed, only to end up dying the day when the czar wanted to meet him and promote him to general.[2] Now we were forced to remain with the delegation, to the great discomfort of the Saudis, who are asking themselves what kind of strange game their hosts are playing. The next day we attended the audience at the residence of the grand mufti, which took place in Arabic (Alexis translated for me and added additional comments in French). We also visited several mosques and interviewed the local mullahs, who spoke very openly, persuaded that they were dealing only with good Muslims. This was a lucky break since my research project then was precisely the religious revival among Muslims in Central Asia, and here I had a front row seat. We noticed that the grand mufti did not say the same things when he spoke in Arabic or Russian—he lived and thought in two registers, not unlike the upper level officials of the Communist Party (in their case it wasn't over Islam but about the grammar of personal relations—a little like the Afghans).

This was truly a rare opportunity for a researcher, and, as you say, a stroke of luck that couldn't have happened under normal research project conditions.

I found here, live, all the classroom teaching of Professor Alexandre Bennigsen who led a seminar at EHESS (École des hautes études en sciences sociales) right up until his death in 1988 on the ways militant and conservative Islam was maintained in the Caucasus and Soviet Central Asia.[3] Since he couldn't travel through the area, he had developed a whole system for analyzing information at a distance (reading between the lines of local newspapers in every local language, interviews with refugees, decoding official speeches denouncing "deviations," etc.). Bennigsen, along with Louis Dupree and Rémy Leveau, were my masters who taught me the art of managing with difficult situations where one is both a researcher, and therefore sticking to professional ethics, and an actor. I confess I am more comfortable in the creative, ambiguous situations that they were accustomed to than in the hair-splitting rules and somewhat artificial ethical regulations that always wind up making research nearly impossible. (For my latest research project, ReligioWest, I had to certify that no animal had suffered as a result of my research. That made me laugh, until a little bureaucrat made a nervous observation, though without insistence, about our possible consumption of halal and kosher meat.) One has to find a certain balance. Bennigsen sometimes went a bit far, but what's important is that the exact sciences have demonstrated how the observation of a phenomenon changes that phenomenon, and I think the same is true in the social sciences.

Why and how did Professor Bennigsen go a bit far?

When we met in 1984, he was working on the penetration of fundamentalist ideas into Central Asia as a result of the Afghanistan war. He made lists of the Islamic publications published in foreign countries, which, passing through Afghanistan, were noticed, confiscated, and often ended up in Central Asia. One day, he called me to his Paris apartment so that I could serve as an interpreter as he interviewed an Afghan commander from the region of Mazar-i-Sharif, a certain Alam Khan of the Jamiat-e-Islami group. And there, while translating, I realize that Bennigsen was quite simply in the process of organizing the printing of religious texts in Mazar (there was also the Bible in Russian) that he then "discovered" in Central Asia. In other words, he contributed to the creation of the phenomenon that he studied. But the researcher could only attest to the result: the war in Afghanistan caused a flow of religious books into the USSR, because, no matter what the true origin of the books was, the impact was the same. I like this kind of story.

And what about the rest of the trip to Samarkand?

After taking leave of my Wahhabite delegation in Samarkand (which is only a shadow of its former self), I arrived in Dushanbe in Tajikistan. It was my first encounter with the Tajik language, a cousin of Persian written in Cyrillic but with lots of false friends (i.e., misleading cognates). Having taken two years of Russian in high school, I was comfortable with Cyrillic. As we left the airport, I see an enormous statue of Lenin with the words, "Glory to Lenin who imprisoned (*dastguiri kardan*) the peasants." OK, either perestroika had gotten a bit ahead of itself here, or something else was going on. *Dastguiri* literally means "take the hand." In Iran it means "to stop" but in Tajik "to help." There was a certain logic to that. In similar fashion, the first sentence that my correspondent uttered as I stepped off the plane left me puzzled: "Can I make trouble for you at my place this evening?" *Taklif* in Iranian Persian means a "duty" (usually onerous). In Afghanistan it means "bother, problem, difficulty," but in Tajik, "invitation." It's true that the protocol of hospitality is often burdensome, as much for the guest as for the host, so one can understand this slide in the meaning, but it did give a surreal touch to the conversation at times.

In Dushanbe I encountered young Tajiks who had served in the Red Army in Afghanistan, usually as translators and experts, including one who confided in me that he translated during torture sessions. They were familiar with the same war zones I had known, simply from the other side of the battle lines. So I learned about their vision from the other side, which often confirmed my analysis of the situation—notably about the alcoholism among the troops. I especially made it a point to meet the mullahs of all categories (Sufi, Wahhabite, Tablighi), and all were happy to speak with a foreigner. They often insisted on speaking carefully in classical Persian and applying themselves to use the Arabic alphabet. I examined their tiny personal libraries, in which I found old lithograph editions of religious texts that dated back to the czarist period (I could read both the Arabic-Persian and the Cryrillic), including the books of my Mawlawi Mirajuddin from Panjshir. My research focused on the transmission of Islam during the Soviet era. I quickly discovered the new Islamists who had come to found the Islamic Renaissance Party. I learned later that some of them had consulted with Afghan mujahideen to know if I was trustworthy. Luckily, their contacts were mostly people close to Massoud, Tajiks like them, who praised me and thereby facilitated my making other contacts.

In sum, I felt oddly at home in Tajikistan, and that's when I started doing my first serious thinking about Central Asia. I later went back two times a year for several weeks each time until 2001. So I lived through the collapse of the Soviet Union and the implementation of new regimes in a context where it was necessary to invent in only a few years entirely new identity references that were more or less artificial.

And did you find yourself in the middle of new wars?

Yes, but this time, though I was not looking to get involved in a war, the civil war that would tear apart Tajikistan from 1992 to 1997, took place all around me. I was no longer in adventure-seeking mode (except, of course, if a door suddenly opened—I couldn't resist). I had a research project (on Islam, nationalism, and the evolution of the kolkhoz system) which would turn into a book, *L'Asie centrale; ou, La fabrication des nations*, that was published in 1997.[4]

I arrived in Dushanbe at the end of April 1992 to pursue my research. Tensions were high between the Islamo-Democrats (an alliance of Islamists from the Gharm Valley and democrats, especially Islamists, from Pamir) and the Neo-Communists from the valley of Kulob. The two camps led demonstrations at each end of the main avenue that traversed the city, but on May 2 civil war broke out. We were staying at the Hotel Tajikistan (formerly the Intourist Hotel), which happened to be the frontline between the two sides. The Kulobis held the presidential palace, and the Gharmis held the National Assembly building. Luckily, there was no artillery, just light tanks, but bullets were flying. The few ex-patriots gathered at the bar of the hotel located in the basement. War correspondents showed up, and some would risk leaving the hotel to try and understand what was going on. The Russian mechanized regiment that had its barracks in the city center right next to us made one sortie to break it up and then turned back. There were no more planes, no more cars, no more buses, and food was starting to run short. But not vodka. Since the Islamists didn't drink, there was a plentiful supply. Eventually, the Gharmis made a successful charge and were able to take over the presidential palace with a few tanks. There was a cease-fire; the Kulobis regrouped into formation under Russian protection and left the city. An old Ilyushin plane was getting ready to leave for Moscow, and I hopped aboard.

Everything changed afterward. The Islamo-Democrat victory was of short duration. An atrocious civil war broke out in the southern part of the country, and in December 1992, the Neo-Communists retook power. The Islamists fled into northern Afghanistan and built camps, dreaming of the day when they would retake power.

Chapter 17

A DIPLOMATIC PASSPORT

So you came back one more time, but wearing a different cap now?

I HAD THE same problem that came up with Afghanistan ten years earlier: what should I do? How was I to avoid being a mere spectator of all this? But as I said, this time I did not want to be part of a war or in the middle of a war.

It so happens that the prospects for chaos at that time within the former Soviet territories were of serious concern in Europe, notably a fear of mass immigration that never took place. In 1993, Sweden was to take on the presidency of the Organization for Security and Co-operation in Europe (OSCE), and all the former Soviet republics were granted the right to join after the collapse of the USSR. As the Swedes are extremely serious and organized people, they prepared for the leadership role one year in advance with a large conference on the post-Soviet era and what to expect. I was invited to this meeting in Stockholm that took place in September 1992. Near the end, I had a meeting with the Swedish foreign affairs minister, Baroness Margaretha af Ugglas. She asked me in excellent French what I thought of the Wahhabi problem in Central Asia. I made a few observations in reply. Three months later, I received a message from the French representative at the OSCE in Vienna. I knew this ambassador, Marc Perrin de Brichambaut from the CAP. He asked to see me immediately. The Swedes wanted to name me the OSCE's special envoy in Tajikistan, with the idea of opening a mission there, which I would be the first director of. I was appointed for a period of three months, July–September 1993. So I returned to Tajikistan in the summer of 1993 and worked in close cooperation with the United Nations and the HCR (where I still had friends); then I returned to Vienna and submitted my report to the Parliamentary Assembly of the OSCE.

Afterward, I returned to Stockholm where the same baroness minister says to me, "Dear sir, my ministry is offering to put you in charge of the diplomatic mission of the OSCE in Dushanbe. Your task is to establish the mission, and your goal is to democratize the country and reestablish human rights—in six months, with one renewal possible." She wrote an elegant nomination letter, in French, for "*Monsieur le professeur Roy, chef de la mission diplomatique de l'OSCE à Douchanbé.*" She further specified that I was to report to the French authorities to obtain a diplomatic passport.

I already had a foot in the door at the French Foreign Ministry thanks to the CAP. I was told to report to the director of political affairs, Ambassador Philippe Lecourtier. I knock on his door, and I'm greeted by an imposing figure who addresses me dryly, "Monsieur le professeur"—I sensed this was not going to go well—"we've learned of the mission conferred on you by the Swedes; but strictly speaking this is a Swedish affair that does not entitle you to French diplomatic status." And yet, according to the OSCE statutes, each member country was supposed to provide a title and salary to its citizens hired by the organization. I therefore insisted on obtaining a salary and diplomatic passport. He sat up in his chair, "What! A diplomatic passport?!" he spluttered. "It's an exorbitant request, Monsieur le professeur, an exorbitant request!" He told me to hold on to my salary at the CNRS, generously offered me a mission stipend for two months instead of twelve, and moved to close the meeting. As soon as I left his office, I went directly to see Bruno Racine, the head of the CAP and someone I knew was close to the foreign affairs minister of the time, Alain Juppé. He received me in his office, cut short my lengthy explanations, asked if I had my normal passport and some photos with me (I did), and told me to come back at 5 P.M. At the appointed hour, he hands me a shiny blue diplomatic passport, and I tuck it in my pocket. Afterward, it was renewed every year automatically (the wonders of bureaucratic inertia) until I renounced it in 2009. I have to say that passport made things a lot easier for me on several occasions.

How did your role as diplomat–nation builder go?

When I arrived in Dushanbe, there was nothing. Since the logistics all passed through the Americans (only the American embassy was open), they assigned me an American collaborator, a career diplomat, to watch over my activities. But the person in question, Daria Fane, was an old friend from my Afghan days, so we actually got along well together. We met up at a hotel in the middle of winter—it's well below freezing and we have no office or staff. Nevertheless, we managed to create together a very competent local team of nice people who were, of course, put under enormous pressure. The mission's role was to influence a government that was composed of a large band of killers whose only goals were vengeance and plundering. There was only one person of some sophistication with whom we were able to work, Vice President Dustov. It was with Dustov that I committed my second big translation mistake between Persian and Tajik.

What was the mistake?

The Tajik government had signed an agreement with the OSCE and was supposed to provide us with offices, which they never did. After one month and with Vienna's urgent insistence, I finally got an appointment to see Dustov. I explain to him that his government is supposed to give us a *daftar*, which in Iranian and Afghan Persian means "office." He gives me a quizzical look and says he'll do his best. As we're leaving, my local assistant asked me very politely, "But why did you ask him for a notebook?" I would know for the future: in Tajik, *daftar* is a notebook, and the word for office is *ofis*, of course! The OSCE never got its office, nor any notebooks either. It was proof of the government's bad faith.

The OSCE was by definition a very international organization?

Yes, I worked closely with the general secretary of the OSCE, Wilhelm Höynck, a German diplomat, and with the representative of the Italian OSCE presidency, Ambassador Francesco Bascone—two remarkable men who spoke perfect French and were used to dealing with complex situations. We established a special system of correspondence: watered-down reports in English were distributed to the entire assembly, and reports in French that were more explicit and critical circulated among a small circle of people. This double use of languages would become a general practice with me: French would be the tribal language of the insiders and convey details and intelligence; English would be the language of generalities and a mushy consensus. Incidentally, I'd like to underscore that my time working with diplomats convinced me that diplomacy is a true profession, with its codes, its logic, and its concrete results, all of which are far removed from the cinematic clichés about embassy receptions in black tie and the like.

You'll talk about your second marriage later, but at this time were you still single or with someone at Dushanbe?

At first I was single and later in a relationship starting in July 1994. Nineteen ninety-four was all the more chaotic because it was the year I got married. Chantal and I had been separated for nearly five years. Her time in Kabul ended badly, and she was then working for the United Nations in Haiti. In late October of 1993, when I was in transit between Dushanbe and New York and passing through Dreux for two days, Martine, the daughter of my Turkish friend, rang my doorbell. I had known her for fifteen years, but we'd always seen each other in the context of family gatherings and never just the two of us. That day, after about fifteen minutes, I asked if she'd marry me. Thus began a series of complex events.

Why complex?

For her to be able to leave her family and join me in Tajikistan, we needed to get married as soon as possible. However, first I had to organize a divorce between a person based in Tajikistan (me) and another in Haiti (Chantal)— and remember there was practically no Internet then. Secondly, there was something more serious than these procedural problems, namely, a theological question: we had to obtain a special dispensation from the Syriac Orthodox Patriarchate in Damascus on account of the fact that I was the godfather of one of her younger brothers—which amounts to incest in many Orthodox churches. Meanwhile, I was continuing with my human rights campaign in Dushanbe, and I was going to New York to coordinate my efforts with the special United Nations envoy for Tajikistan, Ramiro Piriz-Ballon, a Uruguayan diplomat, while at the same time participating as an observer in a first round of negotiations between the opposition and the government in Tehran, from June 18–23, 1994. For the second time—the first was my United Nations adventure back in December 1989—I arrived in that city with diplomatic status, and little by little I developed a network of good relations with Iranian diplomats. A second round of talks took place in Islamabad on October 20, 1994.

When I got back from Tehran, I had a week to organize the wedding—luckily, my in-laws did all the work. This time I invited my parents. We were married on Saturday, July 2, in Tremblay-le-Vicomte by Father Yakoub, the only Syriac Orthodox priest in France at the time, and by Brother Malke, a first cousin of Martine. One of our witnesses was Louis Schittly, the doctor and my companion during my first tour among the mujahideen, and also a convert to the Orthodox Church, my new religion. The service began with a sonorous *Shlomo aleykho* (peace be upon you) addressed to the Virgin Mary, and I found myself in my new, displaced Orient, that of Semitic Christianity. The following Thursday, we landed at night in Tashkent. Then we traveled to Dushanbe for our honeymoon and the continuation of my work (I have no talent for keeping things separate). I had rented a small villa in the Jewish quarter. The lack of security was permanent, but since the attorney general, also a hardened killer, lived in the same street, we benefited from the security offered by his personal militia. The day after we arrived, our female neighbors came by to see the new arrival, and I overheard them saying in Tajik, "But she's oriental, she's like us, so why doesn't she speak Uzbek or Tajik?" In fact, though, with a mixture of Turkish and Kurdish, especially for counting, Martine was quickly able to make herself understood. And here, too, body language played an important role.

We'll discuss later what this marriage meant for you. Tell me how you made progress on the Tajik problem.

As often with me, the threads of my life that ought never to have crossed suddenly came together all at once. The opposition was composed mostly of Islamists who thought well of me because I had been on the side of Massoud's mujahideen, with whom they had taken refuge—though this did not prevent Massoud from controlling the Afghan embassy in Dushanbe. Besides them, a few liberal democrats had joined the Islamists around the idea of the democratization of the country and anticommunism. Among them there was a professor, a true intellectual who possessed a real humane core, named Atakhan Latifi. He became the delegation's spokesman during the peace negotiations. He would later be assassinated in September 1998. One day in Dushanbe, the telephone rang and a female voice said to me in French, "Hello, my name is Gulya Mirzoeva. I am Tajik and we are cousins."

I was dumbstruck but it was true. She had just married Jérôme Clerc, who came from Mouchamps, the same little village in Vendée as my father. I can't remember at what degree of proximity or distance Jérôme and I were cousins, but, of course, I knew his family name. Mouchamps is a small town in Vendée of about two thousand inhabitants, including seven hundred Protestants, who are more or less all cousins if one considers the genealogy over a hundred-year stretch. So they both came to the house, and she says to me, "Oh yes, I forgot, you're well acquainted with my uncle, Atakhan. He's the head of the opposition delegation in the negotiations." All well and good, except that, within twenty-four hours, the entire city had learned that I was related to the head of the opposition's delegation. People in the government let it be known that it was unacceptable for the representative of the OSCE to have family ties with the opposition. However, during the following round, they came up to me smiling and said, "So it turns out you're a bit Tajik now—welcome to our country!" You could say we were sharing in this common grammar of village cousins.

Later, when I participated in the negotiations in Islamabad, it had become something outright positive. The two delegations chewed each other out in Russian and made up in Persian, and we would joke about how the world was getting smaller. It was on the strength of that experience, among other things, that I came to understand true diplomacy: one must construct personal relations beyond the political divisions, that goes without saying, but also beyond the labeling of people as good or bad, worth seeing, off limits, and so on. That said, if I never became a professional diplomat, it's because at bottom there are individuals I wouldn't touch with a ten-foot pole.

Tell me more about your confrontation with the post-Soviet world in Central Asia at that time.

Central Asia was a striking case study. It was an example of colonialism—military conquest, hegemony of the Russian language, an economy managed from Moscow, a double circulation of administrators (whites over the entire USSR, Muslims only in their republics, and so on)—but one that had remarkably co-opted new local elites. The architecture, the urban setting, statues, slogans, shops—everything was Soviet. The Uzbek apparatchik would receive you in the same office with the same protocol as in Moscow; Russian was the normal language at work (often he would not know technical terms in his own language). We would be seated on either side of a T-shaped table. Then, later, at his house, he changes into other clothes, leads you into his guest room covered with rugs, and you're both sitting on cushions arranged along the walls and mountains of greasy rice are served. Then we slip into Tajik or Uzbek. There's only one thing in common: vodka. The Russians trained a local elite that was certainly Sovietized but native, and they held the true power. In wishing to break Pan-Islamism or pan-Turkishness, they developed national entities that took root.

So the USSR invented these nations then?

This easy possession not of two cultures exactly, but of two registers, led me to rethink the problems of syncretism, acculturation, and neocolonialism. All the higher-up administrators viewed the collapse of the Soviet Union as a traumatic event and not at all as an opportunity. Therefore, the Soviet mores of authoritarianism and statist thinking continued in these new nations but without the economic and social underpinning of before. *Homo sovieticus* existed, but at the same time people continued to live in a society marked by traditions and behaviors that were local and characteristic of the south. As the subtitle of my book states—*The New Central Asia:*

Geopolitics and the Birth of Nations—I was especially attentive to the extraordinary invention of these nations. The USSR disappeared, but unlike with the independence of a colonial country, where the history of the colonized replaces that of the colonizers, the only history that remained in these new countries of Central Asia was the one invented by the Soviets. The heroes, for example, were Soviets. We were in a universe in flux where no one knew who was who and in the name of what. People continued to speak Russian because it was the language of the workplace, and yet there were no more Russians. In Uzbek and Tajik, people weren't sure they were expressing themselves correctly. They no longer knew what register to legitimately stand on. Everything was possible. But with an implacable logic, an authoritarian power gradually established itself and locked down the civil society. I saw the borders get changed, and even the colors—of walls, flags, uniforms, signs—and these changes gave each new country its new look. Alphabets grew more different. Each country had its own statuary, and whereas between 1990 and 1993 you could travel everywhere freely, afterward border checkpoints, visas, minefields, barbed wired, and no man's-lands became common. After having barely opened up, Central Asia closed back down, but along new lines of division.

What did people do who were neither Tajik, nor Uzbek, nor Kazakh—the displaced peoples from before the fall of the Soviet empire?

Whole populations just left. The Bukharian Jews went to Israel, the Ashkenazi went to Germany, the Germans back to Germany—even if the two groups got mixed up often. I saw German speakers declare themselves Jews to the Jewish Agency and Germans of the Volga at the German Consulate while waiting for the first visa to become available—a fact which explains how there are new Germans in Israel and new Jews in Germany. The Pontic Greeks, the Armenians, the Lithuanians, the Meskhetians, and Tatars all left. Only the Koreans stayed and converted massively to Pentecostalism. I saw the arrival of missionaries from Tabligh and Salafists, Hare Krishnas, and evangelicals. But here and there one could still see a "Rote Stern" or "Rosa Luxemburg" kolkhoz.

Phantom Soviet towns also survived; for example, a strange ski village north of Dushanbe with concrete high-rise apartment buildings positioned on the dirty snow; or deserted military camps with rows of rusting armored vehicles out front; empty summer camps; and in the most secluded ugly area, a statue falling apart with its surreal slogan proclaiming the union of the peoples of the world. Overnight, history had been rewritten: the great celebration of the victory of the Second World War was presented on May 8, 1996, in Uzbekistan, as a victory of Uzbekistan over fascism but with no further details. The same evening, I crossed into Kyrgyzstan to discover, on May 9, the more familiar celebration of "the great patriotic war of all Soviet peoples" against the Hitlerian Germans.

I think we in the West did not accurately take account of this brutal rupture with a past and a frame of reference when at bottom no one had asked for any of that to happen. One cannot understand Putin without understanding the deep trauma of the collapse of the USSR. Putin is a true revenant, a Soviet phantom, even if no going back is possible.

How did the expedition in Dushanbe turn out?

My mission for the OSCE was terminated at the end of 1994, without human rights or democracy being established in the country, and I went back to France. However, I returned once a year to Central Asia, to Azerbaijan and to Iran. The takeover of Kabul by the mujahideen in May 1992 (the very day when I was witnessing the outbreak of civil war in Dushanbe) gave rise to a new civil war in Afghanistan and left me, and many other members of the Afghan circus, decidedly bitter. The rise to power of the Taliban starting in the fall of 1994—while I was in Pakistan participating in the Tajik negotiations—hardly surprised me. It answered both a demand for order on the part of the local population weary of civil war and a desire for revenge by the ethnic Pashtuns, who had lost power with the victory of the northern coalition. I was not seeking to return to Afghanistan and was completely committed to advancing my research on Central Asia, especially in the Fergana Valley. I was working on the reconstitution of solidarity groups according to a traditional "grammar" in the kolkhozy starting from the decomposition of traditional communitarian systems and the extraordinary forced redistribution of populations carried out by the Soviet system since the 1930s: collective deportations, forced settlements in areas that still lacked basic hygienic norms, arbitrary gathering together of "pieces" of heterogeneous populations into the same kolkhoz—and all of this against a background of official and often superficial multicultural-ism—called the policy of nationalities. The descendants of all these dis-placed peoples told individual stories that were both tragic and extraordinary: the grandchildren of Trotskyists exiled in 1927 and forgotten by the cen-tral power, the Pontic Greeks (on the Black Sea), Polish Jews who had fled the German invasion, Tatars whose grandfathers were the backbone of the KGB in the 1930s. There were also grandfathers but with no descendants: old retired Russian archaeologists, extremely erudite gentlemen who had been surprised and suddenly dispossessed by the USSR, which then receded like the outgoing tide at Mont Saint-Michel, leaving them high and dry on a deserted shore.

On the map Afghanistan is right next door, it even has a common border with Tajikistan, and one finds Tajiks on both sides of it. But you didn't return there?

Yes, I did in fact. At Easter in 1999, when I was in Dushanbe with Martine, who was pregnant and who had made me promise not to take any risks, I learned that a helicopter sent by Massoud was going to airlift a delegation from Dushanbe. I hurried to see my friends at the Afghan embassy in Dushanbe to get on that helicopter—my first ever trip in a helicopter, another aeronautical first for me in Afghanistan! It was a Russian Mi-17, the helicopter of the president during the Communist era, captured in Kabul in 1992. At the controls was the same pilot, a former Communist trained in the USSR. The only ones who knew how to fly those things were the Communists—depending on their ethnic origin, they sided either with the Taliban or with the Northern Alliance. The helicopter flew only 300 feet above the ground to avoid the handful of airplanes the Taliban was using. We passed above the courtyards of farms, and I noticed women dry-ing I don't know what on the roofs of the farm buildings. When we arrived at the foothills of the Hindu Kush, the helicopter rose vertically, staying about 150 feet from the mountainside, and then tipped back down when it reached the pass at an altitude of almost 15,000 feet—the height limit for that model. In the cabin were badly sealed containers of fuel for the return journey. Two months later, that very helicopter exploded in flight. Someone must have been smoking and mislaid his cigarette.

I was happy to see Massoud again. Like always, he reminded me of Comrade Jean from my days with the Gauche prolétarienne. He explained to me that the situation might seem hopeless, but in fact it was really very favorable. The Taliban had reached the limit of their possible expansion, and the northern population wanted nothing to do with them. All that was needed was for the Western powers to commit to viewing the Taliban as truly dangerous, especially because of the Arab volunteers in their ranks who wanted to strike at the West. He said he had good intelligence about al-Qaeda, but no one was listening to him. When he traveled to France in April 2001, he was not received by President Chirac and the Americans refused to invite him to Washington, even though he had precise information about al-Qaeda's development of international networks and about the links between Bin Laden and the Taliban. To show me the control he had in the region, he had me taken by car, close to Kabul, to Istalif to be precise, where I had spent a week in July 1981. Later we returned to Dushanbe in the same helicopter with the same smell of fuel.

On the first of June, my son Samuel was born.

On many of your trips, it seems like many activities are mixed together: diplomacy, research, your private life, hiking, and so on.

It's true I didn't make distinctions among those things. I have only one life—granted, it might be double or triple—and I've always been very pragmatic about these life choices. Sometimes this caused me trouble with various administrators who know how to be good nannies, or with many of my colleagues who also know how to be nagging peers. Both groups could be so sensitive about professional status and administrative rules. For example, many colleagues do the paperwork to request authorization for a professional mission as soon as they leave the center of Paris to speak at a conference in Geneva or Auxerre, whereas sometimes just to exercise my freedom I would deliberately not ask for anything. I changed a bit after having children, for insurance reasons, at least for places like Geneva and Auxerre, but never for tough areas, because they would have been refused anyway. So each time I cobbled together my own mission with a little forcing here and there—Zen boldness is my trusted method. I also learned to take advantage of the inconsistencies and inertia of all bureaucracies. Sometimes with humorous results. In September 1991, just after the collapse of the USSR, the travel bureau of the Foreign Affairs Ministry had not updated its map of the world. I needed to go to Uzbekistan, but for them the country didn't exist and they couldn't find Tashkent on their list of international airports. They only recognized the USSR and therefore refused my mission to Uzbekistan. I went to see another employee at the bureau and dealt with a very nice woman who was not exactly up to date on geostrategy. I explained to her that the USSR no longer existed but that I still needed an authorized mission order. After an hour, she called me back to her office and handed over my passport with a big smile and said, "Here you go." I set off happily for the airport, but when I passed the border checkpoint, I realized that the French Foreign Affairs Ministry had authorized my mission to "*ex-Russie*"—curiously, no one seemed bothered by that, beginning with the Russians and Uzbeks.

Chapter 18

THE EXPERT AND THE POLITICIAN

Did you have other official missions besides the ones to Tajikistan?

I WAS A part of the French presidential delegation when François Mitterrand visited Kazakhstan in September 1993. That trip bumped me up to a new level of travel comfort I hadn't experienced before: we traveled in a twenty-five-seat business jet with leather seats and excellent Bordeaux wine. The president was in another plane. On the return journey, however, the president went up and down the aisle of our plane to shake the hands of those who had been invited along, but I was snoring—probably loudly. I always avoided dealings with the courtier milieu. I've known most of the foreign ministers going back a few years, but I've never dined with any French president. I know several presidents who were in office in 2013 (Hamid Karzai, Moncef Marzouki, Abdullah Gül), but it's because I knew them long before as opposition members at a time when no one would have bet a dollar on their political future. I have attended few if any official dinners in Paris, generally because I behave badly. One day, the head of the German embassy invited me to dinner with his diplomats. I put on my dark suit, dark tie, and cufflinks.

I arrive first like the typical hick. His wife opens the door dressed in blue jeans and a sweater. I conclude that I've made a mistake and that it's an informal gathering. I ask where I can hang my jacket and proceed to take off my tie and cufflinks, roll up my sleeves, and plop down on the sofa. The ambassador's wife disappears with my jacket and tie and doesn't return. Everyone else arrives wearing dark suits, dark ties, and cufflinks—it turns out it *was* a formal gathering, but just for men! And there I was with bare forearms and no tie. It's one of the many reasons why I never wanted to be a diplomat, and perhaps why no one except Bernard Kouchner and the Baroness af Ugglas ever asked me to become one!

In fact, what interested me was to work with true practitioners and understand how to articulate a body of knowledge and elaborate a policy around it. My problem as an intellectual expert was to reconcile a technical request that was coming from politicians and a vision that was both engaged and rational (and if possible ethical) on my part. In other words, the idea that there is a worthwhile objective, a common goal, that one can resolve a conflict, in short that one can implement a "good" policy, or at least avoid catastrophes. Whether it's the integration of Islam in France, the Israeli-Palestinian conflict, Islamism, or *laïcité*, I believe in the reasonable—even if it's only crises and passions that move things along. That's the paradox of policy making. Today policy making is developed and managed via crisis—economic, social, or military. The slow age of international relations, from the Congress of Vienna up to the eve of World War I, no longer exists. Everything is urgent—from the speech writing for a minister to the announcement of a decision—therefore, everything is a bit slapdash, put together at the last minute, and the only coherence is the coherence of the tirade, or the coherence provided after a hasty decision has already been made. A consultant's sentence or paragraph is often used to rationally justify a decision that's already been made but for other reasons.

You have already discussed this point, and as usual you base it on a certain lived experience in the field. So a rational political decision does not exist?

It's a little more complicated than that. Yes, my conviction has always been that as an intellectual one cannot remain nostalgic about some golden age when decisions were rationally made after a period of careful and thorough deliberations. Today one must think about conserving or reviving rationality within a management framework of false urgency. I say false because it is permanent. The long term, if it still comes up, is only thought about as a chain of clichés, whether they come from the liberal Left (rights of man and multiculturalism), the right, or a Jacobin Left (both of which join up with their culturalist obsessions).

Nevertheless, if I stick with politics and policy making, it's because one can, I'm convinced, implement good policy. And there is no necessary contradiction between the national interest and the interest of other peoples. I'm not saying this as some naïve goody-goody. In my view, the national interest of a powerful nation like France, which is living beyond its means, has until now been defined by criteria that are more ideological than truly operational, whereas globalization is neither good nor bad but a fact. Therefore, my link to institutions that make the bridge between knowledge and politics was neither opportunistic or the product of chance, even if each of those elements played a role. One can introduce some rationality into politics. Among the politicians themselves, however, it's less and less certain. One is forced to admit sometimes that politics is becoming hysterical—and here France's Nicolas Sarkozy is more symptom than cause. But at the same time, I remain skeptical of the concept of realism in foreign policy, because it supposes that one is able to clearly identify the relations of force involved, the stakes, and the actors. I've been able to observe the degree to which realists have an imaginary vision of how the world works, because that vision does not correspond to any true assessment of the relations of force, but rather to the image they have of the adversary. What does the Russian policy in Ukraine correspond to if not precisely an imaginary of strength? And what of France's African policy, where colonial nostalgia is turned into a powerful instrument for a world that no longer exists? And then there are the imaginaries about the "Islamic threat" and the "invasion of Polish plumbers."

Is the transition from the engaged intellectual to the expert a recent phenomenon?

No, it's the context of the relationship between expertise and politics that has changed—the link itself is very old. I am fascinated by the relations that French ethnologists and anthropologists had with France as a colonial power (from Germaine Tillion, the model, to Jean Servier, who is hardly a shining figure of colonialism). Obviously, postcolonial studies have a tendency to interpret everything in terms of domination and dominated, but things are much more complicated than that. In the area I know best, I think that an intelligent Western policy toward Afghanistan could be only positive for the Afghans. What I will come to rethink later is the concept of intelligent policy, because the political decision depends on so many other factors, many of them uncontrollable. The CAP was by definition the place for thinking all that through. One was totally free to say and write what one wished—except on "court" topics (Africa, the king of Morocco, the president's friends . . .).

What's more, the CAP put me in contact with the defense and security circles, and this allowed me to learn about the logic behind their operations. My analyses were the same as those written up in my university publications but calibrated to be read by deciders. For me there has never been a contradiction between the university researcher and the expert, even if the latter required a precise intellectual hygiene, if I can put that way, that is, not allowing oneself to be eaten up by the political demands. It also required a certain relationship ethic—namely, keeping one's distance from the powerful. When it comes to this renunciation from worldly gatherings, the only exception I made was to attend three or four Davos summits (though I rather quickly gave up on that) as well as ten or so Bilderberg meetings, but those were not social events at all.

Honestly though, do experts and researchers really play a significant role among leaders?

Consulting is about repetition because it's always immediate: write a piece for the next morning on a topic that you've already commented on ten times, always for the next morning. The repeated request was, "What should be our policy toward Islam?" On this topic, I wrote approximately the same answer for twenty years, namely, that we should stop essentializing; that we should discuss politics and not religion; that we should distinguish between radicals and moderates; that constructive collaboration is possible with the Muslim Brotherhood (even if they're not a barrel of laughs, they can be integrated within a political process). The main difficulty, though it was less a dispute with the Foreign Ministry and more with the office of the president, came from a rule of French diplomacy: it is absolutely forbidden to speak with the political opposition of our "friends" and, in particular, at that time, Morocco and Tunisia, and this was quite unbearable for me. It's a very French way of doing things—the Americans and the British, for example, have never declined to speak with opposition members.

In fact, the big mistake comes with thinking that the expert ought to do politics—it's an old story, from Plato to France's National School of Administration. The expert believes in the rationality of the decision: first, analysis, then weighing the constraints and the possible choices, deliberating, and finally making a rational choice. However, things just never actually work that way. A political act is a decision-making act par excellence, not a time for reflecting. Politics is a performative activity. It creates the real, it doesn't translate it, and what's more, it can ignore it.

Paradoxically, the Fourth Republic, though much criticized, was the golden age of experts, probably because of the relative weakness of policy then: reuniting the territory, the nuclear question, development—in short, everything that had to do with planning fell into the hands of the expert who played the role of Hegel's shaper of history. These policies would not bear fruit until the presidency of Charles de Gaulle, but they had been conceived long before. The technocratic vision that held sway under the Fourth Republic saw in the state the agent of historical reason, precisely because the government's instability in effect handed over power to the high functionaries. One can say the same about Brussels.

Given all the time I've been following the behavior of political deciders, my feeling is that good policy has nothing to do with the reasons for which it was implemented. There are very good policies that are put in place for very bad reasons, and vice versa. If the philosopher could really be king, we would have known about it in Plato's time. The order of politics is not that of the academic or the intellectual—it's about the decision, the immediate decision, the decision with no nuance. Either one intervenes (in Libya, Iraq, Afghanistan) or one does not intervene (Ukraine, Syria)—it's yes or no, all or nothing. The American war in Iraq is an exemplary case. One cannot conduct war with nuances, and Saddam Hussein was turned into the source of all evil, with as a corollary the idea that by killing him one was surely going to create the conditions essential for resolving other conflicts. The experts are then called in—not to weigh the initial hypothesis, now turned into dogma, but to refine how it will be applied . . . and explained.

Politicians are intelligent people—one should not underestimate that fact—but they are not intellectuals—*indecisive* is the worst insult that could be flung at a politician. Intellectuals don't understand that. They always think that they're being asked to cogitate over the goal of a policy because they think that a university professor lives at the summit of knowledge and intelligence, whereas politically he may be stupid (it happens!) or at least naïve.

Would it be too indiscreet to ask for an example?

Yes, but I'll give you one anyway. In 1984, when I joined the CAP, the director, Philippe Costes, told me my job consisted of inviting intellectuals and academics for discussions and brainstorming sessions. So one day I invite a distinguished professor of political science. I told him that he would be in contact with the director of the CAP, who spoke every day with the minister and occasionally met with the president and prepared vitally important briefings. All that by way of underlining (while flattering his self-esteem) that the professor would be dealing with someone as qualified and competent as himself. The interview lasted two hours, during which the professor explained to the director of the CAP why French policy about X was not good while the director listened attentively. Two weeks later, the professor called me up to say that meetings like the one he had attended were useless. I asked why, and he said because nothing about the French policy had changed in two weeks! I was bowled over by just how naïve politically this professor of political science proved to be. Surely, he had taught lessons on political decision making! It demonstrated to me the distance that exists between academic knowledge and political decisions. This gap is even wider in France because of the commonly held notion that university professors are all intellectuals, or ought to behave like they are, and as such it's thought that that they can speak on any topic under the sun. It's different in the United States—there the public intellectual is not a professor. He or she is more likely an editorialist, such as Thomas Friedman at the *New York Times*, or even a novelist.

One of the rare French academics who was remarkably talented at managing these relations between deciders and researchers was Rémy Leveau, the originator in 1983 of the master's degree in Middle Eastern Studies at Sciences Po. The main reason was that he had a lot of personal experience as a high-level functionary with the management of crucial interfaces such as the French institutes of research abroad. Indeed, those institutions constitute the backbone of our intellectual influence when it comes to research on the Muslim world. He always supported me because we shared that hybrid background of the theoretical and the practical.

Can you explain further how that works practically and intellectually? One day you get a call from a decider, you're summoned to the ministry, and you appear and speak without fumbling because . . . why? You feel honored? You're well paid?

One receives neither honor nor a lot of money, at least I never did. When I was a part-time consultant for the CAP, I was paid 800 euros per month (that's less than I made in royalties after 2002, and my CNRS salary was 4,200 euros net per month) to do repetitive tasks, because, as I said, it's not about accumulating knowledge, it's the repetition of the same thing under urgent conditions.

Money is not the problem. A professor in France is paid by the state, though he may not identify with it at all. The problem is the schmoozing. It might be socializing, as is often the case in France (dinners out, club memberships, and the like), though less so in America and Germany. The schmoozing is personally gratifying since it also encompasses receiving honors, indulgent nominations to this or that, literary prizes distributed by one's peers, perhaps even being voted into the Académie française! But as I've said, I'm not that big on socializing. Another type of cozy collaboration comes with all the honorary consulting, such as when a pharmaceutical company confers laboratory missions on a famous doctor or other influential personage. It's not about making them work nor even to have them adopt publicly a certain position or make a decision, but simply to establish the connection, for which there's the prospect of some possible future benefit. I don't go in for that either.

I should clarify, however, that I don't consider collaborations with the state's agencies to be just one more variety of sucking up. The state is the affair of all citizens. If the autonomy and freedom within academia constitute intangible principles for me, they are nevertheless principles, values, but not facts. As Bourdieu demonstrated in *Homo academicus*, the university is a field among others; it is not an enclave exempt from social and cultural determinations or devoid of political stakes. What's more, professors do politics, and have always done so, especially in France. Third, they claim, especially in the social sciences, to have things to say about the society and about public policies, and they want their own professional *oeuvre* to have an impact on the field of politics, economics, social policy, or international relations. So we, the knowledge workers, are permanently crossing paths with politics and politicians.

Unless I'm mistaken, Bourdieu denounces *Homo academicus*'s ignorance of these determining factors, and he claimed, more or less, to be illuminating their false consciousness. Moreover, in France at least, in the name of academic freedom and a certain ethics of research, there exists, I think, a tradition of the university's radical independence vis-à-vis all outside interests—not only business interests, but also those of the state (especially, in the case of Bourdieu at the time he's writing that book, the Marxist critique of the free state that was then still current).

Yes, but I would say just the opposite, namely, that France's problem in this area is the absence of close collaboration between university actors and politicians. Or more precisely, the lack of intellectual overlap—the other kind, sucking up to politicians and socializing happens plenty, as I've already said. How shall we think together? The various categories are difficult to coordinate. A policeman will speak of delinquency and terrorism;

a sociologist or a political scientist will have trouble operating with categories that to them seem so simplistic. That is the difference between the expert, who takes up the categories as given, and the intellectual, who feels obliged to criticize them, or deconstruct them, as one says today. The professor whose opening reply to a politician's request for input is to say, "It's more complicated than that" had better explain very quickly not just why, what, or how it's more complicated but especially *why one*—that is, the decider, not the professor, who is motivated by his own standards of intellectual rigorousness—*ought to take an interest in this additional complexity.* For me, the goal of consulting is to construct with one's interlocutor, the practitioner, a frame of reference, a shared paradigm, that makes sense to both of us, and if possible the same sense even if the context is not viewed or experienced the same way by each party.

This is what, in general, university people don't know how to do. And yet you, a former philosophy professor, do know how?

Let's say that this old prof learned some new tricks—especially from working with diplomats.

For a long time, the diplomatic method seemed rather vain (in all senses) to me. In a situation where it's clear that no agreement is possible for reasons X, Y, Z (for example, one party is convinced it's going to win), what good is it to spend hours elaborating instruments for understanding or interim declarations that are gone over comma by comma within interminable and repeated rounds of negotiations? This was the case for the "Geneva discussion" organized by the United Nations during the Soviet military occupation of Afghanistan. For me, this type of negotiation seemed only intended to legitimate the Soviet intervention, because only a change in the relations of force on the ground could have modified the real situation. It was also the case with the negotiations in Tajikistan. Why would the winners accept the return of the losers, whether they be Islamists or simple refugees (all the more so since the war had as a subtext conflicts over land)? And yet they accepted, and doing so rather increased their power.

What I want to say is that little by little I understand that the goal of such negotiations is not to resolve a crisis at the top but to put in place a framework for formulating the problem, inventorying the possible solutions, defining the stakes and possible ensuing scenarios. In short, it's conceiving of a sort of screenplay whose goal is not so much realism or pragmatism as it is an opening onto a possible imaginary—in other words, to make it so that everything be possible, while testing, through dialogue, the possibility of a solution. Diplomacy has an extraordinary vocabulary for describing transformational paradoxical oxymorons: a "verbal note" is always written; a "nonpaper" is an argument scrupulously written down on paper; an "exercise" is an impossible negotiation that takes place anyway. What appears as simulacrum is more simulation, in the sense that one is eliciting possibilities.

Of course, later on it's always a series of external events that ultimately decides the shape of things: a military defeat, fatigue, a new threat, an economic crisis, a coup d'état, a revolution, and so on. But when this event requires finding a true solution, then all these diplomatic exercises, which may have been going on for years, find their usefulness, even if none of the imagined solutions are taken into account because the reality took place faster. For example, the Soviet retreat or the fall of the USSR took place outside of any planned negotiated framework, but the existence of negotiating bodies (the spokespeople in Geneva, the OSCE) allowed for a channeling of the course of events and for ensuring supervision. That's why I insist that diplomacy as a profession is a real art.

Sometimes I accompanied a United Nations HCR representative (for example, Philippe Labreveux) during negotiations to persuade the government of Dushanbe to allow refugees to return less than one year after the start of the civil war. I didn't believe it possible given the war's violence, the desire for vengeance, and the fear that the refugees felt. And yet, it worked because little by little the HCR was able to build a "structure of mutual understanding" that allowed a reconciliation of each party's interests and fears.

Besides this unexpected but convincing praise of diplomacy, whose powerlessness today is often mocked, what else did you learn from consulting?

These experiences were useful for defining my position in the debate over the compromising collaboration between the researcher and the decider. It's not about selling to the politician a scientific concept nor about allowing oneself to buy into a notion so ideological and confused as terrorism or delinquency. Rather, it's a matter of elaborating a space for mutual understanding, a paradigm that makes sense for both parties, even if each has a different practical perspective. Take the example of deradicalization. For twenty years, politicians, judges, and policemen have concentrated on the theme of the Islamic contagion implying that radical ideas are transmitted like a virus. The carrier of the jihad virus, it was commonly assumed, was a radical imam who, from sermon to sermon, would infect innocent youths. But how and why do young people turn to jihad? The virus model does not help one understand and therefore define what one ought to be fighting against.

The sociologist arrives with a discourse aimed at understanding that tends to annoy judges and law enforcement. He evokes the socioeconomic context, racism, the Israeli-Palestinian conflict, state-sponsored terrorism, American drones, and other factors. Of course, all that makes a lot of sense. But in a way, the judges and policemen are right, because if those were really the causes of radicalization, there would be hundreds of thousands of jihadists. What's especially suspect is the argument that says all that's required to eradicate terrorism is to end the Israeli-Palestinian conflict and racism. That's pure wishful thinking and of no practical use for the functionaries working under any home secretary. Pursuing radical imams is really a trivial pursuit because radicalization doesn't require imams. What one must find is a conceptual model that also corresponds to the lived experience of the police officer, especially since that experience does not match up with the ideological categories that he uses. The good functionaries know because they have practical experience. They end up knowing the young radicals they meet face-to-face, and they understand quickly that what's at stake is not about religion. That's the meeting point where an effective collaboration could begin. But that would presume that one is in agreement about the goal, or at least *a* goal: to prevent a terrorist attack against a civilian population is a good thing, even if it's not enough to repair the world. As for that objective, each is free to pursue it in their own way.

What's important is to avoid offering a mirror argument that not only lacks pertinence but blocks all intelligent approaches. This would be, for example, the grand narrative of the revolt of the oppressed, who are mistaken about the proper means but correct with their legitimate ends, versus the grand narrative of the war against terrorism, the root cause of which would be Islam and therefore its eradication would be necessary. These two narratives are empty. One has to return to individuals, to the actors involved, and investigate their itineraries. One has to go back out into the field.

Chapter 19

MARRIAGE

The Orient Lost and Found

Your marriage could also be said to be inscribed within the context of your relation to the Orient.

YES, AND YET everything happened in the heart of the Beauce, south of Paris. When I settled in the countryside near Dreux in 1974, I made friends with some Turkish neighbors who were farmworkers. And when I moved to the city—that is, Dreux proper—I kept in touch with one of them, who happened to be a Syriac Orthodox Christian and came from the border region between Iraq and Syria. He first brought over his wife and their twins, then his oldest daughter, and finally in 1979 his whole family. I went to pick them up at the airport in a Volkswagen Microbus that I'd borrowed from one of my colleagues. Among the arrivals was my future wife, Marta, renamed Martine by French immigration officials. She was twelve at the time. For fifteen years, I saw all of them regularly at communions, baptisms, and sometimes to lend a hand with their administrative paperwork.

The father, Gabro, a wise raconteur, was a fantastic source of tales and information not only about the Syriac Orthodox Church but about the whole history and way of life in southeast Turkey—in particular the complex relations with the Kurdish neighbors. Although many Kurds participated in the massacre of Christians in 1916, his village was spared thanks to an aga Kurd of the Çelelbi family, for reasons that have more to do with feudal structures in the region than with any sense of religious tolerance.

Similarly, a neighboring village was inhabited by Yazidis, or "devil worshipers," about whom my future father-in-law shared this theological summary: "If God is good and perfect, then there is no need to pray since it adds nothing to what is; on the other hand, for justice to reign over the earth, one must persuade the fallen angel, the devil, to return to God, and therefore it is for him that one must pray." Finally, a rational theology! I spent hours listening to him even though his French remained fairly rough. Yet he was completely fluent in Syriac Aramaic; Kurmanji (i.e., Kurdish, though he refused to call it that so as to distinguish the language common to all from the ethnic group); Turkish, the language of one's military service and the administration; and to a lesser extent Arabic, which was the language of the vast majority of those in the Syriac Orthodox Church and the language spoken to the west of his village. He decided he'd learned enough French to get by and stopped halfway.

I was very attracted to Martine, but I thought marrying her would be impossible and that she'd marry at twenty or twenty-five with someone of her age and religion like other young Syriac women. In any case, we always saw each other at family gatherings, never alone. But at twenty-six she was still single and I thought to myself, well, maybe . . . and that's when she rang the doorbell at my place. Fifteen minutes later, I asked her to marry me.

All's well that ends well!

No, troubles began for an unexpected reason. As I said, I was the godfather of one of the twins, her younger brothers, and there's a religious interdiction among the Orthodox against any marriage between a godfather and all those who are related to his godchild. It's considered a form of incest. A dispensation was necessary, but the Syriac Orthodox bishop for Western Europe, Bishop Çiçek, who lived in Holland, refused to grant one. When Martine attempted to get him to change his mind, he suggested she get herself to a nunnery, specifically a new convent he had opened in Holland and was trying to fill. So we had to make our request to the patriarch in Damascus. But who would advocate in my favor to this distant pope? No one in the community dared approach him. It then occurred to me that, since until then I had never asked the French Foreign Ministry for any personal favors, I might make this one request for help. I called the French ambassador in Damascus, Jean-Claude Cousseran, whom I had met at ministerial meetings in the past, and told him my problem. He asked me, "But which patriarch are you talking about? There are seven! Ah, the Syriac Orthodox one, his holiness Zaka I, perfect! I've not yet met that one. I will pay him an official visit as the ambassador of France, the country that protects Christians of the Orient, and I'll bring up your case. Write me a note telling me what to say." I wrote the note—I'd had plenty of practice at that sort of thing.

So as the ambassador of the ultrasecular French republic, Cousseran negotiated a theological dispensation authorizing my marriage, a document called in Syriac Aramaic a fatwa. The patriarch also asked that I write a "note," in diplomatic language, or a "supplicant," in the language of the Church, telling him what to say. My religious training came in handy at that point, as I wrote the following: (1) there is no sin unless there is knowledge, and being ignorant of this rule when I acquiesced to being a godfather, I could not be classified as a sinner in this matter; (2) baptism effaces sin, and I was requesting therefore to be baptized into the Syriac Orthodox Church. One month later, a courier from the Foreign ministry arrived by motorcycle to hand over to me a document with the red seal and keys of Saint Peter stamped on it. It restated my two arguments and gave me the right to be married religiously. By coincidence, Martine's cousin, Malke Urek, had become a monk within the Church, so it was he who married us along with Father Yakoub in the church of Tremblay-le-Vicomte on July 2, 1994.

Later, Martine's cousin was named bishop and inaugurated in Adiyaman, the first Christian bishopric in Turkey since the fall of Constantinople. In fact, the Ottomans were tolerant people, but the slow decline in numbers of Christians, accelerated by the massacres of 1916, led to the escheat of most episcopal seats of all Christian denominations.

Meeting Martine was obviously an event in your private life, but its ties with your intellectual itinerary were striking even to you.

True. Once again my personal and family history overlapped with the themes of my research. While working on the subject of conversions and new religious movements, I entered into contact with a cousin who became a bishop precisely because people were converting in high numbers. But even though he was Syrian and spoke Syriac Aramaic, he was placed at the head of a parish where no one spoke Syriac (the converts were Turks, often distantly Greek or Armenian in origin, but who spoke only Turkish). In short, I was experiencing, live, the central theme that would provide the framework for my book *La Sainte ignorance*—namely the disconnection between religious faith and cultural identities. This theme was unfolding before my eyes at the very moment that the debate about a "clash of civilizations" was defining this link as intangible. Paradoxically, the renewal of faith (the conversions and the born-again phenomenon) was taking place against (or, more accurately, with total disregard for) the grain of ethnic-linguistic identities.

Was your relationship an opportunity for new travels, new research, or at least a pilgrimage to the village she and her family came from?

For travel, of course, but it had taken twenty years. The first trip back to their home village happened in 2005. Research? No. A golden rule among researchers, even if it's not always followed so well, is that one must never study the object of one's affections or fall in love with the object of one's research. Besides that, my wife, though not renouncing in the least her family or her origins, does not want to be defined first as Syriac—she is what her choice has made her: French. I am the one who brought her back to her village. She didn't want to go back there. It's me that's always wanting to rediscover the Orient, something others are, when it comes right down to it, happy to have lost.

So I'm not going to launch into an anthropological analysis of any of that. I could speak of it only elliptically, but this ellipsis coheres with the situation of a tiny community that only ever existed in the shadow of a dominant group, with a memory that has not always been theirs to control and with a future that borrows its imaginary from others—Armenians, Kurds, Christian Arabs, and Iraqi Chaldeans. The Syriacs of Tur Abdin were created by history but never got to make it. In Turkey, they were killed following the massacre of Armenians who constituted the vast majority of Christian Turks, but all one ever hears about is the Armenian massacre. In their own Syriac Orthodox Church, the inhabitants of Tur Abdin, who are Syriac Aramaic native speakers and from rural backgrounds, are a small minority compared to the mass of faithful and clergy who are Arabic-speaking and city people (and therefore generally more educated) and mostly live in Syria. In Europe they arrived along with immigrant Kurds, with whom they share the old and new social framework, the culture, and professional niches (from factory work to kebabs), and with whom it's easy to confuse them in the poorer suburbs of Paris, whereas they have constructed a lengthy narrative of their centuries-old conflict that pits them against the Kurds over land, language, and religion. They arrived in France as part of a workers' immigration, leaving wives and children in their villages—a reality that has little in common with immigration as a flight from religious persecution. But today, when the second generation wanted to construct an identity that meshed with the times—a time of diasporas, ethnic groups, nations, and multiculturalism—it borrowed the software, so to speak, of ethnic nationalism from the Assyro-Chaldean Iraqis, who were far more numerous and much more plugged in to the identity discourse, which, however, excludes the Syriac religion and Church that are the only real links among the members of the Syriac community—and this because the Iraqis are Nestorians, or Uniate Catholics. Ah, the antiquarian charm of the Christological quarrels that date from the Councils of Ephesus and Chalcedon, that is, not that long ago, in 431 and 451!

So is Syriac vitality mainly thanks to emigration?

We have to say *was*. Martine's village, which today has about three hundred inhabitants, was the starting point of a diaspora of thousands of individuals dispersed across Germany, Sweden, Holland, Belgium, Switzerland, and Ukraine—and that's not counting those in the Paris region, in Australia, New Jersey, Florida, California, and even Bethlehem, where some first cousins of Martine Arabized and Palestinized themselves, all the while remaining Christian. This causes certain problems for us at the Tel

Aviv airport and additional problems for them at Israeli checkpoints and with local Salafists.

I've been reading, over a thirty-year period, about all the changes common to many villages in the Mediterranean world from Turkey to Tunisia. First, now is the end of emigration—something Europe has yet to understand. Mediterranean emigration due to demographic pressure is over, for Christians and Muslims alike. The question of political refugees is another matter. There is no longer pressure on the land, because the young have left, birthrates are dropping, and in any case it's no longer profitable to farm the land—agribusiness took care of that. The Kurdish neighbors emigrated to Turkish cities and found work there. The countryside is losing population, the traditional village is disappearing, high-speed Internet is everywhere, emigrants are building themselves secondary residences, and young people of the second generation are sometimes returning to start small businesses.

As for the religious question, in Turkey, contrary to the widely held belief that Islam and Christianity are at war, or that only an aggressive secularism can protect Christians, the government of the AKP has been more favorable to Christians than the secular Kemalists. The AKP returned lands to the monasteries (lands that had been seized with the help of Kemalist authorities) and did away with the mention of religion on personal identity cards. The AKP also speaks of the massacre of Armenians, something the Kemalists would not do, and sent representatives to the ceremony celebrating the new bishop. A final point: something that is common to the entire Mediterranean world is an increasing tension everywhere between new religiosities and the identification between a religion and an ethnic group, or else the transformation of a religious group into a neoethnic group, as with the Egyptian Copts, where identity replaces faith. The world is changing, but the story told about the world is not changing. Finally, just about everywhere, one-way immigration is being replaced by the circulation of people in all directions. But it's not just people who are moving. It's words, signs, labels, beliefs, and senses of belonging.

PART V

CULTURES AND THE
UNIVERSALLY HUMAN

Toward *Holy Ignorance*

Chapter 20

THE CRISIS OF CULTURES AND
THE UNIVERSAL

**Listening to you, one has the impression that the guiding thread
of your *parcours* is not Islam, even if it is present, but more and
more the question of culture or cultures, would you agree?**

I BECAME GRADUALLY uncomfortable with the gap between the professional image that had built up around me (specialist in Afghanistan and
then specialist in political Islam) and what really interested me most of all,
namely, an old philosophical question: is there liberty, and how shall we
think about it, within the determinism of various kinds of ties of belonging? The theme of identity, even in the apparently more flexible form of
having multiple identities, the choice of *my* identity or of a negotiated identity, has become the conceptual tool of a large portion of the Left as a way
to think about immigration and diversity within the movement in favor of
multiculturalism. This trend disappointed me even more since another
segment of the Left found no other alternative than to fall into a kind of
phobic defense of *laïcité* [France's version of secularism], which could be
imposed in an authoritarian way only through a strengthening of the
state, and therefore to the detriment of personal freedom, as one sees with
the proliferation of laws passed in the name of defending *laïcité* that are all
more or less repressive. In sum, these two parts of the Left swerved to the
right, jumping from identity talk to authoritarianism and back again. I
therefore found myself to be a *liberal* in this area.

What influenced you to go in that direction?

In my last year of high school my philosophy teacher, Jean Dyonet, was a Sartrean who made a big impression on me. In my next to last year, I went to see him to ask how I should prepare for his class. I had three weeks in the thermal spa town of Luchon ahead of me that summer, in other words, three weeks of boredom, and I wanted to at least read. He suggested that I read and take notes on *L'être et le néant* (*Being and Nothingness*). So that was my first experience reading philosophy, and like with one's first love, one never gets over it—except that the book was really uninviting, which was hardly the case with my first love affair. What I took away from it (the book, that is), was that liberty requires never being trapped by an identity. Therefore, I'm interested in moments of truth that prevent identity from functioning as a comfortable armor. War is one such moment; so are all varieties of crisis and rupture: the step into action (into crime or terrorism), and into faith (especially conversion). Reading Dostoyevsky with Sartrean glasses—that was me! In the other direction, you could say, this explains why I always liked presenting false identities, circulating with false papers. (I even once had a real false passport and traveled under the name Michel Renardin, but that's another story.) I liked to pass myself off as someone or something else—an Afghan refugee, for example—as though I needed to experience the contingency of believing oneself to be something, or to *be*, period.

As Sartre showed, rupture, or at least the possibility of rupture, is a necessary condition for freedom. In a synopsis that he wrote on my case for a professional journal, my psychoanalyst noted the fascination I had with rupture. For him, it was a negative symptom, a problem I had inserting myself in the real; whereas for me (and yes, one can win an argument with one's shrink and I interrupted my analysis rather abruptly over this disagreement—a rupture over the narration of rupture) it was a question of freedom, especially when dominant doctrines, in sociology or political science, are being presented as doctrines of the impossibility of freedom (from Foucault to Bourdieu). Moreover, for these two thinkers, freedom is also thought in terms of rupture, often named revolt, but an ephemeral revolt:

a strike or religious revolution in Foucault, and various battles against powers, including symbolic powers, in Bourdieu.

I never turned that into a research project, but from an intellectual perspective I'm interested in just about everything. Details, anecdotes, conversations, life narratives, anomalies, derailments and unravelings, bizarre and mad episodes—they've all been interesting to me. Doing everything in my power to keep from being imprisoned by the serious and from taking myself too seriously—that's important to me. As Montaigne says in one of his *essais*, "Most of our business is farce. . . . We must play our part properly, but withal as a part of a borrowed personage; we must not make real essence of a mask and outward appearance; nor of a strange person, our own" (*Essais*, book 3, chapter 10). That was the passage I cited in my letter to the director of teacher inspections.

If I may use Sartrean language, your analysis of terrorism appears more existentialist than political.

I think I was one of the first to say that the question of converts was a key to understanding al-Qaeda. It was the organization that contained the largest number of converts; no other group even came close. And it was the only Islamist group that assigned roles with important responsibilities to those converted individuals. I was able to compare al-Qaeda with other organizations, like France's Gauche prolétarienne from the 1970s, so I knew what I was talking about. I saw very clearly how the logic of radicalization and madness could dominate within a group of young people thirsty for breaking away. To understand the pathway that could lead to al-Qaeda, I never thought that I ought to look to the Koran for causal explanations. The Koran as an explanation is a useless hypothesis that leads nowhere or else gets one sidetracked. Why would it have taken until the 1980s, fourteen centuries after the Revelation, for terrorists and experts to suddenly discover a theological justification for terrorism that no one had noticed until now? But if al-Qaeda is not the result of religious tension, neither is it the expression of Muslim anger in response to Western acts of aggression. The reason is that the radicals don't come from the heart of the

Arabic Muslim societies, but from their margins. While the Right and the Left wanted to see the Israeli-Palestinian conflict as the epicenter of the Muslim mobilization, one should note that the targets, battlefields, goals, and zones of recruitment for radicalization tell a very different story. The Arab Spring is the latest and clearest demonstration that the logic of these movements is now internal to each society and has nothing more to do with any false essentialization of an imaginary Muslim world. In sum, both the Left and the Right, both the parrots who speak of a clash of civilizations and those who talk about postcolonial resentment have understood nothing about the radical changes throughout the Muslim world, its fracturing, its globalization, and especially its secularization in the wake of an apparent wave of Islamization. For example, to come back to al-Qaeda, the explanation is not to be found vertically (from the Koran to Bin Laden via Ibn Taymiyya and Sayyid Qutb[1]) but rather by taking a horizontal perspective: individualization, the crisis of cultural reference, the growing autonomy of the religious person and their deculturation, and a new intergenerational crisis.

In short, while I do not deny the *cultural fact* (and this book demonstrates it), I do consider *culturalism* (mono- or multi-) a lazy, redundant explanation. Multiculturalism is only cocktail party shorthand for *the world*.

Yes, but humanitarian workers, for example, must have felt the cultural differences?

Yes, of course. Concretely, in Afghanistan, when I was translating for doctors, we found ourselves confronted with some specific problems: the reluctance to give blood (something that really perturbed the young doctors); a severely wounded person who preferred to die rather than have a limb amputated (the Salafist doctors accused their French peers of being too quick to amputate); a village that brings in a foreign doctor on horseback in the middle of the night to treat an old man who's coughing but doesn't have the doctor treat the newborn who is dying in the house next door (the reply given to the doctor, who expressed his indignation: "It takes nine months to make a baby but ninety years to make an old man"); a woman whose husband leaves her to die rather than let her be treated by foreign doctors. But here, too, people tend to lump together under the label culture a number of heterogeneous elements, and the thoughts expressed by the actors themselves about their behavior is routinely ignored. The events mentioned above were always followed by discussions, just as in France, where different views can be shared about euthanasia, abortion, or the refusal of overly intrusive medical care. It's a debate about values and norms where not everyone—in France or Afghanistan—shares the same opinions. But people tend to deny those from the Orient the possibility of debating their norms and instead they get presented as passively reproducing their cultural habitus.

For me, if culture exists, it is always being put into question by the actors within it; it is always up for discussion and never objectively given. Note, in fact, that one often gives the name culture to that which is merely a collection of codes (like codes of manners or politeness), especially ones that are less and less connected to a meaningful social universe and that escape or are exempted from the control of the actors themselves. In that sense, one can speak of a universal within a shared framework of discussion. Many people behave as though between a logical cultural ordering and an action there were nothing—and yet in actuality the man or the woman who does the translation between the two thinks, speaks, and discusses. Especially when he or she argues over their culture or religion, in other words, when they introduce a certain self-reflexivity, when they translate the determinism that is imputed to them into a discourse of personal choice and decision making and send back to their culture or religion the message of its invariableness, a message that third-party observers are only too happy to receive as confirmation of their negative prejudices.

Of course, all this causes problems. I always felt ambivalent about so-called ethnopsychiatry as practiced since Georges Devereux's work up to that of Tobie Nathan. I don't at all deny the cultural factors—the fact that symptoms are meaningful only when expressed in a framework of precise cultural and linguistic references. I don't deny the cultural fact, but today it has become a false fact, or let's say, to avoid the oxymoron, it is being used in lazy ways. I'm thinking in particular of that threadbare doctrine that claims etymology defines not only the deep sense of words but the usage that one makes of them. For example, if the etymology of the Arab word *dawla*, used to designate the state, goes back more to the idea of dynasty and cycles of power, that would mean that Arabs have no concept to designate a transcendent state! It would be as if we said that the French are culturally vegetarian because to talk about a quality cut of meat they were obliged to borrow an English word, *beefsteak*. Or that the Turks have a problem with sexual identity because their language does not recognize a masculine-feminine distinction. Etymology is the lazy person's explanation machine.

One gets the impression that you insist more on the idea of a universal that's a work in progress or, to put it another way, on a modernity that universalizes human behaviors.

Yes. When I studied the humanities, I was immersed in the humanist vision of an eternal human nature. When we were translating as seventeen-year-old high schoolers the speech of Lysias, an Athenian lawyer in ancient Greece, our professor underlined the extraordinary humanity of those texts, and it was really true (the jealous husband who kills his wife's lover, the foreigner who requests naturalization, and so on). But it's not that sort of permanent humanity that interests me—even if, after having been the center of the literary humanist vision (the heart of the human soul), it is returning in a paradoxical way today through neuroscience research that is attempting to define a permanent, precultural human nature based on studies of the human brain.

My research is more directed at the effects of deculturation that are linked to globalization. There's a contrast between, on the one hand, the development of a culturalist coaching session—"Learn to understand the cultural predisposition of your customers, business partners, foreign colleagues, and enemies"—which probably comes down to us from American strategies during the Second World War, and, on the other, a homogenization of practices and codes. I'm thinking, for example, of François Jullien, who explains Chinese culture to French businessmen. It's not absurd, but it can give rise to silly situations such as when the French CEO who has been taking classes in Chinese culture and how to behave in China happens upon a Chinese person who attended the Harvard Business School, speaks exclusively business, and thinks it oddly quaint that this Frenchman is reciting lines from a Chinese poet about whom he could care less. Today we're in a situation of cultural metalingualism: there are people who have understood that modern-day communication derives more from codes than from culture, and then there those who persist in sounding the depths of the Slavic soul or the Asian mentality.

And yet it is said that cultures persist even when everything has been forgotten.

Of course, cultures have not disappeared, but they are in crisis—if they weren't, we would not be indulging in so much mourning over lost identities. As soon as one starts identifying with some identity, it's a sure sign one has lost one's culture. Can one imagine Proust talking about identity? Cultures are no longer fully taking on their status as cultures, that is, as a content that is never reducible to its own self-representation. Today cultures are transcended by code systems that are univocal, in other words, devoid of any implications or ambiguity and therefore perfectly poor in value. Today's smiley face and the resulting set of emoticons are perfect examples. There you have a finite list of explicit feelings that can be universal in a way that is not the case for seduction, allusion, the come-on, and everything that lends itself to illusion and without which life has almost no meaning. Also of importance here is body language such as American-style hugging or the high five, which one now sees being practiced among young Chinese and Iranians. We are in a crisis of cultures, a conflict between traditional cultural codes that are implicit and modern codes that by definition have to be explicit and are therefore poor. A language is rich because it contains the implicit (double entendre, allusion, connotation); a code is explicit and therefore poor. Driving rules and road signs are not open to interpretation—something is either plus or minus, yes or no, on or off. "Come on, I don't hate you at all" is not translatable into a code.[2] This is also why broad, high-octane sarcasm has won out over irony, which has the elegant refinement of turning against itself.

I have worked a lot with Iranians who are also very Westernized, but it is clear that there remains an *atavistic* Iranian culture, codes of recognized acceptable behavior, just as there are in Arab countries. Afghans and Iranians, for example, have a typical way of negotiating: it would be very impolite—this is important—to get right to the point; whereas among Americans, as soon as one has said hello, no time is lost and everyone sits down at the table (of course, I mean the negotiating table—no other kind exists). On more than one occasion, I've participated in negotiations between Afghans or Iranians and Americans. When the former, after a long moment of unimportant small talk, begin to slowly and softly get around to talking about important matters, the Americans think it's over and say, "Very interesting (when in fact they were bored and disappointed), goodbye, see you soon." But what I have discovered in thirty years of such meetings is precisely how Afghans and Iranians have integrated this double register and play with it—at one moment imitating the Texan negotiating an oil contract, at another retreating into unfathomable cultural difference and overacting to fool their interlocutor.

Sticking with traditional codes can become very misleading when it comes to encounters with others. If, when I was in Istanbul, I had asked the young students I met to go to a typical, old-fashioned café, they would have laughed in my face and never come with me. It would be like an American tourist in France asking to be taken to see the women of Paris. You might laugh in his face or tell him to cut the crap. I readily admit, however, that the Japanese have a very particular self-centered culture, but there, too, one ought to take note of the process of uniformization that is under way to the detriment of the alleged authentic culture.

Is it necessary to speak of uniformization?

I prefer to speak of a modern form of universalism that goes on above and beyond cultures. There are certainly other registers of voluntary universalism with decultured and deculturing ideologies such as Marxism. I remember a book that fascinated me, *Sans patrie ni frontières* (Without homeland or borders) by Jan Valtin (the alias of Richard Krebs). It told the story of a German officer of the Comintern in the 1930s.[3] This man, who speaks many languages like all secret agents at the time, tells of his travels around the world without ever alluding to local cultures. He's sent to organize a strike in Java and he talks about his activities there, but at no time does one learn what the Javanese lifestyle is—what they eat, how they're dressed, how they speak, or what they talk about outside of union meetings. In fact, they probably ate and dressed like locals, but for the Soviet agent all that was of absolutely no importance for carrying out his mission. He was addressing proletarian worker-comrades, and his words fit the times—the time, that is, of the International Brigades.

I also think of Paul Nizan in this regard. Nizan was another individual who fled Normale sup' to encounter an Orient that was never for him a vehicle for an imaginary construct. In his book *Aden, Arabie*, he tells of finding in Aden a concentrated form of economic exploitation, not the perfumes of the Orient. He describes both colonizers and the local inhabitants as entirely devoid of any cultural dimension that could inscribe their antagonism in a symbolic register where signs and meanings would be at stake. It's only with postcolonialism and the advent of cultural studies that the culture of the dominated will be ascribed a militant dignity of resistance, even if unconscious to the actors themselves. Valtin and Nizan describe only the nakedness of social beings.

It seems to me, though, that Valtin and Nizan are the exceptions within this literature. In general, things are told the other way around.

They are not as exceptional as many might think, but in an unexpected way, it's not on the left that one finds universalism today. The indifference to cultural context in favor of direct relations with the other as an immediate, universal subject (just as the bourgeois or the proletarian was for the Marxist) is what one finds among evangelical Protestant preachers for whom it is precisely the chasm between believers and heathens that founds the universality of man. All the believers resemble each other, brothers and sisters in Christ. What makes a heathen a heathen is his refusal of Christ, not his attachment to this or that cultural practice of no interest. These preachers travel about the world like the apostles in the eastern Mediterranean: all cities are the same, all converts behave the same, and everything happens as though everyone spoke the same language (which was probably the case with the Greek language called Koine that was spoken in the Middle East in Jesus's time, and is often true today with English). It's the nakedness of souls. In fact, the metaphor of stripping is a constant in this preachy literature. One must strip down, be reborn, be a new man, be like a newborn baby. Nizan will describe his own spiritual journey in Aden as a descent into hell followed by a stripping down, a peeling off, which is then followed by a rebirth.

One of the constants of my work since the 1970s turns out to be decul-turation, or a theory of deculturation, and for this, religions are wonderful prisms for analysis, as I tried to show in *Holy Ignorance*.

So in fact there is no uniform passage from traditional past to a decultured modernity.

Correct. One must show the complexity and the paradoxes of this passage. For example, one could say that communism was only a varnish or lid of sorts, and that it touched only the surface of the culture (be it Russian or Oriental or something else). When it collapsed, the older cultures seem to have reappeared as if by magic, and so communism then seems like no more than a long parenthesis. But that's false. Sovietism also created codes of behavior. The Uzbek apparatchik, for example, had his marching orders, which were as Soviet and bureaucratic as his homologue in Moscow—and what's more, he kept on functioning that way after 1989. In fact, he lives according to a double code, but one thing must be immediately under-stood: in general, the West sees this as a situation of conflict or as internal contradiction or as a form of syncretism. The Westerner uses pejorative terms to designate this situation as abnormal, or to denounce abnormal play between codes or cultures. I think, on the contrary, that this vision needs to be reversed. Instead of saying "There is first a fundamental culture that represents a structuring element and afterward the encounter between this culture and other codes that leads to *métissage* (mixing of cultures)," we ought to begin at the periphery and not from a core cultural heart or body that no longer exists (if it ever existed). It's the relation that counts, not the essence.

Chapter 21

WHAT WAS GOOD
ABOUT ORIENTALISM

In a posthumous book, *La construction humaine de l'islam*,[1] Mohammed Arkoun declares his admiration for the work of Edward Said but also his disagreement. According to Arkoun, Said forgets that the Orientalists, who were enormously erudite, disseminated a lot of important knowledge about Islam that would not have come into common circulation without them.

HENRY LAURENS MADE a similar critical observation about my work when he served as a member of the jury during my *habilitation*.[2] He said the work of Orientalists was remarkable and produced a true body of knowledge—and he's right. If it had produced only falsehoods, how would it have permitted the Occidental countries to control the Orient? Unless perhaps the Machiavellian plan was to control the Oriental by making him interiorize a false vision of himself constructed by the Orientalist? But that is again defining the dominated as the one who is unable to escape alienation and false consciousness, even when he claims to be doing just that. If the supposed culture of the Oriental is an alienating construction imposed by the dominator, then what is the true culture of the Oriental, if, that is, there is one? Either everything is a game of mirrors, or else there is a hidden authenticity. It's a vicious circle. In fact, Said's critique was above all a political stance, and paradoxically it contributed to a political polarization of Islamic studies in the Middle East and the United States (the other actor in this regard is the pro-Israel coalition for which the site Campus Watch operates as the leading policing force).

We ought to recognize that we're in an area of subtle and complex distinctions. For example, one could just as easily ask, If the Orient of the Orientalists does not exist, then what are we talking about?

That's exactly the problem with a certain anti-imperialist Left that you've put your finger on. The Muslim is alleged to be a construction of the West, with, then, two possible conclusions. The first, in good Marxist tradition, is that at bottom religion does not exist; it only expresses something in a language of alienation. But this analysis, secular and universalist, is overlooking a fundamental fact: for the believers, religion is obviously important, and to take it from them or contest its importance amounts to contesting their autonomy. This is what we see, for example, with the secularist's refusal to consider women who wear the veil as exercising their freewill. The discourse of emancipation begins with the disqualification of those who one claims to want to liberate. (The same observation could be made about the recent discourse around liberating prostitutes.) The second possible conclusion, such as in François Burgat's *L'Islamisme en face*,[3] goes in the opposite direction and says, "Face it, the Muslim speaks Muslim because Islam is the way the oppressed express themselves, they can only speak that language, it's their identity." But the problem again here is that the religious person is always made into something else. Even though the believer may claim to have a religious identity, for him, religion is never simply that identity. It's much more than that—and the whole challenge for the social sciences is to understand this *more* that goes by the name of *faith*, among other names. This is the problem that the Left has with Islam today, and I would add with every religion: either they speak in terms of alienation or in terms of identity. But in both cases, they duck the fundamental question: what does it mean to be a believer?

The fight against Islamophobia, which seeks to construct a concept analogous to anti-Semitism, rests on the same paradox. It takes up the Orientalist construction, but this time in the context of how European

Muslims get talked about: making Islam into the unvarying component of the category "descended from immigration" and separating it from all explicit belief. A Muslim always gets categorized as Muslim even if he is atheist, and therefore only the Westerner has access to the universal—which is moreover precisely what populist movements do (Frenchness, Welshness, native born, Englishness, Dutchness, and so forth).

Shouldn't one recognize that Said was right to point out that our perception of Islam remains for the most part essentialist? It is this, it is that, it won't change, and so on. Is the essentialist definition of the Muslim Other a Western malady?

About that, Said's analysis is still correct—perhaps more than ever. Essentialist talk has become stronger and stronger in contemporary Western discourse, despite the critiques of Said and other authors. Max Weber, although a culturalist, never says that culture is the cause of social practices; he prefers the subtler and less deterministic term *elective affinities* between a culture and social practices. However, with Huntington (at least as he gets handed down and passed around) and contemporary essentialism, one could think that today's Muslims walk around with Koranic software installed in their brains that orders their every movement.[4] This gap between the exterior vision of Islam and its actual functioning explains the difficulty of understanding the Arab Spring, which owed nothing to Koranic software. But when we watched those revolutions stall, some immediately interpreted that halt as the return, the reassertion of that software: the Arab Spring was merely an ephemeral bubble. Islamists inevitably regained power—the Koran that went out the door came back in the window in their telling.

But in reality, Islamists did not regain power. On the contrary, they have been forced to give up power, as one sees in Egypt and in the latest developments in Tunisia. The evolution of the Muslim Brotherhood in Egypt is interesting since it shows that the myths about Islamists are false. For example, the idea of an International Muslim Brotherhood preparing the caliphate. Who went to demonstrate on their behalf in front of the Egyptian embassy in Paris or London? No one. Nowhere in the world have we seen signs of any Islamic revolution, though its existence is widely claimed. Did the Ennahda movement in Tunisia help the Muslim Brotherhood? It did not. Many spoke of the secret army of the Muslim Brotherhood; in fact, they found themselves isolated and disarmed when faced with the military repression that occurred. People would talk about their control of mosques and Islamic institutions, for example, but those established groups took advantage of the Arab Spring to assert their autonomy and did not seek help from the Muslim Brotherhood, a group that, at bottom, faced the problem of not knowing what to do with it once they had power in Egypt. They ended up mostly breaking friendships and distributing government positions, just like every winning party after elections. There is no Islamic International. The Arab Spring recast Arab societies around a closed nationalism that has lost interest in the fate of Palestinians. As for al-Qaeda, their uprooted and unkempt band of followers tramps from jihad to jihad like rolling stones without ever taking root anywhere—just like the revolutionaries of the Far Left who made the rounds with their "just causes" forty years ago.

Chapter 22

AGAINST THE SECULARISTS'
ESSENTIALISM

Doesn't a society require secularization before there can be democratization?

NO, I DON'T think it's a precondition. Thinking so is what I call the theological prejudice—the idea that political culture evolved directly from theological categories and norms, but that with Islam the link remained unbroken. Yet one sees how in France Catholic theology, which is remarkably stable because the Church was always obsessed with control and with orthodoxy, has coexisted alongside an extremely diverse set of political cultures at different times and places. Theology is turned to when the social and political environment changes to give a theological explanation for this change. For example, we quote the line "Render to Caesar the things that are Caesar's" (Mark 12:13–17) when in the twentieth century the Church finally accepts to be separate from the state, and then we talk as though the Church had always accepted that separation, which is certainly not the case. The separation is explicitly condemned in the Syllabus of 1864, and in 1905 the Church—in Rome at least and in France mostly as well—was absolutely opposed to the separation that was voted into law that year. The key thing is really the evolution of religiosity, not the theology; in other words, the way believers live and eventually conceptualize to themselves their relation to a religion.

The idea that with Islam an intangible corpus of doctrines passed on since the closure of the *ijtihad*[1] in the ninth century directs relations between believers and the political sphere is quite simply contradicted by both the actual history of the Muslim world and by studies of the religious practices and utterances of believers. In sum, the theological question gets limited to an internal debate among ulema, just as it was frozen by Orientalism.

What's changing or what has changed?

To understand the religious, one must distinguish between religion (a normative corpus) and religiosity (the way the believers live their religion). We act as though the first is the key to the second when really it's just the opposite. The Koran says what Muslims say it says. One can easily study religion by going to a library, but to understand religiosity, you have to go out into the world among its practitioners. You have to be interested in those people. Studying religiosity is the only way to understand how religion translates into social practices.

For those with eyes to see, the changes in religiosity in the Muslim world are clearly evident: the individualization of faith, traditional religious authorities' loss of legitimacy, a reformulation of the links between religious markers and cultural markers, and so on. This is the research I report on in my books *Globalized Islam* and *Holy Ignorance*. These changes have a simple but essential consequence: the religious field is diversified and becomes the space of a debate between equals, because everyone can talk about the religious. And this has nothing to do with a liberal theology—the Salafists, as fundamentalist as they may be, are big debaters and highly individualistic. It's largely because of them that the Muslim Brotherhood lost the monopoly that they had arrogated to themselves when it came to the religious in politics. The choice that the Salafists made in Egypt to align themselves with the secularists and the army against the Muslim Brotherhood shows that the concept of political Islam has exploded and left behind a religious space that is diversified and more open.

But isn't a certain degree of secularization necessary, a middle class, or at least elites detached from religious practice, or perhaps something else?

It's important to go back to the historical example of the United States. They did not have first secularization and then democratization. It was a religious society that democratized itself while totally accepting the presence of the religious as part of its diversity.[2] It's the whole sense behind the First Amendment: no established religion, therefore a diversity within the religious space. This creates a homothetic situation alongside the development of democracy. If, in the religious sphere, every individual is completely free, then democracy is possible. Even if, in the religious sphere everyone continues to believe that true sovereignty comes from God and not the people, the democratic game is accepted by all, either for empirical reasons (one must still govern society while waiting for the Last Judgment) or because the retreat of God from politics has been theorized. But approaching the matter this way is discredited by ultrasecularists as insincere and duplicitous (*un double discours*). I, on the other hand, see the Salafists as comparable to fundamentalist American Christians who practice democracy but don't make a dogma out of it. It's *laïcité* that makes republicanism (more than democracy) into an ideology. In short, one can be a democrat without being liberal and, vice versa, be liberal without democracy—as one sees with those who want to eradicate Islamism or chase religion from all public space. Militant secularists in France or in Tunisia always think that an authoritarian secularization is necessary as a precondition for democracy to take hold. That's just false, and really it only results in dictatorships, as we see now with Sisi in Egypt, and he's not even really a secularist since he reestablished blasphemy and apostasy as crimes.

You have discussed the United States, Egypt, and Tunisia, but can you specify how your analysis of those cases helps understand the French situation?

I am always blown away by the way unanimity reigns supreme, on the right and the left, on the essential questions that are treated via the imaginary. It is the case in France with the problem of disadvantaged suburbs, the infamous *banlieues*. All evil supposedly comes from the *banlieues*, which are said to be splintering away from the republic into communitarianism, and this is further claimed to be the catalyst for the Islamization of the society. The Right and the Left make the same diagnosis but disagree about the remedy—though in fact less so recently. An authoritarian *laïcité* backed up with muscly police raids seems now to be the doctrine of every French interior minister. But the diagnosis is false. Why? Because the *banlieues* are ghettos, and ghettos have never constituted a threat. One never leaves the ghetto, or if one does it's via social promotion. The aspects that are viewed as negative (gangs of youths, Salafist groups) are really part of what I call autoconstraint: they live crammed together in a territory or small community. But of course, logically, the corollary of the ghetto is the phantasm of riots that originate from the ghetto—youths who take the regional RER train en masse from their ghetto to the city center to attack the Champs-Élysées. Yet, as Olivier Mongin[3] and others have shown, there is no such exit from the ghetto of that low sort because the ghetto autoconstrains itself. There's no need to place lines of CRS riot police around the bad neighborhoods because the young people congregate in that territory on their own. No one denies the violence, the vandalism, the juvenile delinquency, but the problem is not the ghetto. It is rather the exit from the ghetto through social promotion that one does not want to face up to, because that would put into question the racist clichés and the bleeding-heart hand-wringing over the misery of the young people in the *banlieues*. And yet one sees today a whole generation of young French Muslims who belong to the middle class, who are professionally integrated, and who have frequently entered into mixed marriages and taken up residence in the city center. But those individuals are totally ignored. The French prime minister, Manuel Valls, and his followers don't see them, and that explains in part the Socialist Party's disappointing electoral results of late. And yet these successful Muslims are hardly invisible, and one can get to know them empirically. On this score, most sociologists, with a few exceptions, are not doing their job.

They'll tell you that they don't have the right to gather statistics based on ethnicity.

But they don't even need to do that! All they need to do is look at a city like Dreux and work on marriage licenses and other civil status records. For example, according to the demographer Michèle Tribalat, mixed marriages are in decline, even though she claims to not be able to work on ethnicity-based statistics. It's debatable. All you have to do is consult the lists of births mentioned in the local paper in Dreux and the names of the parents. Granted, it's forbidden to gather national statistics, but there is no law against gathering local statistics. In Dreux a quarter of couples with an Arabic name are mixed couples involving both men and women in roughly equal numbers. It is true that when young women marry non-Muslims, the latter are supposed to convert. That happens sometimes, but it is almost always a convenience conversion that carries no obligations. What's more, young women go off to get married without consulting their fathers. If the British have established within their Foreign Office a special agency to combat forced marriages, it's because there are more and more of them— but that is precisely the sign that the young women are leaving home and therefore the end of their resigned acceptance of former ways in the name of tradition. In the past, it was called an arranged marriage—a girl married without protest the spouse chosen by the parents. But today they no longer want to, and so a certain number are dragged into forced marriages. In similar fashion, in Germany honor crimes are cited as proof of the noninte-gration of Muslims (who are in fact almost always Kurds in the cases in question—yet another example of Islamization from the exterior of a purely ethnic phenomenon). However, this is precisely the sign that if the parents may not integrate, the daughters do. That's the essential point— the future is those young women. Once again, what is actually proof of inte-gration, of a changing mentality in the younger generation, is presented by the media as a resurgence of tradition. One sees with this example the force of the culturalist prejudice that makes a social fact say the opposite of what it means.

Could you say a bit more about local statistics?

Here's a personal statistic for you: at the hospital in Dreux, the only Arab name when I arrived in that city in 1973 belonged to the Lebanese Maronite intern who treated me. The heads of all the wards had typical French names, and one could recognize a few Jewish names, mostly Ashkenazi and a few Sephardic ones. Now, though, there's a high percentage of Arab names. Of course, one cannot conclude that these are all devout Muslims. There may even be Middle Eastern Christians in the lot as well as atheists. But it's clear that there is an increasing number of Muslims who belong to France's middle classes. And the same is true across all sorts of professions: business people, lawyers, journalists, high school teachers, financial advisers, tele-communications engineers, and so on. Twenty or thirty years ago, men who married Muslim women often studied Islam or had some other profes-sional connection to it. They were sometimes fellow researchers. This is no longer the case. In Dreux it's locals, such as someone from the Beauceron family, who are marrying Arab women.

Here's another example. People ask about the loyalty of French Muslims in the event of some future foreign conflict, as though it were a potential problem the country needed to face now. One forgets that the answer has already been given: 15 percent of those enlisted in France's all volunteer armed forces are of Muslim origin. They fought hard in Afghanistan and in Mali against Islamists—and in neither place were there any desertions or sabotage (a fact that ought to be compared with the French army's per-formance in Indochina and Algeria, where desertions and sabotage were fairly frequent). In short, ideological questions are being asked that have already been answered by the facts and by the people concerned. As for jihadists, there, too, one must underline (1) their isolation within the milieu in which they are operating, including within their families (including some who are ready to sue the state for failing to bring back their children), and (2) their motives, which resemble more a revolt of rebels in search of a cause than they do a religious radicalization.

Let me play the devil's advocate on the essentialist side for a moment and ask you about veils and headscarves.

There, too, we've fallen into a misunderstanding. The upsurge of religious symbols in public spaces, a change that is clearly in evidence in this genera-tion compared with the last, does not signify a return of religious people toward a society that would have existed in the past, but on the contrary a growing rupture between the religious and the cultural or social environ-ment. Sixty years ago, in postwar France and in the Algerian departments of France, religious signs were integrated into the landscape—one could see nuns with wimples and priests in cassocks in the streets of Paris and women wearing haik in the streets of Algiers. When L'abbé Pierre was elected to parliament in 1946, he arrived at the National Assembly in his cassock, and no one found that scandalous or bizarre. Today it would be unthinkable. What makes the religious visible today is its disconnection from the dominant culture, and that is as true for Christianity as it is for Islam. The signs are erected against the culture as proof or symptoms of the autonomy of the religious. The veil that has provoked scandal in France has no traditional roots. Like the Turkish or Egyptian veil, its role is really to mark the entry of pious women into public space and the labor market—and their exit from the traditional setting of the housewife.

With the generation of so-called Lustiger priests, one finds the same irruption of militant religious forms, but with Christians, in public spaces. Belonging to the Church and the functions of the Church are prominently displayed: cassocks are worn, crosses are erected, bells are rung, processions long abandoned are revived, and even public demonstrations are organized (*"La Manif pour tous"*—the demonstration for all).

And that's irritating?

Yes, but what's not noticed is that this reaffirmation of the religious is reaching its outer limits: the implosion of Islamism (and Salafism) in Egypt following the Arab Spring, the total absence of any passage into politics of Islam in France, or of Catholicism, and the failure of any expansion of the *Manif pour tous* into secular contexts. The election of a less intransigent papal leader such as Pope Francis goes along the same lines. I remember a cartoon by Plantu from twenty years ago, at the time of John Paul II. One sees a French family in front of a television broadcasting a speech by the pope, and the mother says to her husband, "Quick, take the children out of the room. He's going to talk about sex again!" As everyone knows, Pope Francis has announced that he would like to move away from the image of the Church as the staunch defender of rigid norms that tend to revolve around questions of the body (sexuality, reproduction, abortion, euthanasia), and women's bodies in particular, to the detriment of charity and shared values.

Is it appropriate to speak of a *liberal Islam*, to cite a controversial term among religious people today and for some time?

I'm not sure that the concept of a liberal religion makes any sense. It's not for the religion to be liberal—it's up to the believer. In the Muslim world, too, contrary to superficial received ideas, we notice a deep crisis around the discourse of norms, a discourse incarnated by Salafism. If there is a marginal movement (in numerical terms, perhaps a few thousand people) from Salafist jihadism to al-Qaeda, the others (those known as quietists or scientific in Egypt, for example, have formed themselves into a political party and are running in elections. And, of course, after a few months of talking about sharia, they've been drawn into political squabbles and their message becomes inaudible. Moreover, for the first time the publication of an article on atheism in Egypt was allowed. The authors are a small group of young atheists who performed in this way their coming out—an unthinkable action twenty years ago. In another example, Moroccan and Algerian *dé-jeûners* (fast breakers), announced on the Internet that they would break their Ramadan fast in public. In Tunisia and Egypt *sécularisme* is freely declared as a public stance. The conversion of Muslims to Christianity has also ceased to be taboo, if one judges by the increasing number of Protestant churches that have been built to accommodate the influx of converts, a phenomenon one sees in Algeria, Morocco, Turkey, and in France.

There is still legitimate discussion of the death threats that hang over certain apostates, but one doesn't see that tens of thousands of apostates live in Muslim communities without anything happening to them. The Tunisian Constitution of 2014 explicitly recognizes the right to change religions (*hurrya al-damir*, "freedom of conscience," and not simply the freedom to practice the religion of their fathers, *hurrya al'atiqad*, "freedom of belief"). This is why religious freedom is not only the precondition of democracy, but the very definition of what it means to affirm religious belief is what's at stake. By seeking to confine the religious to the private sphere, today's *laïcité* in France not only has no understanding of the religious and betrays the spirit of the church-state separation law of 1905, but feels obliged to behave in authoritarian, nondemocratic ways.

One ought to look at the recent evolution without blinders and see it within a longer time frame. This is not easy to do, even for people who have a lot of experience in the field. The Muslim world is going through a crisis of the religious sphere. The stories of groups who openly break with Ramadan is but one symptom. Those are courageous actions, but they would be impossible if a certain tolerance in the society were not already established, and if quite a large number of people were not already in a position to say why not? Of course, it would be impossible to carry out the same public rejection in Kandahar in Taliban territory. The Muslim world is very diverse and changing all the time. The Moroccan authorities cite the possible disruption of public order if they don't arrest the *dé-jeûneurs* because otherwise they could provoke violent reactions against what constitutes an attack against the Moroccan "national identity." Except that the only riots are caused by excessive police zeal and by no one else.

How does one explain the extremely diverse set of opinions among specialists about what Islam is becoming?

In part one needs to speak about the crisis within the social sciences. Studies in this area are being conducted more and more in amphitheaters where students are taught theory, and they spend less time out in the field. We're constantly interposing filters to understand what some people think— through opinion polls, for example—and these practices always strike me as dubious, even when they are statistically well done, as in Europe. In Egypt and some other countries, the results are laughable. With these filters, one isn't in touch with reality because the answer is in the question. Of course, when I say that X is going on and use some lived or observed fact as evidence, I'm told that I'm being anecdotal or relying on empirical observation, and this is meant as a put-down. Personally, and going in the other direction, the only thing I really admired about Bourdieu's method was the interviews or qualitative investigation. *La misère du monde* (1993, *The Weight of the World*) is his greatest book. The actual reality in the field is what counts there—and yet one notices that the book is increasingly ignored. Besides fieldwork, intuition remains very important to me, and yet it has no scientific legitimacy within the social sciences, even though epistemologists are the first to underscore the role of the imagination in scientific discoveries. I published a small book in 1978, now out of print, on that topic, *"Le nouvel esprit scientifique" de Bachelard*. When the social sciences want to imitate the physical sciences, they take on the dogmatism and forget about the fuzziness, subjectivity, and the imagination that are commonly known to be at the center of all creativity, including in the so-called hard sciences.

The problem is that Islamologists have a tendency to reduce Islam to a summary reflection of what the ulema say—in effect a transtemporal corpus of norms and concepts. Even though, as one would expect, historians report on the great diversity within the history of the Muslim world, it's not enough to dislodge the ideal type that constitutes Islam. Sociologists and political scientists have trouble, as I've said, thinking about religion as religion, and instead they treat it as an identity marker or as ideology. The only researchers who have managed to work on Islam as something diverse are anthropologists and ethnologists. They noted early on the many different Islams—Indonesian, Moroccan (I think of the work of Clifford Geertz, of course),[4] and so on. But they analyzed this diversity through the interpretive grid of culture, and by seeking to deconstruct the paradigm of a normative, transtemporal Islam, they reinforced the culturalist vision, namely, the idea that there really is an implicit cultural software that determines Muslim behavior. The surprising upshot of the ethnologists' work is to have handed the New Right a differentialist discourse that is less unsavory than biological racism.

However, little work has been done on what I call religiosity—the personal relation believers have to their faith and their personal way of inscribing themselves in the world.

Why did the anthropological angle on Islam swing from the Left to the Right?

The anthropological discourse of the 1950s, exemplified by Claude Lévi-Strauss, was very progressive, even though he himself held conservative personal opinions. The progressive stances were equality and the shared dignity of all cultures, each person being at bottom a particular incarnation of an invariable human essence. Professional anthropologists held to that position, while refining it along the way, of course. The question was how to think of diversity under the overarching positing of a universal.

Immigration didn't change the anthropology of the anthropologists, but it did change the way anthropology was used in public debates. One notable case is the influence exerted by what was called the New Right organized around the research team GRECE (Groupement de recherche et d'études pour la civilisation européenne) under the leadership of Alain de Benoist, who borrowed in astute ways from the writings of Gramsci. That Marxist philosopher thought a political revolution could take place only if the cultural field (in the most general sense) reflected the values and norms of the new society to come. The dominant class was thought to hold the reins of cultural hegemony, and the new ascendant class was to put an end to that cultural hegemony before embarking on revolution. With his efforts to revive thought on the Far Right that had been discredited by Nazism and Pétainism, Alain de Benoist thought it was necessary to draw upon modern anthropological concepts to justify a *différentialisme culturel* without associating it with biological racism. Culture takes the place of biology, and ethnicity replaces race. One thereby uses polite concepts.

Jean-Marie Le Pen's National Front, which is now led by his daughter, Marine, takes up the same idea. Of course, this doesn't mean that the experts or essayists who are constantly talking about culture wars identify with the National Front. But we are in a Kulturkampf that the Left didn't understand or know how to deal with other than by resorting to a moralizing, normative discourse (antiracism or now its inverse opposite, militant *laïcité*) before eventually falling into the trap of the communitarian phobia—not realizing that it was handing over to the Far Right the cultural hegemony that the latter was seeking to conquer. Obviously, the Left is careful to play the good guy by combating concepts rather than rejecting a whole population. But in a curious accident that is hardly accidental, the combat against—take your pick—Islamism, fundamentalism, communitarianism, sexism among the young, delinquency, anti-Semitism in the *banlieues*— always targets the same collection of individuals who have one part of their origin story in common: immigration from Muslim countries. All the intellectuals who eagerly jump to the question "Why don't Muslims condemn terrorism (or anti-Semitism or sexism or . . . fill in the blank)?" have fallen into the trap of essentialism. Why should the Tunisian green grocer at the corner be summoned to write a communiqué about Bin Laden, if Bin Laden means nothing to him? We're asking this shopkeeper to distance himself from a link that we've ascribed to him from the outside. We're demanding that he confirm, through a forced confession, that Bin Laden is truly the quintessence of Islam.

But would we, for one second, entertain the idea that the Protestant Federation of France ought to publicly distance itself from George W. Bush or the Tea Party? Would we ask the French Catholic Church to repent for the support that was given to Franco by the Spanish prelates? Would we ask the Dali Lama to condemn the massacre of Muslims by Burmese Buddhists? I know that there is also the tendency to require every Jew to first condemn the Israeli policy in the occupied territories before he can express any opinion, but that is wrong. I am vigorously opposed to the boycott of Israeli universities—campuses I personally would visit more often if the Israeli police made less trouble for me at the border.

To conclude this discussion of anthropology, it's not at all by chance if in 2013 the Catholic Church seized on the anthropological argument against gay marriage, which says that the heterosexual couple is the anthropological foundation of our society . . . instead of the theological argument—God created man and woman. Anthropology here becomes an ideological pretext, whereas in reality it's diverse and does not confirm, at bottom, the universality of heterosexual marriage. Lévi-Strauss himself had perfectly well demonstrated the relativeness of sexual ascriptions in the matrimonial bond.

In the 1980s and '90s, you linked the problems of immigration in Dreux to your reflections on globalized culture.

True, I moved between these two poles. I was still residing in Dreux, and that city was always a home to me and my observation post. The birth, youth, and growth into adulthood of the children of immigrants, the crisis and persistence of the *cercle laïque*, the aging of leftist elites, and the arrival of new elites of immigrant origin all profoundly changed the public space, but in the sense of renewal more than replacement. The latter term alludes to Renaud Camus's obsessive interpretation which seems to forget that if one wants to assure the continuity of a population, one needs first of all to make babies. That's also why I'm in favor of PMA (*procréation médicalement assistée*) for homosexual couples. In November 2012, the *cercle laïque* organized a meeting in Dreux outside the city center in a southern suburb near the "tough neighborhoods." The evening meeting was coorganized by a youth association in the area that included several teachers. Some of these teachers spoke about Muslims in moderate but religious terms while also praising their elders in the *cercle laïque*. Those elders, who are free thinkers, were in a way pleased to witness the continuity of their efforts, except that it was through Muslims who were not at all antireligious and had daughters who wore headscarves and yet were also modern and dynamic. In short, one got the impression that the old *laïcards* didn't really understand what's going on today, though they could see that it included some continuity.

Locally, bridges exist, everyone knows each other, people do things together, and these undertakings go well—whereas Parisian elites on the left who no longer have any local anchor spout ideological interpretations that are out of touch with the mutations of *French* society. I insist on that term, because most of the young people we're talking about live as French, despite the opposing efforts of the Moroccan and Turkish consulates, which are bizarrely seconded by the French Ministry of the Interior, and which do all they can to keep them under the influence of their country of origin. But as the affair swirling around the Baby-Loup daycare center shows, the secularists don't understand that the new religious situation in the country creates another positioning of *laïcité*, and they therefore latch on to *laïcité* as a tool to expel the religious from public space, which is in total contradiction with the intent of the law of 1905. Far from being a guiding principle for living together, *laïcité* has turned into a pseudoideology and especially a phobia of religion. It's not surprising to see *laïcité* be taken up by the extreme right-wing party, because I think one of the fundamental characteristics of the Far Right is precisely a tendency toward phobias, with biological racism being only occasionally expressed in that phobic register. It would be helpful to return to the spirit of the law of 1905: the state is neutral and seeks only to regulate religious practices in the public space, not exclude them. The law of 1905 never says that religion ought to be a private matter. It proposes regulating religion as a public matter, which is entirely normal and exactly what it should do I think.

Chapter 23

THE DECADE 2000–2010

Where Were You on September 11, 2001?

Why talk about decades?

IT WAS NEVER something I decided, but I realize looking back that I have changed lives every ten years. After a certain amount of time spent living in a country or working on a country, one gets stuck in a rut and imprisoned in one's intellectual and political reflexes. You get categorized in this or that camp. You defend certain positions and end up repeating yourself a lot. I would be incapable of spending my whole life studying a single country or a single topic as many researchers do. Fatigue comes over me after ten years of specializing in the same area. I have the feeling that I've been there, done that—even if many questions remain. I prefer to set off into new territory, both geographic and intellectual.

The 1990s were my Central Asia decade because that's mostly where I was traveling and living. I wound up writing a book about these little-known republics that curiously enough has held up rather well. I was expecting that another comprehensive study would replace it rather quickly given all the changes in this part of the world. But fifteen years later, no newer general study has appeared, not even in English. However, more specialized studies have appeared. It was starting in Dreux that I began to think about globalized Islam, globalization, the back-and-forth between local and global and related issues. Looking back, I was lucky that my book *Globalized Islam* did not appear before September 11 because I was able to add an important and necessary chapter on al-Qaeda. The book was published in 2002. It has aged well, in the sense that it shows that globalized Islam is no longer linked to a culture and that it has entered into a process of global deculturation. It was after 9/11, with the flood of events and statements that followed, that the idea of what I eventually called holy ignorance came to me. A portion of the material in that book already appears in *Globalized Islam*. I forced myself to generalize about intuitions that were already present in earlier books, while at the same time broaching a new corpus—Christianity.

The first decade of the twenty-first century opens with the attacks on the World Trade Center. Where were you at that time?

I arrived in Dushanbe at the end of the day on September 9, 2001. I was to meet with Massoud in a few days. My last meeting with Massoud had taken place a month before the birth of my son Samuel (June 1, 1999), and now nearly a month had gone by since the birth of my second son, Nicolas (July 30, 2001). Massoud was killed, however, that very morning—two days before the attacks on Tuesday, September 11. Monday and Tuesday (remember that with the time change it was already the evening of the eleventh in Dushanbe when the attacks happened in New York) were spent making condolence visits at the Afghan embassy, where people were stunned and miserable. Everyone was expecting an immediate Taliban offensive on the northeast stronghold, now that its charismatic leader was dead. I saw Abdullah Abdullah, Massoud's special envoy, who had come to my home in Dreux. I then went to the hospital to see my old friend Massoud Khalili, who had been wounded in the attack but survived. He didn't accept that Massoud was dead and claimed he was in intensive care. And then, as I was going back to the headquarters of the French NGO ACTED that served as our inn, I saw the two towers on fire on a Russian television that kept reshowing the same images with no subtitles. I did not doubt for a moment that this was the work of al-Qaeda and said so in an interview published in *Le Monde* at the time. Massoud had forewarned this was coming. I understood that we were entering a new phase of history, first for Afghanistan but more generally for Islam. It confirmed my hypothesis about the deterritorialization of Islam and the uselessness of territorial wars against these new forms of terrorism. The odd thing was my Afghan friends at the embassy had cheered up a bit. Like me, they understood that the Americans would now attack the Taliban and that for them the time for revenge had come. The next day, I got a call from Hubert Védrine[1] and his ministry director, Pierre Sellal, asking that I help them take stock of the situation in Afghanistan and think about what was to come.

What were the consequences of the September 11 attacks for you as an expert?

The four years that followed were mostly spent wrapped up in endless tense debates with the Americans. I was already well known in those neoconservative circles. Those who led that movement had first become active in the 1980s to promote the efforts of the Afghan resistance, and at the time I had collaborated with them in arming the mujahideen and in criticizing the CIA's management of that aid. Now I was shocked by their totally ideological and abstract approach to the situation. I questioned all this in two books, *Les illusions du 11 septembre* and *Le croissant et le chaos*.[2] One encounters here again the sticky matter of the rationality of political decisions. Responding to September 11 by invading Iraq was totally irrational. But that's something the Far Left cannot accept: imperialism is always rational, so the Americans had a precise agenda; for example, control the oil fields— a logic that was obviously absurd—but it blocked all political intelligence and left only a confusion of tangled conspiracy theories.

Meanwhile, France's refusal to intervene in Iraq—announced with panache or grandiloquence, according to your point of view, by Dominique de Villepin at the United Nations General Assembly, created very strained relations with the United States. I attended many meetings, sometimes independently, sometimes as part of French delegations, conducted by the American administration or think tanks.

What did September 11 mean when it comes to terrorism?

What interested me was less the vertical genealogy of Islamic terrorism (from the Koran to Bin Laden), a topic that occupied plenty of researchers, and more its horizontal dimension and its Western genealogy. As I've said, those who started from the Koran to eventually wind up at Bin Laden were doomed to fail. This terrorism was born in the 1980s and has nothing to do with what was done, said, or written fourteen centuries ago. During that long lapse of time, Muslims did not experience terrorism—violence yes, but not terrorism. On the other hand, I was acquainted with terrorists from my days with the Proletarian Left, where actual terrorism stayed at the level of temptation, as well as being familiar with Action directe, the Baader-Meinhof group, and the Red Brigades. Even after having broken away from the leftist universe, I continued to closely follow these phenomena. Going back further, there were the Russian populists and the European anarchists at the previous turn of the century. It's also generally forgotten that Malraux wrote some remarkable pages on terrorism in *La condition humaine* around the character Chen.

Farhad Khosrokhavar revisited in his analyses the logic already presented by first Dostoyevsky, then Malraux.[3] The terrorist thinks that this world is so rotten that one ought to blow oneself up. He has no wish to live to see the beauty of his actions because every revolution will fall again into corruption. These are the reference points one must study to understand Islamic terrorism, and not the mad ravings about seventy virgins promised to martyrs. The martyr, let's remember, does not *choose* death, he *meets* it, whereas the terrorist *seeks* it. The pseudointellectual ramblings about the Koranic origins of terrorism are worthless. One needs only to read the testament of Mohammed Atta, one of the September 11 pilots, to see that his relations to women were shot through with phobia.

How did you react afterward to the Western intervention in Afghanistan against the Taliban?

I considered the October 2001 intervention in Afghanistan to be legitimate. I had high expectations, whereas I expected nothing would come of the intervention in Iraq. So I started participating again in meetings as an Afghanistan specialist, and I accompanied the French army when the government sent its contingent there. General Py, who commanded the ISAF in 2004, asked that I come to make an on-site evaluation, and for that trip I traveled form Cologne to Kabul with the German Luftwaffe. I also gave lessons to American National Guard soldiers who were going to Afghanistan to help with civilian programs—and this despite the disapproval of the American Anthropological Association, which was opposed to all collaboration with the government and the army. It was the old debate about the relationship between expertise and power that I had already lived through with my friend Louis Dupree. In reply to this absolute refusal to collaborate, I countered that it was important to know what the army was actually doing. Either it would do a good job and demonstrate that it was possible to fight against the Taliban (and for that I didn't see why we shouldn't offer our help and our talents), or it was a mistake, a quagmire, and in that case, it would be necessary to construct solid arguments in favor of a pullout on rational grounds so as not to be viewed as the ideological condemnation of an imperialism that in any case had lost its rationality, like the Soviets one decade earlier. The time of imperialism is over. We're now in a world of unhinged financialization that is totally uninterested in the control of resources and territories. It takes some time to understand that the deterritorialization of the economy leads inevitably to a deterritorialization of strategy. The Russians and Chinese have yet to understand this.

I would like to point out that the act of taking sides never cut me off from the people on the other side—the Russians in Afghanistan, Iranians in the government, hard-core Islamists, and even the Taliban—whom I encountered occasionally through their representatives up until 2013. Those individuals are also in the logic of confrontation/negotiation and to that extent they like having across from them someone who knows them and who also maintains ties with their enemies. Sooner or later one has to negotiate, and one usually negotiates with one's enemies, not with one's friends. I'd like to underscore that the Taliban are not a superficial phenomenon in Afghan society. They were not just a ragtag band of terrorists who wandered in by accident; they were the interlocutors with whom one had to accept discussing things. On the other hand, al-Qaeda was wildly different because its leaders were not involved either in politics or in any real society, be it Afghan or Syrian.

How do you explain the provocative destruction that started in 2001 of the Buddhas of Bamiyan by the Taliban and the indignant reactions in the West, where they were definitively classified as barbarians? Also, the Taliban did not destroy the tombs of the Muslim saints but took aim at the patrimony of another religion.

Well, the Taliban *did* also destroy the tombs of Muslims that they considered pagans. As for the Buddhas, the Taliban's reasoning was symptomatic of what I've called holy ignorance. To the few diplomats who were able to meet with them (among them Ambassador Pierre Lafrance, who speaks fluent Arabic and Persian, and who in his reports on the Buddhas spoke eloquently of the *crise iconoclastique*), they said this: If the Buddhas were religious symbols, they would not touch them, but there are no more Buddhists in Afghanistan; therefore, the statues no longer represent anything religious. If they're only about culture, then they have nothing to do with any religion, and we're not in any way limiting religious freedom if we blow them up. (The argument is somewhat similar to the Swiss claim that wanting to get rid of minarets in their country is not about limiting anyone's religious freedom.) In short, what they were attacking, they said, was not other religions (they did not harm the synagogue in Kabul, nor the Hindu or Sikh temples in the city, because there were still believers who frequented those places), but the idea that there could be a culture that would be autonomous vis-à-vis the religious—this they could not accept. For example, they attacked the Pashtun code of honor—the Pashtunwali—and traditional Afghan games likes combats with animals, but they had nothing against volleyball or soccer, on condition that close-fitting uniforms be forbidden, and of course women's teams.

In 2008 *La sainte ignorance* proposes a comprehensive analysis of the contemporary religious context.

With this book, I was trying to understand religious mutations in general. Since the culturalist and differentialist approaches do not work, another approach has to be found to understand today's events. Of course, that means everything that touches on Islam, but also John Paul II, the Tea Party, American Evangelicalism, neo-Buddhism and neo-Hinduism, Jehovah's Witnesses, religious conversions in every direction, and also the tense debates around *laïcité*, reasonable accommodation, multiculturalism, and so on.

There is no return of the religious, but there is a mutation of the religious. Secularization has isolated the religious, which constructs itself as a community of faith—in other words, a community of primordial believers who put religion out front—and this community lives its life surrounded by a dominant culture that is not simply profane but more precisely pagan. The religious person's religious life is no longer in harmony with the dominant culture, which is no longer merely a secularized religiousness. Since the 1960s, values diverge (in particular, values about sexual freedom, procreation, the family, and women's bodies) to the point where one could speak today of two different anthropologies. For the dominant culture, man is the measure of everything—the rights of man or, as one says today, human rights, sacralize man, and a new notion of freedom puts in question what was formerly considered as nature and natural (sexual differences, procreation).

At the same time, globalization puts in place a universal marketplace, and among other goods a marketplace of the religious. In this marketplace, it's the religions that have accepted their deculturation (Evangelicalsm, Salafism) that win big. Conversions are the sign of new marketplace relations. At the same time, it's the most fundamentalist forms that triumph because fundamentalism, instead of being the expression of traditional cultures, is, on the contrary, a product and an agent of deculturation. Finally, and this is the last point of my argument, since there is no longer any cultural evidence of the religious, the religious signs and symbols frighten or upset people (from veils to church bells). The religious is no longer familiar, and therefore people ask the state to hide it, even if it means ignoring what the law says about religious freedom. Therefore, it's left up to the court system to format and configure religiousness, to give it a definition that will reestablish if not harmony at least a social order. But this effort to renormalize religiousness disrupts the incantations of frightened *laïcité* extremists.

Coexistence risks returning, therefore, as a normative or even authoritarian system that then produces further tensions and fear. Hence, the quest for identity—the new lullaby, the new security blanket, the new pacifier of our childhood terrors.

PART VI

THE IMPORTANCE OF A
RELIGIOUS GENEALOGY

Chapter 24

PORTRAIT OF A YOUNG
PROTESTANT IN THE
1950S AND '60S

If I may ask, what is your own religious genealogy?

I AM AT the intersection of several religious genealogies that are all
Protestant and rural. My mother's family was from the Tarn in the southwest. A distant relation, a nobleman named Calvayrac, was forced to
renounce his Protestantism at the moment of the Revocation of the Edict
of Nantes in 1685 to keep his title and lands in Espérausses. But the monar-
chy, being suspicious, put in place a surveillance system, and the priests
were forced to fill out police forms that were then transferred to the royal
supervisors, the intendants, who kept files on people. Another distant
cousin (but a close friend), Michel Miaille, inherited a portion of the estate
and discovered the file of our mutual ancestor Calvayrac, in which the local
priest, evidently exasperated by him, had written, "Talkative and badly
converted"—I would gladly accept that as my motto! The priest was right
because as soon as the Edict of Toleration became law in 1787, the Calvayrac of the time, a descendant of the half-converted chatterbox, returned
to Protestantism along with the majority of the inhabitants of the valley.
When the young pastor Augustin Barraud, himself the grandson of a
republican deprived of a republic after 1852 and a painter of porcelain and
supporter of the Tour de France under the name Sanglier la sagesse (the Wise
Wild Boar), is given his curacy in Vabres in 1913 just after completing his
theological studies at the Protestant seminary in Montauban, he marries

the young parishioner Émie Mercier, a descendant of Calvayrac. Just before he retired, in Limoges, one of his students in Sunday school was my colleague and superior, Jean Bauberot, a well-known sociologist of religions.

On my father's side, and more precisely on the side of his mother, Élise Dion, the home turf is rural Vendée. There, little Protestant communities had survived the European wars of religion, the Revocation of the Edict of Nantes, and, despite being republicans, the massacres perpetrated by the hated revolutionary troops, who did not distinguish between a Catholic Vendéen peasant and a Protestant Vendéen peasant. In the village of Mouchamps, where one of my first cousins has kept the family farm, one can see, thanks to Google Earth, a physical trace of this history. Although it's been a long time since the lands were sold to bigger Catholic landholders and fifty years since the hedges and roads were smoothed over to make larger parcels and allow tractors to roll on them, cultivating hundreds of meters in straight lines, you can see in the aerial photo one point where the lines are oddly pushed out, as though avoiding an invisible something before returning to their straight path. In fact, that something is the place where over a century ago my ancestors, who were forbidden cemetery rights on account of heresy, were buried at night by their loved ones. This practice continued for a long time, in Vendée and in the Tarn, but by daylight, even though by then the secular municipal cemeteries were open to everyone. This tradition of persecution and resistance certainly contributed to turning many young French Protestants into defenders of other religious minorities. I might mention that this little village was the birthplace of three future directors of contemporary research at the CNRS, Jérôme Clerc, Marc Gaborieau (whose family was Catholic), and myself. As it happens, our thee areas of research form a geographic continuity: the Persian-speaking world in my case, the Turkish-speaking world for Jérôme, and the Indian subcontinent for Gaborieau.

In Martine's Syriac village, I rediscovered this phenomenon of a little rural religious minority united around a story of persecution. Curiously, our villages have another feature in common: the presence in the area of another, even more dissident religious community—a community even smaller and in agony: the Yazidis, who pray to the devil for the Tur Abdin, and the Little Church of Courlay in Vendée (though situated in the

Deux-Sèvres Department), a small dissident Catholic town that broke with Rome in 1802 over the pope's signing of the Concordat, since they viewed it as collaboration with the devil (Napoleon I), whom they certainly were not going to pray for. The Little Church carries on a purist strain of Catholicism with no clergy. As the alchemists of the Renaissance used to say, there are microcosms that are the reflection of the world.

So Protestantism, in particular of the Calvinist Reformation, is a tradition that goes back a long way for you.

Yes, but it's not true for all of my ancestors. My father's father, Alphonse Roy, a teacher, was also a convert. He came from a very devout Catholic family. I remember my great aunts exchanging tips about the best saints to pray to, depending on what one was angling for—a perfect example, in the eyes of good Calvinists, of Catholic paganism! My grandfather found in Protestantism a good synthesis among his rationalism, his sense of ethics, and his desire to preserve a certain spirituality. And incidentally, it was the only way he could marry my grandmother—that was serious business in those days. His conversion cost him six years of ostracism from his own family and angry conversations all his life with his brothers. Being myself ten years old at the time, I didn't miss a single word of their tense debates about papal duties from my hiding spot under the table.

So this discord between Protestants and Catholics has also been one of your religious experiences.[1]

I was always struck by how much the memory of the Wars of Religion persisted. When I was fifteen, my aunt and my godmother took me aside one day to speak of serious things. I was old enough, they told me, to date—*fréquenter* was their term—and as such, I was to avoid going down the road toward a mixed marriage, which in those days meant a marriage between a Protestant and a Catholic. To hear them tell it, such marriages were doomed to fail and hence best avoided altogether. The only time I was ever punished at school was at the end of a history lesson, when I attempted my own remake of Saint Bartholomew's Day with a little Catholic kid.

Does speaking of a Protestant education still mean something specific today?

It might be best to say it did mean something specific until now. In my day, it was more than just a school education—it was a training in a way of life, a *Bildung* or *Erziehung*, as they say in German, which took place within a certain milieu and a certain subculture.

Of course, there are specific characteristics related to the postwar period and others that are specific to Protestantism. That time was dominated by youth movements that mostly came into existence in the 1930s, developed thanks to the Popular Front, and began to wane at the end of the 1960s: Cub Scouts, Boy Scouts, guides (*éclaireurs* was the Protestant name), youth groups (never adolescent groups) all stood on a religious or political foundation— not to mention the numerous overnight summer camps (*colonies de vacances*). Within the Catholic Church groups, the JOC, JAC, and JEC (Jeunesse ouvrière chrétienne, working-class youth; Jeunesse agricole catholique, farming youth; and Jeunesse étudiante chrétienne, Catholic youth) played an important role. The Communist Party also had its youth groups as did, on their side, the hard-core secularists defending *laïcité*. Communists and Socialists often mingled together within the Fédération des oeuvres laïques (Federation of Secular Good Works). They would organize overnight camps, day camps, and secular study (not Bible study!) circles. Each chapter had its own theater troupe and movie club, where screenings were followed by debates on social problems of the day to frame—*recadrer*, they would say—the film according to the community's values. This is why today's vehement denunciation of communitarianism makes me roll my eyes and chuckle since French republicanism has always defended tooth and nail—or, more often, comma and semicolon; that is, in speechmaking and tract distribution—its communitarian prerogative.

So the hearts and minds of the younger generation became a political battlefield?

Yes, and it was the product of several phenomena: the advent of free time (the vacation and the weekend, but also urbanization, which meant that young people were not automatically corralled into doing farm chores once school let out); the expanding autonomy of young people as they cease to be considered as miniature adults and they're accorded their own psychology; and finally, the rivalry between ideological movements (communism and fascism), which turned young people into a political constituency, a fact that obliged Christians to also position themselves as one political culture among others.

For Protestants, did the principle of secular schools (*écoles laïques*) pose a problem?

No, of course not. But it needs to be understood that the supposed neutrality of the secular school system left the door open to a parallel training program in ideology and culture that built up the school's instructional curriculum in a direction whose goal was to make sense and not just transmit knowledge. Among the most active of the Reformed French (but one could observe the same Protestantization and lifestyle among militant Catholics in the 1960s, and even as early as 1950), what mattered was to give meaning (*donner du sens*)—and being responsible for oneself and the world, and ultimately orienting one's life not so much around faith but around social and political values. One was supposed to be personally called out to (*interpellé*) by the large problems of the day. This responsibility was situated, first of all, at the level of the individual and not the community or the Church. At bottom, it was a more personalist perspective than that of a believer. One had to give life meaning, *build* a marriage, and breathe meaningful life into a professional practice. People weren't anxious about being saved. They were anxious about meaning and the meaning of meaning. Pleasure was not forbidden—far from it—but from hiking to sex, all activities had to be inscribed within some scheme of transcendent meaning, a transcendence of self, and the achievement of an ideal. That at least is what we were told. Obviously, we had the habit of indulging in pleasure first and accepting participation occasionally in some debate about meaning with the instructors and priests as the price that had to be paid to gain admission to the club. But we were all the same marked by the culture, and I ascribe to that process what would become my puritanism: not the refusal of the flesh, but the simple acceptance of the fact that desire is never a reason on its own nor a good in itself.

This could also be observed in the Catholic Church during the 1950s. What was typically Protestant in your case? What role did theology, and in particular Calvinist theology, play?

That's an important point. In political philosophy, one sees the thing to do now is to connect a social behavior to a theological paradigm—predestination and capitalism, for example, or a Weberian vocation—*Beruf*—and service to the state or, in the case of Islam, the status of the Prophet and the nonseparation between religion and politics. What doesn't get explained is how this connection gets made, how the theology *descends* into the political, so to speak, by what vector does a concept change into a practice? How does an idea developed by theologians or philosophers become an explanatory paradigm of a collective behavior? The sociologist of religions who's interested in the behavior of believers is also ignorant about the link between faith and practice. This explains why the treatment of religions in the social sciences and political science is often of such poor quality. The practitioners in these disciplines typically do not understand the internal functioning of religions—the spiritual motives and constraints that one finds in the practice of religious individuals.

What are they not seeing exactly?

Often we're overly impressed by theology because it's written down in books, whereas religiosity is harder to see. But the true training of the believer does not happen in theological studies. Believers (or their era or their school) choose, in fact, what they want from the theology. One day when I was about twelve, my grandfather, a pastor, took me aside and shared with me that he didn't believe in predestination (an essential element in Calvinist theology) because, he said, it went against his conception of God as love. Father Bosiger in La Rochelle had great difficulty explaining to us how God could be so arbitrary in his decisions. I remember in particular the story of Gideon and his three hundred men chosen, without explanation, solely on the basis of how they drink water (Judges, chapter 7).

Why are you so sensitive to religiosity?

Maybe because of the Protestant socialization as I experienced it. True religious culture was acquired by us in a banal daily setting: in sermons, debates in groups, recommended readings, the way we were told to verbalize our feelings and behaviors (especially with regard to our affections)—in short, through the definition of a practical *doxa* and ethics, a register of words and references where we would recognize each other immediately. This confirms that all religions are made up of subcultures that religious people often like to refer to as different sensibilities to maintain the myth of the unity of faith and of orthodoxy. This area between theology and social life is the true explanatory factor of the believer's behavior, whether it be within Christianity, Judaism, or Islam. And this is what makes it possible for believers to be both purists and fundamentalists and yet adapt themselves and live their faith in an open system of relations with the surrounding world.

Yet no sociologist of religious people is really interested in these phenomena—and that neglect is even greater in the field of political science, which is no longer interested in anything but itself.

If Catholicism, especially on the left, and Protestantism share common features, what was for you the specific contribution of a Protestant upbringing?

First, an intellectual education with true teaching: Sunday school before the service, Thursday classes on the history of Protestantism, retreats every other month, summer youth camps that included debates and Bible study, and participating in public group debates like those organized at cinema clubs. I acquired a solid grounding in the Bible and an initiation to philosophy. A typical exercise was Bible explication. Starting at age thirteen, we formed small workshop-style groups. The priest would give us three passages from the Bible taken from various places, and after two hours of reflection and discussion in the group, we had to make a presentation on the similarities and differences among the texts. Pluralism of opinion was allowed and even encouraged. In this way, we learned to read and analyze texts, to compare and contrast, contextualize, and debate.

Indirectly, it was also an introduction to politics. For example, the pre-1967 Protestants were enthusiastic Zionists, especially because their concentration on the Old Testament favored a pre-Zionist culture. From that perspective, the Holy Land definitely belonged to the Israelites, and the Philistines were definitely the enemy. We became acquainted with the map of Palestine with the Hebrew names. But this was also the continuation of a philo-Semitism that dated from the end of the nineteenth century and the alliance among Protestants, Israelites, and republicans to implement *laïcité* in France. In the pre-1967 teaching on Israel, the Palestinian Arab simply did not exist. Everything was presented as though the Jews had returned to a desert that they turned into a cornucopia and the hordes of Arabs from Egypt, Syria, and Transjordan were attacking the borders of this new garden. Certainly, it was just a small minority that got involved in militant Zionism, but it did happen, even in France. As late as the early 1980s, when I left for Afghanistan, one of my first cousins enlisted in the Israeli reserves in southern Lebanon. The 1967 war changed everything. Now suddenly there was the Palestinian as indigenous inhabitant and later as political actor. This change was consistent with a shift toward Third World and anticolonialist sympathies that became visible within the Church in the 1950s. But this raised the question of how to revise thinking about the colonial period. How should one now think about the Protestant missions in the colonies? In the 1950s, our parishes, just like the Catholic ones, had a lot of experience with missionaries making fund-raising presentations at Sunday-school sessions, and these would include presenting short black-and-white amateur films that showed black catechumens singing hallelujah with wide-open mouths before a bearded white missionary. But what was one to think when the anticolonial revolts erupted at missions—like the one in Madagascar, for example—that were Protestant? And what were we going to do in Indochina and Algeria?

One can imagine that this divided religious communities?

Yes, the Reformed Church of the 1950s was divided. A small right wing survived in the southwest around the Free Evangelical Church. One of my great uncles, Gaston Mercier, had recouped the lost particle of the Calvayrac *de la Tourette* family and had royalist and Pétainist sympathies. The centrist majority was more progressive, liberal, bourgeois, and intellectual. Finally, the young leaders of the student movements and a few priests, often sons from good families, enthusiastically joined the leftist, anti-imperialist, militant PSU (Parti socialiste unifié).

These divisions also rocked La Rochelle, with, on one side, the supposedly bourgeois parish in the city center (though our youth group was socially very mixed because the parish was too small to be effectively organized along class lines) and, on the other, the parish of Laleu-La Pallice, known as the Fraternité. This was really a mission in a working-class neighborhood and not at all a traditional parish. It was started in 1946 and was to become an example of evangelical, populist, missionary Protestantism, except that its priests, in particular Pastor Benjamin Atger, were very leftist at the time. Atger came once a month to preach in the bourgeois parish church and spoke out vehemently against French internment camps in Algeria, against colonial wars, shameless capitalist exploitation, and against the silence of the *bien-pensants* (conformists) seated in front of him.

The Algerian War was the big political ordeal of the 1950s, including for the Protestants.

Yes, it was around the Algerian War that I discovered the political life of adults, but without really knowing what to make of it—at least not until the attacks by the OAS (Organisation armée secrète) that provoked a general rejection of the extreme Right.[2] Politics was considered the business of older people—I was born in 1949, so I was five years old when the war started. For me it remained in that inaccessible adult realm until the presidential election of 1965, when, even though we couldn't vote ourselves, my cousins and I tried to persuade our grandfather the priest to vote for Mitterrand. He accepted, but one week before election day, he called us together to declare solemnly: "My children, my principles forbid me to vote for Mitterrand!" "But why, Grandpa?" "I've just learned that Mitterrand has mistresses, and de Gaulle does not." We didn't really see the connection.

And what about the celebrated Protestant principles: faith alone, grace alone, Scripture alone?

They were there, but real Protestants don't spend their time endlessly repeating these words. They live them in the concrete situation and historical moment in which people find themselves. For me, that Protestant education, with its principles, took shape through a particular figure, a priest who focused our attention on a dilemma: thinking about absolute evil and absolute faith.

We were between thirteen and eighteen years old when Pastor Roger Bosiger, recently elected by the local consistory, took charge of the youth group I belonged to and promptly organized cycling summer camps. It was during my time with this group that I learned what the Shoah was. Of course, we didn't use that term yet. But it's important to remember that in the 1950s and '60s, the specific details about the destruction of the Jews were kept secret—it was inscribed and obscured within the official discourse about Nazi atrocities and the *déportation* in general. There were a few rooms devoted to the concentration camps at the museum in La Rochelle, with testimonies by survivors who had been deported—but everything was presented as though, at bottom, the Nazis had deported all resisters. Many may remember the film *Nuit et brouillard* (*Night and Fog*, 1955) by Alain Resnais and the song of the same name by Jean Ferrat (1963), both of which aligned themselves with the unique explanatory framework at the time, namely, seeing Jews as one set of victims among many. But Bosiger had lived another experience. A brilliant math student, he volunteered in 1945 at age seventeen as an ambulance worker helping convoys bring home the surviving deportees. Bosiger had German-Swiss and Alsatian origins and spoke fluent German. He therefore was able to hear direct testimonies about the Jewish genocide. Having decided that one could not live a normal life after that, he chose to become a priest after completing his mathematics degree.

This tragic side of his vocation expressed itself in simple language: life is good (he was neither an ascetic nor a maniac about morality), but there is something essential, something that makes life a mere contingency, a diversion that turns your attention from what may be at once an absolute horror and absolutely sacred. In 1963 he guided us through a reading of *Le Vicaire*[3] by the playwright Rolf Hochhuth. He also made us study the Shoah by watching films about it and reading testimonies and other texts on the topic—all this at a time when the official school curriculum totally ignored the subject. The gap between absolute evil and daily life haunted him and worked its way into his Calvinist vision of faith. The absolute has a hard time finding a place in daily life, and yet daily life retains its dignity only so long as it never forgets God or evil. He regularly preached against conformist religion. As a good Calvinist, he believed that faith signified the death of former man and the advent of the new man—born again, even though he kept his distance from the Evangelical movement. He advocated both a strong involvement in the civil society that surrounds us as well as a radical break that comes with the absolute of faith.

When the first Evangelicals appeared in La Rochelle, and not just in the working-class parish where they were already present, he greeted them as a new ray of sun—but for us they were the beginning of new troubles and especially a new boredom. Of course, we had entered the youth movement for all kinds of reasons, many of them overtly profane—including the fact that it was the only mixed milieu composed of both young men and women in the entire city. We turned the club of folkloric dancing into a general dance club, and we flirted softly in between two Biblical explications.

With such a demanding pastor, how did the courageous faithful react?

The upshot of Bosiger's position was, as one would expect, a tension between faith and culture. He was asking, what exactly does culture amount to when confronted with this exigency over an absolute? This also held for evil. He loved German culture, but what to make of that culture in the face of the Shoah? What possible or impossible return might one contemplate toward the pre–World War II humanist culture? In a way, an entire

Huguenot culture was constructed to render useless the demands of faith in favor of a simple ethics. This passage from faith to ethics was characteristic of Protestantism at the time, but it caused problems for our pastor. He probably did not believe in the possibility of founding an ethics without God.

Worse still in his eyes was soft conformity. He never stopped complaining about tepid behavior such as the religious faith that is limited to Sunday services. From his pulpit, he upbraided the conformity of his parishioners, but in vain. He took us to meetings of the Salvation Army where a youngster of our age would get up on stage, slap his hands together, and launch into his tirade: "My father was alcoholic, my mother was a prostitute, and I was a thief. . . . But I've found Jesus and since then my life has meaning, I no longer drink or smoke, and I converse with Jesus. . . . " We were a bit shocked by what looked to us like the naiveté of this presentation, but the pastor was moved by the faith of the *charbonniers*. When an Evangelical Protestant (the first I ever encountered) who was my age and had been converted by American missionaries joined our group, it caused a panic. He insisted that we greet each other with a loud "Christ is risen!" to which the other was to reply, "Hallelujah! Christ is risen!" But this didn't work because we simply found it ridiculous.

The pastor sighed but let it slide. And then one June day during my last year in secondary school, he leaned forward in his pulpit toward the somnolent public, dressed in their Sunday clothes, and asked, "Why are you here if you have no faith!" At that moment, before the entire parish assembly, I stood up along with a friend, and we filed out down the central alley and never returned. Of course, he invited us to meet with him the next day so he could say, a bit sadly, "But I wasn't talking to you, I was addressing your parents!"

That time, I may have chosen the wrong door, but I didn't miss the exit.

Chapter 25

CAN ONE THINK ONE'S OWN LIFE?

This description of your youth touches on all the themes contained in *Holy Ignorance*—especially the disconnect between faith and culture and the question of pure religion. Does that mean that at bottom your academic conceptualizations are the reflection of a lived experience more than the result of fieldwork or intellectual research?

I DON'T THINK making distinctions among those categories makes much sense. Intuition and practical experience are at the heart of all intellectual endeavors. As I see it, the big mistake of the social sciences is to want to eliminate everything even remotely subjective and, we could add, *philosophical* in today's research and instead favor quantitative analysis (statistics, measurements, and the like), which in fact have only a weak explanatory power because everything interesting really follows from the quality of the question being asked at the outset. The pseudoneutrality of the measuring tools lends only the appearance of objectivity. That's why the social sciences are turning in circles today with their American university approach—because the actual terrain disappears behind the obligation to start out from existing theories and place the brick of one's own scholarly contribution into the university edifice.

But what one builds with bricks is a wall, not thinking. We're only borrowing *form* from the hard sciences, and we're forgetting that they are also made up of *questions* (that must be asked first) and also of intuition, errors, and a gradual feeling one's way into a problem. Maybe, like Kant, we need to dare to think, as his injunction *sapere aude* (dare to think for yourself) instructed us to do. The commentary on Gaston Bachelard's *Nouvel esprit scientifique* that I wrote in 1978 was not just a school exercise in epistemology. I was very interested in his discussion of the relation between science and the imagination, between measuring instruments and "cold" theories. People often forget that every form of measurement is already a closed system of theories and presuppositions. University work is too often simply making the university gears turn, instead of trying to understand the real. Theses and theories are too often carried out with an eye on career advancement and displace opportunities to report back from the field or, to put it in more highfalutin' language, to pursue the exigencies of thought.

I'm not speaking here about my French colleagues. In France, working in the field and individuality are still respected. This is why in the social sciences French PhDs easily find jobs abroad because they have superior training in the field compared with their American counterparts, for example. American universities are not stupid; they know where to recruit. What I'm especially criticizing is the new system that's been put in place following the model of the Anglo-Saxon PhD program, where people are paying more attention to the caliber, conformity, and capacity to duplicate the system and not to intelligence, discovery, or risk taking on a material, intellectual, or political level. This conformist model is spreading and becoming the norm, even in France, sadly.

What's the connection with holy ignorance?

I was very sensitive in my parish to the tension between faith and culture—culture in the sociological sense of a social group. I didn't theorize about it at the time, of course, but as often in my life, I turned a lived experience into a sort of notecard that I kept in the back of my mind (or now on my hard drive), with the idea that it might be retrieved when it made sense in a different context months or decades later. This is what gives my life a sort of repeating spiral appearance. I relive, revisit, and update segments of the past according to what occurs in new, present circumstances. The past, therefore, takes on a new meaning, a new depth, and the present acquires a certain thickness and resonance that raises it above the simple status of event or anecdote. It's afterward that I understood the relationship between faith and culture that is constitutive to Abrahamic religions (I'm thinking of the character Polyeucte in Corneille), and which takes on a new meaning in the context of secularization and globalization.

During the century from 2000 to 2010, you attain a stable situation: CNRS director, division director at the EHESS, consultant at the CAP, married and the father of two children, and still living in Dreux. You're working a lot on terrorism, the Iraq War, and you publish *Holy Ignorance*. But overall your life is calmer. Bernard Kouchner offers you the chance to head the Direction de la prospective with the Foreign Ministry at the Quai d'Orsay, but you turn it down. You resign from the CAP, you go on leave from the CNRS, and you leave for Berkeley, then Florence. Is this again an expression of your rupture syndrome—leaving the peloton to make a breakaway?

It was certainly the sign of a certain fatigue, a certain lassitude brought on by the tenseness of the intellectual debates in France, the shift of a portion of French elites toward a bitter style of conservatism that was preachy and intellectually vacuous, the incapacity of the Left (what's left of the Left) to extricate itself from a phobic obsession with *laïcité* (now enthusiastically taken up by the National Front), and the dereliction of the radical Left, which is stuck in a multiculturalist trance or in complacent conspiracy thinking. Life now seems to scare everybody. Sarcasm has replaced irony, and an increasingly sticky, hate-driven muck has displaced all lightness of speaking or being. France has become a country of resentment and rehashing. I am deeply European, and therefore what's talked about as a return of the nation and national sovereignty is to me a sign of the provincialism of little frogs in even smaller ponds within the intellectual landscape. Witness the desperate folks celebrating with sausage and red wine, the new secular Eucharist, as the quintessence of French culture resisting globalization and Islamism while forgetting that a true culture would be more open because in no way unsure or nervous about itself.

I also wanted my children to learn foreign languages, so I accepted an invitation to be a visiting professor at Berkeley for one year in 2008, after which I accepted a post at the European University Institute in Florence. At least I'm coherent when it comes to my European identity.

I also feel the need to avoid getting too locked into a character, most recently the character of the expert being constantly solicited and interviewed. With every crisis that touched on one of my areas of expertise (terrorism, integration, Islamists, Central Asia, the Middle East, Afghanistan, or Iran), in other words about twice a month, the telephone would ring every ten minutes. I was appearing on television talk shows constantly. Journalists offer an easy hospitality, but since they don't have much to say, they stack up experts like dominos and have them say everything and nothing, and they call the result balanced reporting. After a while, I was repeating myself too much and it was time to stop.

I left for Florence on August 30, 2009, the day of my sixtieth birthday, with my whole family packed into our little car—if all went well, we'd sign on for a new decade. My office now sits among olive trees on a Tuscan hillside in a Dominican convent without a single monk left. A faded fresco that tells of their activities in the Baltic survives, but religion is declining all around like an autumn sun setting slowly and beautifully. And yet in Florence, at least culture is overflowing. The weather is pleasant, there's plenty of good food, and perhaps a little less neurosis than in some other places. The intellectual work with young researchers, men and women who have come from all over the world, is also a pleasure. My sails caught new wind just as I had hoped.

EPILOGUE

A Story to End All Stories

SOMETIMES THINGS ARE easier than one thinks.

For years I told my students a story taken from a chapter in an anthology entitled *When They Read What We Write*.[1] The story talks about the aftereffects of the theories elaborated by anthropologists on the people they've studied. The time of impunity for anthropologists is long over. The Trobrianders and Nambikwara have learned to read, and people no longer hesitate to sue for damages against the person or group that dares to write about them. The book's starting point is a lawsuit brought by the Polish community in Chicago against an anthropologist who dared bring up the question of alcohol consumption! Here's my favorite story.

A young anthropologist arrives in the Pacific islands—Tuvalu or Nauru, I can't remember which ones—which gained independence between 1968 and 1978. The focus of his research is studying a small event within the perspective of the "total fact," with the idea that by analyzing one by one the different aspects of the small event he will bring to light the entire warp and woof of a society that until then had been opaque. The event chosen for study is the murder of a young woman by her husband. Of course, this murder puts into evidence the matrimonial link, the relation between the sexes, the attitude toward violence, authority, rights, and so forth. While the researcher studies the reactions of the relatives, attends the trial, listens to the witnesses testify and the lawyers litigate, one notices as one reads that the very fabric of this small society is being revealed little by little. This small event seems to illuminate the soul of the world. The author systematizes all the diverse elements and turns it into a big book of analysis and synthesis entitled *Culture, Sex, and Violence in the ___ Society.* In no time, a university names him to an endowed professorship.

Three years later, he receives a letter from an Australian prison where a murderer is serving his sentence because there is no prison on his little Pacific island. This polite letter says in effect: "Dear Professor, I've recently come upon your book in the library of the prison where I am incarcerated for the murder of my wife. Your book is truly erudite and interesting, but, you know, if I killed my wife, it's simply because she was sleeping with the postman."

It's a beautiful story—the one thousand and first of my lost Orient, and my last.

The only problem is that when I wanted to do a more precise analysis of this chapter for my students at the European University Institute in 2013, I discovered that this text was not in the book I had remembered it in, and that in fact it was nowhere—there was no such text.

But as one says in Italian, *se non è vero, è ben trovato*—"if it's not true, it's a good invention."

NOTES

FOREWORD

1. Olivier Roy, *La sainte ignorance: Le temps de la religion sans culture*, Collection Points Essais (Paris: Seuil, 2008). Published in English as *Holy Ignorance: When Religion and Culture Part Ways*, trans. Ros Schwartz (New York: Columbia University Press, 2010).
2. Olivier Roy, interview by Olivier Mongin, Joël Roman and Hermine Videau-Falgueirettes, "Paris-Dreux-Kaboul: Itinéraire d'un chercheur," *Esprit* 282 (February 2002): 6–34.

1. HITCHHIKING FROM PARIS TO KABUL: A LOOK BACK AT A DEPARTURE

1. Translator's note: *khâgne* is the customary way to refer to the second year of a two-year preparatory program (*prépa*) for a *concours* (exam competition) that is the prerequisite to admission to many of France's top business and engineering schools, known as the *grandes écoles*. Students in *prépa* typically take classes in a lycée building, but they have already graduated from high school with their baccalaureate diploma in hand. *Hypokhâgne* refers to the first year of the *prépa* program.
2. Paul Nizan, *Aden, Arabie* (1931; repr., Paris: La Découverte, 2002).

3. LOUIS-LE-GRAND, NORMALE SUP', AND THE CRISIS OF THE HUMANITIES

1. The Victor Hugo (1802–1885) poem under discussion is "Pasteurs et troupeaux" (Pastors and their flocks), from his *Les Contemplations*, Book V.
2. George recounted his experiences in several articles that were published in *Les temps modernes* in 1972, and later as a book, *Prof à T* (Paris: Galilée, 1973).
3. On February 25, 1972, Pierre Overney, a militant Maoist, was killed by a security guard in front of the entrance to the Renault factory at Boulogne-Billancourt. 200,000 people participated in the funeral procession on March 1. On March 8, GP activists kidnapped Robert Nogrette, a Renault executive. He was released two days later on orders from Benny Lévy.
4. A rival student political group on the far right.

5. RETURN TO THE FOLD

1. Translator's note: It is important to clarify that the *agrégation*, of which there are several in various subject areas, is not merely a set of tests (*examens*), but a *concours*, that is, an exam competition. This means one is not tested simply on what one knows but on how much one knows and how well one presents that knowledge, in writing and orally, *compared with other candidates* who are also competing for a specific number of government teaching posts (i.e., lifetime employment within France's National Education system) and this varies from year to year. The philosophy *agrégation* is particularly difficult and selective because the number of teaching posts is lower than for, say, French or English professors for the simple reason that philosophy is taught only at university and in the last year of high school, called the *terminale*. To my knowledge, there is no comprehensive history of France's *concours* system, of which the *agrégation* is but one type within France's vast civil service recruitment machine. French people learn the ropes from parents, older siblings, friends, and high school teachers (and later special *prépa* teachers) who lead the chosen through the proper channels and grooming exercises. The *concours* system is a major component of France's meritocracy, the central tenet of which is that one gets what one deserves and deserves what one gets.

6. POSTCARDS AND AMERICAN POOL

1. Edward W. Said, *Orientalism* (New York: Pantheon, 1978). Published in French as *L'Orientalisme: L'Orient créé par l'Occident* (Paris: Seuil, 1980).
2. The lyrics are from the Robert Schumann (1810–1856) lied "Widmung" (Devotion), the first in his song cycle of 26 art songs for voice and piano, *Myrthen*, op. 25.

7. PROFESSOR AT DREUX: LEFTIST, AWAY FROM PARIS, AND HAPPY

1. Hervé Hamon and Patrick Rotman, *Les années de rêve*, vol. 1 of *Génération* (Paris: Seuil, 1987); Hervé Hamon and Patrick Rotman, *Les années de poudre*, vol. 2 of *Génération* (Paris: Seuil, 1988).
2. Translator's note: The term *harki* designates those individuals who accepted (or were forced) to side with the French army and fight against pro-independence Algerians during the Algerian War, 1954–1962. Despite their service to the French nation, many of them were held in internment camps in France after the war; many others who were unable to leave Algeria were considered traitors and brutally killed. For more information, see Vincent Jouane, "La Littérature des Enfants de Harkis: Mémoire et Réconciliation," (PhD thesis, Washington University, 2012, available at http://openscholarship.wustl.edu/cgi/viewcontent.cgi?article=1700&context=etd. In English, see Vincent Crapanzano, *The Harkis: The Wound That Never Heals* (Chicago: University of Chicago Press, 2011).
3. Translator's note: In France it is possible to hold more than one elective office simultaneously—it is known as the *cumul des mandats*.
4. Daniel-Cohn Bendit was an emblematic student leader during the May '68 protests; he later became a member of the European Parliament.
5. Dieudonné M'bala M'bala (b. 1966) is a controversial French actor, stand-up comedian, and political provocateur.
6. Jacques Rancière, *La nuit des prolétaires: Archives du rêve ouvrier* (1981, repr., Paris: Hachette Pluriel, 2012). Published in English as *Proletarian Nights: The Workers' Dream in Nineteenth-Century France*, 2nd ed., trans. John Drury (London: Verso, 2012).

7. Michel de Certeau (1925–1986), most noted in the United States for *The Practice of Everyday Life*, trans. Steven Rendall (Berkeley: University of California Press, 1984). Published in French as *L'invention du quotidien*, vol. 1, *Arts de faire*, Collection Folio Essais (1980; repr., Paris: Gallimard, 1990).

8. See Olivier Roy, "Le fantôme de la culture; ou L'inculture des professeurs," *Esprit* 53, no. 5 (May 1981): 99–110.

9. The Russell Tribunal, also known as the International War Crimes Tribunal or Russell-Sartre Tribunal, was organized in 1966. Russell's book *War Crimes in Vietnam* was published in 1967.

10. Olivier Roy, "Dreux: La démocratie de justesse," *Esprit* (May–June 1983): 291–94.

11. Translator's note: These were priests of the generation of Cardinal Jean-Marie Lustiger (1926–2007), a charismatic leader eventually named archbishop of Paris.

8. OUT OF SCHOOL

1. Virginie Linhart, *Le jour où mon père s'est tu* [The day my father stopped talking] (Paris: Seuil, 2008).

2. Translator's note: The French sentence, which reads, "*Moi et votre professeur, nous sommes entre pairs, p-a-i-r, bien sûr,*" contains a multidimensional witticism, since *pairs* (peers, equals) is a homonym of *pères* (fathers). So Ms. Dreyfus spells out the word *pair* to avoid (or commit?) the Freudian slip of stating that she and Professor Roy are "between fathers"—whatever that might be supposed to mean.

9. ONCE AGAIN, AND FOR REAL, AFGHANISTAN

1. L'Institut français de polémologie was founded by Gaston Bouthoul in 1946 to study the origin, nature, and functioning of war. It was closed down in 1993.

2. Translator's note: "Centrale" is the nickname for the École centrale des arts et manufactures, one of France's oldest (founded in 1829) and most prestigious engineering schools, and one of the group of so-called *grandes*

écoles that admit students via *concours* after two years of *prépa*, like for the École normale referred to earlier.

3. Jean-José Puig is the author of the authoritative guidebook to fishing in Afghanistan, *La Pêche à la truite en Afghanistan* (Paris: La Martinière, 2005).

10. ON FOOT, ON HORSEBACK, AND WEARING A BURKA IN WARTIME AFGHANISTAN

1. The *naqshbandiyya tariqa* (Naqshbandi order) is one of the four largest Sufi congregations. *Madrassa* is the Arab word for schools of the secondary and university levels, which may be either secular or religious, but most madrassas in Muslim countries are, in fact, religious schools.

2. Michel Seurat, a sociologist and researcher affiliated with France's Centre national de la recherche scientifique (CNRS) and a specialist on Syria (see his book *Syrie: L'État de barbarie* [1982; repr., Presses universitaires de France, 2012]), was kidnapped in Lebanon by an Islamic organization probably connected to Hezbollah. In 1986 he was not freed with his fellow hostage, Jean-Paul Kauffmann, and his body would be discovered only in 2005 outside Beirut. Doubt remains surrounding his death—assassination or illness?

3. Ulema, also spelled ulama, is a body of mullahs and is the guardian of the legal and religious tradition in Islam.

4. In English these titles are as follows: *Islam and Resistance in Afghanistan* (Cambridge: Cambridge University Press, 1986); *The Failure of Political Islam* (Cambridge, MA: Harvard University Press, 1994); and *The New Central Asia: The Creation of Nations* (London: I. B. Tauris, 2000).

5. A mining center in the Democratic Republic of Congo (ex-Zaire) located in the Haut-Katanga region. In 1978, the town was taken over by Katanga rebels opposed to Marshal Mobutu, and they took Europeans hostage. The town was liberated by a parachute regiment of the French Foreign Legion commanded by Colonel Philippe Erulin. The operation was considered a great success, even though it caused the death of several Africans and Europeans.

6. Cornelius Castoriadis, "Vers la stratocratie," *Le Débat* 5, no. 12 (1981): 5–17.

7. See the presentation of the works of these thinkers in Farhad Khosrokhavar and Olivier Roy, *Iran: Comment sortir d'une révolution religieuse* (Paris: Seuil, 1999).

12. THE FAILURE OF POLITICAL ISLAM

1. Olivier Roy, *The Failure of Political Islam*, trans. Carol Volk (Cambridge, MA: Harvard University Press, 1998).
2. First printed in 1941 in the Argentine literary magazine *Sur* and later reprinted in the collection *Ficciones* in 1944.
3. "À la recherche du monde musulman" [In search of the Muslim world], *Esprit* (August 2001).
4. Emmanuel Todd, *La Chute finale: Essai sur la décomposition de la sphère soviétique* (Paris: Robert Laffont, 1976). Published in English as *The Final Fall: An Essay on the Decomposition of the Soviet Sphere*, trans. John Waggoner (New York: Karz, 1979).
5. Olivier Roy, "L'énigme du soulèvement: Foucault et l'Iran" [The enigma of the uprising: Foucault and Iran], *Vacarme* 29 (2004): 34–38.
6. Farhad Khosrokhavar, *L'islamisme et la mort: Le martyre révolutionnaire en Iran* [Islamism and death: The revolutionary martyr in Iran] (Paris: L'Harmattan, 1995).

13. WAR EXPERIENCE: PRISONERS AND BANDITS

1. Saba Mahmood, *Politics of Piety: The Islamic Revival and the Feminist Subject* (2005; repr., Princeton, NJ: Princeton University Press, 2011).

14. JIHAD

1. The Catholic Community of Sant'Egidio was founded in Rome in 1968 by a layman, Andrea Riccardi. Its mission is to fight against poverty and the death penalty, to help AIDS sufferers and the elderly, and fight for greater access to education. It is especially well known for organizing international interfaith conferences and for its role as a mediator of international conflicts.
2. Sunni-inspired schools common in Pakistan, India, and Afghanistan. The Deobandi are fundamentalists in their approach to texts, favoring

and teaching in the madrassas an Islam that was rather apolitical and traditional.

15. THE AFGHAN CIRCUS

1. Jean-Christophe Notin, *La Guerre de l'ombre des Français en Afghanistan* [France's shadow war in Afghanistan] (Paris: Fayard, 2011).
2. *L'Étoile du soldat*, directed by Christophe de Ponfilly (2006).

16. A SOVIET INVITATION TO CENTRAL ASIA

1. Translator's note: A French newspaper founded in 1904 by the Socialist Jean Jaurès and long associated closely with the French Communist Party.
2. Iouri Tynianov, *Le Lieutenant Kijé*, trans. Lily Denis, Collection Folio Bilingue 94 (Paris: Gallimard, 2001). Published in English as Yuri Tynyanov, *Lieutenant Kijé / Young Vitushishnikov: Two Novellas*, trans. Mirra Ginsburg, Eridanos Library, no. 20 (New York, Marsilio Publishers, 1990).
3. Translator's note: EHESS is a prestigious institute of higher learning founded after World War II as an offshoot of the École pratique des hautes études. EHESS has a special status that allows it to operate outside the rules of ordinary French universities, with notably the permission to have selective admissions.
4. Olivier Roy, *The New Central Asia: Geopolitics and the Birth of Nations*, rev. ed. (2000; rept., New York: New York University Press, 2007).

20. THE CRISIS OF CULTURES AND THE UNIVERSAL

1. Ibn Taymiyya (1263–1328), theologian and Kurdish jurist, a Sunni Muslim, and member of the radical Hanbali movement that inspired

contemporary Islamic tendencies; Sayyid Qutb (or Qotb) (1906–1966), Egyptian thinker of an Islam ruptured from the modern world and a member of the Islamic Brotherhood movement. He was condemned to death under Nasser and in prison in 1966.

2. Translator's note: The author's French example, which tests the skills of the translator, is "*Va, je ne te hais point.*"

3. Translator's note: Jan Valtin was the alias of Richard Hermann Julius Krebs (1905–1951), a writer of German origin, during the interwar period. The book mentioned was first published in English as *Out of the Night* in 1940.

21. WHAT WAS GOOD ABOUT ISLAM

1. Mohammed Arkoun, *La construction humaine de l'islam* (Paris: Albin Michel, 2012).

2. Translator's note: France's *habilitation à diriger des recherches* is a mid-career evaluation of university professors who, if successful, are then declared qualified to direct doctoral dissertations. The procedure consists of an oral defense of a "*document de synthèse*" or other unpublished research text. Roy's was entitled "Individu, communauté et société civile dans la reformulation religieuse de l'islam contemporain" (Fondation nationale des science politiques, Paris, 2001).

3. François Burgat, *L'Islamisme en face* (Paris: La Découverte, 2007). Published in English as *Face to Face with Political Islam* (London: I. B. Tauris, 1999).

4. Samuel Huntington, *The Clash of Civilizations and the Remaking of the World Order* (New York: Simon & Schuster, 1996).

22. AGAINST THE SECULARISTS' ESSENTIALISM

1. *Ijtihad* means "effort to interpret" (by the ulema and Muslim jurists). When it comes to the decline of Islam, some incriminate the closure of the *ijtihad* in the ninth and tenth centuries (fourth century of the Hegira).

2. Translator's note: Tocqueville says as much in volume 2 of his *Democracy in America* (1840).
3. Mongin has published many articles and books on the city, notably *La ville des flux: L'envers et l'endroit de la mondialisation urbaine* (Paris: Fayard, 2013) and *La Condition urbaine: La ville à l'heure de la mondialisation*, Collection Points Essais 585 (Paris: Seuil, 2007).
4. Clifford Geertz, *Islam Observed: Religious Development in Morocco and Indonesia* (Chicago: University of Chicago Press, 1971).

23. THE DECADE 2000–2010: WHERE WERE YOU ON SEPTEMBER 11, 2001?

1. Translator's note: Hubert Védrine (b. 1947), a graduate of France's École nationale d'administration (ENA), was a political ally of François Mitterrand and minister of foreign affairs under Socialist prime minister Lionel Jospin from 1997 to 2002.
2. Olivier Roy, *Les illusions du 11 septembre: Le débat stratégique face au terrorisme* [The illusions of September 11: the strategic debate in the face of terrorism], Collection La république des idées (Paris, Seuil, 2002). Olivier Roy, *Le croissant et le chaos*, Collection Tapage (2007; repr., Paris: Fayard, 2013). Published in English as *The Politics of Chaos in the Middle East*, trans. Ros Schwartz (New York: Columbia University Press, 2008).
3. Farhad Khosrokhavar, *Les nouveaux martyrs d'Allah* (Paris: Flammarion, 2002). Published in English as *Suicide Bombers: Allah's New Martyrs*, trans. David Macey (London: Pluto Press, 2005).

24. PORTRAIT OF A YOUNG PROTESTANT IN THE 1950S AND '60S

1. Translator's note: In the French, the word *expériences* appears in quotation marks, thus signaling that the interviewer is likely playing on its two common meanings: *experience* and *experiment*, which correspond to

being the actor and the observer, respectively—the point being that Roy is frequently a bit of both.

2. Translator's note: The OAS was a clandestine French political-military organization created on February 11, 1961. Its members launched a series of bombings and assassinations in Algeria and metropolitan France, with the goal of keeping Algeria part of France.

3. *Der Stellvertreter* in the original German, *The Deputy* in English. This tragedy started the polemic, still ongoing, about the silence and responsibility of Pope Pius XII with regard to the Holocaust.

EPILOGUE: A STORY TO END ALL STORIES

1. Caroline B. Brettell, ed., *When They Read What We Write: The Politics of Ethnography* (1993; repr., Westport, CT: Begin & Garvey, 1996).